EDUCATION, LITERATURE AND ISLAM

EDUCATION, LITERATURE AND ISLAM

Writings by Mohammad Mujeeb

Edited by

Akhtarul Wasey

Farhat Ehsas

SHIPRA

ISBN: 978-81-7541-395-5

First Published in India in 2008

Education, Literature and Islam

Published by :
SHIPRA PUBLICATIONS
115-A, Vikas Marg, Shakarpur, Delhi-110092 (India)
Tel. : 91-11-65277210, 22500954, Fax : 91-11-22458662
Email : info@shiprapublications.com
www.shiprapublications.com

To

Mr. M. Hamid Ansari,

Vice–President of India,

who represents many qualities that

Mujeeb Saheb cherished

Preface

Early years of the twentieth century saw many changes slowly but surely sweeping the Indian society. This movement of history was not as visible on the surface as it should have been but nevertheless many structures and patterns of thought and action, traditional views about the world and universe and perceptions about social values and objectives of life were under intense stress due to new ideas and thoughts impacting the western-educated middle class people in the country. What later came to be termed as a clash of tradition and modernity has its origins in the same period. Undoubtedly the great Indian renaissance had already revolutionized the Indian mind during the nineteenth century and it had left many lasting marks on the traditional thinking and living. But tradition and the age-old customs were still intact to a very large extent and they did not encounter any prominent threat to their survival. But one thing was no doubt very disturbing even at that time. It was the unsettling effect of new ideas on the religious faith, at least of an extraordinarily intelligent and perceptive section of the urban Indian youth. This section not only started questioning the validity and rationale of the religious beliefs and customs but also tried to evolve altogether new forms of religious ideas and experience.

Hindus having being much ahead in receiving western education were the first to get influenced by these changes in thought pattern and views of the life and society. Naturally then, this section of society was much more prominent among Hindu middle-classes. The twentieth century came with new promises for this section which made itself much more prominent and expressed itself in many forms.

Muslims were no doubt much more tradition-bound and tied to their religious faith in a manner that no winds of change could be able to touch their inner core of religiosity and traditionalism. But the impact of rationalism driven by the enlightenment that Sir Syed

Ahmad Khan heralded among Indian Muslim left at least a more mentally alive and strong section of the Muslim society open to the changes that were becoming inevitably necessary. It was this section comprising energetic and promising Muslim youth which soon assumed the role of intellectual and cultural leadership of Indian Muslims.

This intellectually strong and demanding section of the Muslim society had a few skeptics, even atheists but taken as a whole most of its representatives were strikingly balanced in their orientation towards tradition and religion. These intellectually and spiritually challenging people reinterpreted their religious and cultural tradition in a very creative manner and thus reinvented their relationship with their past. Sir Syed being the starting point, this movement towards re-energizing the heart and mind of the Muslim civilization in Indian subcontinent had Mohd. Iqbal, the poet philosopher, as its most brilliant exponent. People like Zakir Husain represented another very enlightening feature of this movement that found expression in institution-building, among other things.

Prof. Mohd. Mujeeb belonged to this group of extremely intelligent and sensitive individuals who wanted to do something new and lasting in impact. They had questions in their minds and their hearts longed for something that they may call their own creation. They were not satisfied with all that their past and tradition has bequeathed to them. They wanted to choose the living and throbbing elements of their tradition and weave them into new patterns of thought and action.

Prof. Mujeeb was one of the most brilliant stars of the firmament of new ideas that the group led by Dr. Zakir Husain spread out on their head at the Jamia Millia Islamia, which was both the birth-ground of a new educational philosophy and practice and a battle-ground of new ideas necessary to lead the Indian Muslim into a future of intellectual and spiritual freedom, a happy balance of faith and rationalism and a constructive synthesis of core Islamic and Indian civilizational values.

This book tries to represent as much as possible all the shades and hues of the astonishingly diverse intellectual and academic expressions and achievements that Prof. Mujeeb was known for, which I believe will become a starting point for a process of reappraisal of his ideas that is long overdue.

Akhtarul Wasey

Contents

Introduction

Professor Mohd. Mujeeb was one of the most intellectually gifted, morally upright and spiritually correct Indian Muslims, who made themselves prominent in the twentieth century. He was a quiet and unassuming person who always tried to remain withdrawn in himself but the more he withdrew the more his creativity and intellectual talent became prominent. He lived the life of a thinker mediating upon the fundamental questions of human life, society and universe. He also lived as a Sufi continuously trying to enrich himself and others spiritually. All his life Professor Mujeeb remained a seeker of knowledge but to him knowledge did not mean merely knowing of facts and having information about things but acquiring a deeper understanding of men and things and processes of life, knowing things from within. He was gifted with an extremely inquisitive and analytical mind and a turbulent spirit. He could not accept anything—faith, values, ideas, postulates, doctrines—as given and without putting it to a severe intellectual questioning. And once he was convinced about the rightness of any idea or view he took it as an articles of faith and practised it to the end.

Professor Mujeeb belonged to an affluent aristocratic family. He learnt Arabic and Persian at home and then studied at a Roman Catholic School, Loreto Convent in Lucknow and later at Cambridge Preparatory School, Dehradun. He was given the mandatory instruction in the holy Quran but at that stage he had no interest in it. This disinterest in the formal religious education proved to be an excuse for him to rediscover his faith in Islam later in fife. In 1919, when he was 17 years old, he went to New College, Oxford where he graduated in Modern History in 1922. After completing his education at Oxford he didn't know what to do next. A friend suggested to him that he should go to Germany to learn printing. He went to Germany and remained there till 1926. There he learnt German, French and Russian language besides trying his hand in printing. In Germany young Mujeeb had interactions with a cross section of people which helped him to have a deep understanding of German culture and literature. In those days Dr Abid Husain was also in Germany. Dr Zakir Husain came to Germany in 1922. Mujeeb met him and soon he developed a strong liking for him. Dr Zakir Husain talked to him about the Jamia Millia Islamia. Mujeeb showed interest and offered to join the Jamia. Dr Zakir Husain tried to dissuade him from joining the Jamia saying that it would be a tough job for him to do. But Mujeeb remained firm. In 1926, he came back to India and joined the Jamia as a teacher of History and Politics In 1948 he was appointed its Vice-Chancellor, a post he held till 1973.

Life at Jamia was an altogether new experience to young Mujeeb. There were hardships but he faced them all with courage and determination. His habit of hard work and self-discipline came handy. Moreover, Jamia had come to him as a challenge and he was not scared of challenges. Rather he welcomed them, to test his abilities and talents. It is not that Professor Mujeeb had completely submitted himself to the Jamia. He was too individualistic and lover of freedom to do that. He always tried, and successfully so, to keep a part of himself, the core of his individuality, untouched from anything of the outside world, Jamia included. It is in this kingdom of privacy that he reigned supreme. He had many opinions and views that were not in consonance with the general climate of opinion at the Jamia campus or in the Muslim community at large but he never allowed this divergence of views to affect his bond with the Jamia, which was complete and irrevocable. The kind of relationship he had with the Jamia can be understood to some extent by what he had himself told about it :

> I joined the Jamia over thirty-nine years ago, and I have remained there since. Many people admired my colleagues and me for having asked for seat in the leaking boat of national education when other crafts were available. I know I offered to join the Jamia on an impulse and have never been able to explain my action even to myself. But I have always hated looking around for the better job, and the line of least resistance has led me to seek whole-hearted satisfaction in the choice I made.

> I think I liked the Jamia Millia best because it demanded creditable performance in return for admittedly meagre compensation. . . . And so service in the Jamia Millia meant really giving without question all that one could give and accepting without question whatever was doled out in return. . . . But please do not imagine that I am thinking of self-sacrifice, of dedicated service to great causes. I am not. . . .

Professor Mujeeb adds that he felt embarrassment at not knowing whether he was wanted or not wanted in the Jamia. He further says: 'working in the Jamia Millia made me feel that I could live a full life even if, according to any reckoning, I was classified as unwanted. I can, therefore, be happy with my ideas even it they are, like me, classified as unwanted. I do not need to make a system out of them, or even to argue in their favour.'

There was a symbiotic bond between the Jamia and Professor Mujeeb. Both enriched and sustained each other. He made the Jamia into his laboratory of ideas on history, education, art and culture and fundamental issues of human civilization. It is at Jamia that he wrote his magnum opus, Indian Muslims which deals with the intricate social, economic, political and intellectual processes that shaped the destiny of Indian Muslims. It offers an entirely new creative and critical interpretation of the Muslim experience of India. Professor Mujeeb calls this book as the embodiment of an 'inward experience of the past'. He emphasizes the Sufi side much more than the political side of this history as the Muslim rulers exploited Islam to strengthen themselves and in the process distorted it. Professor Mujeeb condemned the Partition of India for it inflicted a grievous injury to India's socio-cultural unity and spelt disaster to Muslims left in India. He was a severe critic of the religious orthodoxy among Muslims which never allowed them to come out of their narrow self-image and enlarge their area of consciousness. The Muslim cultural identity can be kept intact, according to him, only if it is brought back into harmony with the humanist ideals of Islam.

Professor Mujeeb had extremely diverse interests and concerns as is evident from his articles contained in the books, Education and Traditional Values and Islamic Influence on Indian Society. Here his restless and creative mind grapples with many themes ranging from human values, essence of Islam, education, moral values, conscience, culture, democracy, architecture' etc. He wrote brilliantly and with a new vision on Ghalib's poetry. Professor Mujeeb considered only the creative aspect of poetry worthwhile as against the value loaded aspect containing a message. He liked the free flow and flight of imagination in poetry and to him Ghalib had it in abundance. We hope this will help in forming a clearer and more unified picture of the multi dimensional genius of Profssor Mohd. Mujeeb.

Akhtarul Wasey

1

Speaking for Myself

I think I have improved now, but for a good part of my life I have been an extremely nervous person who most of the time kept on asking himself the embarrassing question, am I wanted or not wanted? I could, of course, hide myself from the question, or turn my back on it, or in a way look down upon it in a spasm of dizzy self-confidence. But it was always there. Even now at parties when I do not see known faces I feel I am not wanted, and if I misunderstand a person or a situation and am made in some way to realise it, I feel like the guest at a hotel who has by mistake walked into the wrong room. And really, if I am not as nervous now as I used to be, it is because I have been too long in the world already for the question of my being wanted or not wanted to have much relevance.

This is just a preface to my confession of an utter failure to understand life or anything about it. I have not, however, allowed my intellectual curiosity or my sense of freedom to be smothered beneath the weight of a borrowed philosophy or of plain despair. I think, those who have tried to prove that existence is an illusion, have merely deceived themselves and others. I have never had the desire, like Ivan Karamazov, to return my ticket of entry into the world. I have lived, I have wanted to live and I have enjoyed life. If I have not understood for myself the meaning of existence or accepted on trust any traditional interpretation, I have not felt that I was walking in the dark. Tolstoy made a moving story out of the question. How much land does a man need? Why can't one make a whole life of spiritual discovery out of an answer to the question? How much light does a man need? It's just a matter of

From *Education and Traditional Values.*

how far and how clearly you want to see. The sun can never be bright enough to efface the limits fixed by distance on the human vision, and the light of a few matches will help one to get up and down dark and winding stairs. The wisest of men cannot see even into the immediate future, and a little commonsense properly used is guidance enough in the present.

So why kick against the pricks? If God alone knows what the future of the world, of India, of the Indian Muslims, of the Pakistani Hindus, of the Jamia Millia, where I have spent the whole of my adult life, is going to be, and He does not want to or cannot, without showing flagrant favouritism, share His knowledge with me, I do not wish to be importunate. I do not know what success is and I have not tried to find out. I do not know what is the right thing or the good thing to do. The question is just too complicated. So why not say that we cannot measure success with any confidence, that we cannot know what is the right thing to do; we can only hope that we shall have the good sense not to do the wrong thing and the courage to examine what we have done without partiality towards ourselves.

I joined the Jamia Millia over thirty nine years ago, and I have remained there since. Many people admired my colleagues and me for having asked for seat in the leaking boat of national education when other crafts were available. I know I offered to join the Jamia Millia on an impulse and have never been able to explain my action even to myself. But I have always hated looking around for the better job, and the line of least resistance has led me to seek wholehearted satisfaction in the choice I had made.

I think I liked the Jamia Millia best because it demanded creditable performance in return for admittedly meagre compensation. Work under this condition did not carry with it any social status or moral prestige. On the contrary, we had to justify continuously the existence of the Jamia Millia, to remove suspicions, to withstand ridicule. And so service in the Jamia Millia meant really giving without question all that one could give and accepting without question whatever was doled out in return. There is a principle involved in this the ramifications of which I have been discovering for myself, and the more discoveries I have made the more confident I have become about its value. But please don't imagine that I am thinking of self-sacrifice, of dedicated service to great causes. I am not. I am talking at the ordinary level of human nature, the level of mere biological persons, undivided and indivisible into a higher and a lower self. For me the principle, know thyself, is not a call to be spiritual, to dive into the depths of the real and the unreal, but a straightforward matter of discovering my own nature, of finding out pragmatically what exercises my faculties to the utmost, what gives me the greatest amount of satisfaction over the greatest length of time. I have been engaged in finding this out. In this process I have not felt the need to ask others what should make me feel satisfied, and though I have admired persons, this admiration has not induced me to deny my own nature or to attempt what it is not in my nature to achieve.

The one-sided bargain which the Jamia Millia offered kept people away. We never had enough workers for a reasonable distribution of the total work, and so everyone had to try his hand at everything. I was no exception, and my failures made me sharply aware of my shortcomings. These failures, fortunately, were part of a long and continuing account. Being aware of them did not produce despondency or feeling of inferiority; it just corrected my perspective. The joy in doing what I could became keener and I saw, at the same time, that the shortcomings of others were as natural and inevitable as my own. But what has been most helpful to me personally is the habit of freely admitting my mistakes and of inviting others to do the same.

If you remember what I said at the beginning about the embarrassment I used to feel at not knowing for certain whether I was wanted or not wanted, you will understand my telling you now that my ideas have not solidified into a philosophy. Working in the Jamia Millia made me feel that I could live a full life even if, according to any reckoning, I was classified as unwanted. I can, therefore, be happy with my ideas even if they are, like me, classified as unwanted. I do not need to make a system out of them, or even to argue in their favour.

But is not this attitude, you may ask, individualistic, narrow and even unsocial in the larger sense? Perhaps it is. I have a right, however, to adopt all reasonable measures to maintain the status of a sane and normal person. I am afraid I would be charged with insanity or worse if I advocated openly the principle that we should all aim at the highest excellence in our work and accept without question any compensation offered in return. We all know that this is the operative principle in communism, and will have to be freely and sincerely believed in and practised by us if we hope to realise our own ideal of a democratic, cooperative and socialistic society. But who dare ask a citizen of our democratic state, not to put himself first, when he, his salary and his allowances are so much more important than anything else. It would be still worse for me, I might even render myself liable to prosecution if I attempted to publicise my view that all our communities and groups should think only of what they can give to each other of goodwill, opportunity, security and trust and ask for nothing in return. I know that there are innumerable persons who as persons have all the goodwill towards other persons that one could ask for. But generous instincts have to be set aside in public affairs, set aside, that is, where they really matter. There they are condemned as expressions of foolishness or treachery. So I would much rather keep to myself the habits of thought that I have acquired in a lifetime, and regard them as unwanted but not conceal them deliberately. I realise, of course, the supreme significance of basic moral and social principles. We cannot have a just social order without a concept of justice. But statements of lofty principles and definitions of ideals are not enough. You would agree with me that they are rather like light thrown into the eye than the light of the eye itself; they do not improve the vision or illumine the mind. So why not have your own private light, not so bright as to hurt the eye, but bright enough to gather a few people around and create the feeling that all is not strange or dark. Why not imagine a country with glimmering land scapes of such lights, each encircled by people with thoughtful faces and hearts at peace?

2

My Schooldays

The first school I went to was the Loreto Convent at Lucknow. Schools of that kind are now even more popular, perhaps, than in my time, and for the good reason that they are serious about the fulfilment of their functions. But if we assume that there is an Indian way of life, a distinctive culture which each generation believes it should transmit to its successor, the inconsistency of an Indian Muslim boy being sent for education to a Roman Catholic school is obvious. It was more obvious in my case because my father wanted me to be brought up as a good Muslim. So I learnt how to close my mind to alien influences, to learn English and other subjects from Christian teachers without becoming favourably disposed towards Christianity. But my real teacher in those days was an illiterate villager, Ramzan, whom I called Nan for short, whose business it was to take me to school and escort me back. It was on my way to school and back that I learnt what I still cherish. Ramzan had an incredibly wide range of interests—growing vegetables, training dogs, making ornamental walking-sticks with his knife, fishing, hunting, watching out for parasitic growth on fruit trees, searching for edible wild fruit, chasing monkeys and jackals, killing snakes. He had a ear that caught the sound of every bird and understood its meaning, a love of dogs which enabled him to follow every movement of their minds. Nothing could repress his passion for open air life, not even the anger of my parents or the sarcastic remarks of his fellow-servants. His pet dog saved my mother's life, and he himself was such a successful snake hunter that, living on the wild outskirts of the

---

From *Education and Traditional Values.*

city as we did, we could not but feel indebted to him for preserving us against snake-bites. Ramzan, however, transgressed too flagrantly in following his own inclinations, and I was his only admirer. I only watched him doing things, still I feel that but for him I would have had no interest in making things with my hands, birds and animals would have meant nothing to me, and I would have passed by the most graceful tree without giving it a look. I would also have had no idea of the free life, for Ramzan is the only person I have known who could do only what he liked, and he had a passion for doing a large number of things.

My other teacher was Robert Talbot Dalby, Principal of the Cambridge Preparatory School, Dehra Dun. The school was an enterprise of three or four Muslims who could not raise funds but were desperately anxious to do something to provide education in English style for the sons of well-to-do Muslims, mainly landlords and lawyers. Their ideas of education were not only vague; they were silly. The school lasted as long as it did only because Dalby was able to carry the whole burden of teaching on his shoulders. He taught us English, Latin, Mathematics, Physical Geography and the Bible. He had a fine library of his own, and it seemed to me that he possessed all the knowledge a man could possibly acquire. I was not his best student, except perhaps in Latin, and sometimes he got so annoyed with me for my negligence or unpleasing behaviour that he would not talk to me or turn his face away if he did, but from the beginning I was filled with the aspiration to be like him and he could not have helped noticing it. He was a theosophist and I became interested in theosophy. I read the *Bhagwadgita*, several books of Annie Besant and other theosophists because of him, and devoted special attention to Latin, a subject in which he was particularly interested but which none of the other students liked. He felt elated if I did my homework well or answered questions correctly in the class. He forced me to take what is called Higher Mathematics in the Senior Cambridge syllabus, though even elementary arithmetic was something beyond my capacity, purely for the reason, I think, that he felt that a man should be equal to any task. He never said so, as far as I can remember, but his conviction must have been transmitted to me in some intangible form. I have failed in many things—mathematics, music, business, short-story and play-writing, administration, gardening—but I owe it to my teacher that I have always wanted to try.

In my home life, what left a real impression on me was a type of discipline which my father imposed. The occasion for imparting this discipline was breakfast time. All the children living in the house had to be present at this meal, or their absence had to be explained. We had to talk, to talk refined Urdu, and each of us had to make his or her individual contribution to the conversation interesting enough to evoke some form of appreciation from father, on whose face our eyes were continuously focused. If anyone used a wrong word or idiom, the others were asked in turn to give the correct word. We laughed at each other's attempts, but it was a serious matter if none succeeded, because then mother would be accused of having spoilt our speech by always talking in her '*purbi*' dialect. When she was no more there to take the blame, the reproach of being indifferent to language had to be borne by all of us together. Circumstances have changed, of course, but the fear of laughter or reproach is still there, and I feel that the use of the appropriate word is a moral command.

My sisters were privileged persons. Father was very fond of them and made it quite obvious. He did not deprive his sons of anything due to them under Muslim personal law or custom or social practice, but we saw that his daughters were more a part of his life than his sons. There were two stories of my childhood which father was never tired of repeating. One evening, while driving home from the city I asked the coachman to stop, and when father asked me why, I said I wanted to buy some sweets for Sabira—my younger sister—who had not been able to come with us. This was an outburst of affection for which I got full credit. But I could also be resentful. Once father was teasing me with remarks about daughters being better than sons and I countered by asking, 'What about the daughters of King Lear?' He was highly amused and I, of course, felt ashamed at what I had said. Later in life my attitude has been somewhere between these two extremes. But it is because of father that I cannot even now understand why a father should not be closer in spirit to his daughters than to his sons, and it is because of him that I think men must want to give women more than their just share of everything. I have found that all talk of 'reverence' for womanhood is due to hypocrisy or anaemia. I have no such reverence, but only a full and frank acceptance of my father's attitude and its implications for his sons, and, in principle, for all sons. A sister has no right to ask for more than her due, but he is no brother and no man either who does not want and does not try, at least sometimes with success, to give her more than her due.

It used to be the talk of the family that father was quite unnecessarily interested in other people. It was said that he had gone out of his way to help lawyers in mofussil towns to come and establish themselves at Lucknow and look! Were they showing any gratitude now? They were behaving like big people, making money, showing off, regarding the man who made their careers as someone not half as clever as they! This was true. But father could not help giving talent any support it needed and being happy at the success of anyone who had ever come into contact with him. Family and community had nothing to do with it. It was sheer goodwill towards all who honestly worked for success, and he valued this success more highly than his own. I have not been in the same position so far as helping others is concerned, and I have no right to look around for expressions of gratitude. But I owe to my father the interest I have in the happiness of other people and the gratification I feel for any success that they achieve.

3

Right and Wrong in Education

I have been pleading with all and sundry to accept my statement, made in all honesty and sincerity and without any sense of false modesty, that I cannot speak with any authority on education. I have not studied the subject, I have felt I was a very poor teacher. And on me my fate and my friends have chosen to confer the singular honour of delivering the Foundation Day address of the Central Institute of Education. There is an inexplicable quality in the circumstances that has beaten me completely. I am not only honoured; I am overwhelmed.

The Central Institute of Education is celebrating its tenth anniversary. Its record is magnificent, almost incredible. Government institutions, once the enthusiasm that led to their establishment is diverted elsewhere, survive without effort, but have all the dilatoriness of government machinery, all the lofty indifference of successors to great enterprises and achievements turned against them. The Central Institute has defied all precedent. Indeed, to me it has never looked like a government institution, its Principals and teachers have been so ardent, so full of the feeling of personal responsibility, so determined to succeed. I remember my first visit to the Institute, when it was housed in a building not much larger and far less impressive than its bus. I remember seeing the present building go up, and the look of the traveller-in-the-waiting-room on Dr. Basu's face. You can see from Dr. Pires' Report that the present building must be already too small. The Institute is more active than a beehive, overflowing with honey gathered from all the flowers of the meadows and the gardens of education.

From *Education and Traditional Values.*

Its pupils have already carried to different parts of the country the habits they learnt here. This beehive is producing other beehives, and transmitting to them its sense of urgency, its energy, its virtue of planned, persistent activity. Within ten years the Institute has not only grown, it has become an example of rapid and healthy growth. I shall not repeat here all that Dr. Pires has said about the scope of the Institute's work. But I am confident, as all who know Dr. Pires and his colleagues would be, that the Institute can carry its present burden and much more with ease and grace.

This Institute has succeeded so well, it represents trends whose forward pull is so great that slow-moving minds like mine, which assume dangers and difficulties and a certain ratio between the possible and the impossible are disturbed by an uncanny feeling of having left the stars behind. Once upon a time men set their courses by these stars. Sometimes they lost their way, and even the quickest and surest took time to reach their destination. Now we seem to have laws of space and time operating in the world of education that make it possible to arrive before being quite ready to start. We seem to have an entirely novel way of looking at things, to have changed our values without being aware of it ourselves. I have confessed already that I am not entitled to speak on education. My subject is history, which further hinders my understanding of educational problems. In a place, and on an occasion like this, I should have exercised my right to remain silent. But it is also in a place like this, where knowledge and competence and earnestness have produced an amazingly rich harvest that one can express doubts without fear of shaking the convictions of others and imagine how things might have been somewhat different without being held to have disparaged achievement or damaged illusions. It is in the hall of knowledge that it is most appropriate to inquire into the nature of knowledge.

One reason why I feel diffident in talking about education is that I do not understand its current language. It does, indeed, bear some resemblance to a language I have learnt, but every now and then, in an otherwise intelligible context, I find ensconced a term my eyes and ears are not used to. The dictionary does hot help me, being, after all, only an English dictionary. I have to seek illumination from my friends. They smile and explain. I am resentful. I feel that language has taken a short-cut to avoid and circumvent, even to obviate thought. I fear that the habit of taking these short-cuts will make a mystery of even the elementary facts of education. We may not have Pandits reciting *mantras*. We may have something very much worse—the whole of our life, our future, our humanity reduced to formulas used automatically by those who apply them frightening the intelligence of those on whom they are applied. The educational expert might soon become something like the medical expert, diagnosing, prescribing, observing and repeating this process till the educational objective is attained. The disastrous feature of this will be that the educational expert will not treat the diseased but only those in reasonably sound health.

My study of history reminds me of parallel situations, when living ideas were reduced to concepts and concepts to technical terms, and these terms made into goods of intellectual traffic. When these goods were examined, they were found to be camouflaged emptiness. Are we not today filling our minds with things history will one day disown and philosophy brush aside? And are we not, till this reckoning has taken place, denying ourselves the pleasures and rewards of contemplation, of discovery, of intellectual fulfilment by contenting ourselves with terminology. We may say that contemplation, discovery, fulfilment are the privilege of a few, the many must depend on what language can convey. But must the many be induced to borrow even the little they could themselves have earned? Must we add to their shortcomings the sterility of a make-believe knowledge?

The borrowing of terminology becomes a more serious issue if we see it in its historical and sociological context. We are involved in an almost worldwide movement to rationalise education. We not only produce for profit as well as need, we have fallen so completely under the spell of the bourgeois capitalist mind that in organisation, in methods, in aims we are disposed to adopt, almost for its own sake, the rational in place of the traditional, the inorganic in place of the organic. Education has become a process of transmission and reception, and the more smooth-working the machinery, the more satisfactory the results. Consider the rich variety of methods, the ever-improving techniques, the abundance of aids, grouped under the hideous word audio-visual, and it will be apparent that the tendency to mechanise education cannot be stopped. It is so convenient if education is a measurable quantity? We can prepare questionnaires that will convince us that even its quality is measurable. We are sure of things. We have proofs. We have at one end society, which is considered a knowable factor and which statistics are rapidly converting into a known factor. We have at the other end the individual, whom we analyse so constantly and so carefully at all ages and under all circumstances and collect and sort and file our findings so scentifically that there seems to be nothing more obvious and determinable than human nature. Then we coordinate the two factors, society and the individual, through education. Our difficulty is lack of statistics or of the availability of mechanical means, and of course of the financial means required for the continuation of research and the enlargement of its scope. It does not occur to us that all our assumptions may be only relatively true, and the little difference between truth and error may make all the difference in education.

But perhaps I am wrong in saying that we do not realise that our assumptions might be only relatively true. We do realise it. But we have no longer the freedom of choice. The bourgeois capitalist mind is a matter of history now. Applied science and technology, the creations of this mind, have become a force we can neither resist nor think of resisting. We talk of technological impact, of social change, as we would of a thundering procession of wheeled vehicles, and of almost mechanical hands steering these vehicles. It needs not only courage, but an utterly unattainable stupidity to believe, and act and think as if we were free agents, able to resist the fascination of the latest mechanical appliance and its accompanying methods, to question the value of the research which led to its inventions, and to the further research that its adoption involves. Truth was long ago declared to be relative; applied science and technology do not need philosophical stilts and supports. They have become so powerful that they can do without a discussion of values. We have to accept the assumptions they require us to accept. We have to do what they require us to do.

We have to assume that society is a known factor because any other hypothesis would hamper the operation of economic and technological forces and the intellectual system they have built up. We have to assume that the individual is a knowable factor, because otherwise he does not fit into his environment. He may become a rebel, and the destructiveness of man's rebellious spirit is incalculable. It can even destroy other destructive forces, such as economies that prevent man's spiritual growth, and bombs that endanger his survival. Education must, therefore, be as precise as possible. We must have methods so sure and measurements so accurate that education will fit a man in society as nicely as a manufactured part fits into a machine.

I cannot resist this logic. But I am sure the Central Institute can. I shall be accused of confusing history and political philosophy with existing reality if I say that society is a concept, not a physical fact; that while we must be willing to drink hemlock because of our ideal of society, we must become gadflies, if necessary, to the men among whom we actually live and move. But the Central Institute could raise the question as to whether Indian society today, meaning the actually living and thinking people, can serve as a standard for purposes of education. It would have means of showing, in a way that would accord with the prevailing methods of psychology and sociology, that there are fundamental doubts and uncertainties which must be removed, patterns of living, shattered by accident or decayed through neglect, which must be rebuilt before the Indian educator can say with any confidence that he is clear about the purposes of education. The Central Institute could advise against all glib talk about cooperation between school and community by showing how today the one tends to drag the other down. It could claim that the task of the school is to guide the community, and it should, if necessary, assert its independence. What applies to school and community applies also to education and society. It is for the Central Institute to declare that it will not allow society to dictate what standards education should accept, that it will freely exercise the right to reject. Between acceptance and rejection is the determination of what should be emphasised, and to what extent. It is not only to persons and societies living today, and not only to current educational philosophy and practice that the Institute should look for guidance in the ordering of values. Its field is all history, all philosophy, all art and, I do not hesitate to say even in this technological age, all religion. It should reach out beyond true statements to assertion of truth, beyond books and teaching to categorical imperatives.

But is all this possible for a college of teachers' education? Would it not be accused of producing preachers instead of teachers, men attempting to perform a social and spiritual function inconsistent with their vocation, and sacrificing formal education to social reform? I admit there are grave dangers here, and I would not have suggested the possibility of change if I had not felt that our present attitude to education is leading to disaster. The teacher cannot be disinterested, indifferent, neutral. His enthusiasm for particular means and methods can only lead into a blind alley if he is incompetent to look beyond his allotted task, beyond formal education, beyond the school and beyond society. He must have something that makes him bigger than his surroundings, something that cannot be imprisoned within routine tasks and conditions of service, something that makes him feel that he is not an employee only but also a free agent, that he has not only duties to others but also to himself.

In other words, before we can have the teacher we want, we must have a different concept of society and a different concept of the individual. Education must not accept without serious qualification the view that society is the environment to which the individual must adapt himself. On the other hand, while measuring individual aptitudes, it must insist that such measurement has a purpose as limited as the calculation of normal food consumption for the organisation of a kitchen. Measurement of aptitudes should have about as much to do with the idea of personality as the amount of food consumed by a person has to do with his endurance, his physical and moral courage, his creative power. We cannot take man's measure, even for the purposes of school education, unless we look beyond the measurable to the immeasurable.

I have not heard anything more depressing in all the wise talk about education than observations on personality. I know, personality is derived from person, and everybody is a person. But I have felt that 'personality', as we use it now is only another word for the individual, for the machine-part to be fitted into a machine, for the unit to be absorbed into the mass. Sometimes my imagination paints an even darker picture. We glorify the individual as 'personality' only to induce him to accept his fate; we wrap the body in a shroud, to give an appearance of decency to the burial. I am sure our world is not yet quite as gloomy as all that. But I am afraid there is little to convince me that we are not, in our education, anticipating by quite a century what might happen if we have in India a society conforming in every detail to the technological societies of today. Before we have appreciated the moral implications of the decision, we have begun to think in terms of masses, we are already training the young to fly from their selves, from all those values which foster the moral independence of the individual, from all that acts as a normative force in society. Where tradition gave the command, 'Know thyself', we create the fear that the external world is the only subject of study. All our knowledge is born of this fear, is nourished by this fear and lives in this fear. We impress the external world so deeply on the mind that the world within the growing individual, if it does not fade out of experience and existence, is reduced to a wilderness where the spirit feels lonely and haunted, in a country where man found the fullness of life in the solitude of his spirit, we educate as if everything not visible and tangible and conducive to the acceptance of a prescribed harmony of social relationships and a higher standard of living was tainted with decay and death.

Of course, I have nothing to say if it is argued that what was supposed to be the self within a man died years ago and it was not considered important enough to deserve an obituary notice. But can educators seriously take up that position in this country, with all its Parsees, Christians, Sikhs, Muslims, Hindus, believing, praying, hoping? Where can education begin, where can it lead, if we ignore this belief, this prayer, this hope? As citizens of a secular state we are enjoined not to vitiate and deform our citizenship through intolerance, prejudice, discrimination. We are enjoined by implication to learn to understand religious values as human values, to generalise particular interpretations of truth. Has the Central Institute of Education no function in this context? Should it not take the lead in the search for meaning, should it not consider the process of education to consist in the attempt to combine and harmonise the objective mind with the ever-unfolding, seeking, subjective spirit? God said, Let there be Light, and there was Light. We say, Let there be Research and there is Research. But must we keep Light and Research apart, merely because Light was created by God? Must we insist that research should add to knowledge, but not to wisdom, that it should be a search for truth, but should not have a moral intent?

I am not suggesting a revision of aims, but only an addition to them. The immediate addition could be a study, of personality, of those qualities in his inner struggle and growth which make man into a moral being. Applied psychology is far from enough. It is a corrective to what may be called speculative psychology, but cannot replace it, Man cannot be understood by being reduced to the smallest measure when he is already writ so large in history, in art, in religion. We may kill him but we cannot comprehend him if we cut down his personality to physical urges and physical needs. It will not be a romantic assignment but a sober performance of its function if the Central Institute devotes its experience, its desire for precision, its objectivity to a study of the processes of self-knowledge, of revelation and self-realisation, of the wider functions of the imagination, of the creative powers of the spirit. Such a study may or may not produce books on educational philosophy. It will have served its purpose if teachers graduating from the Institute carry with them a conception of the dignity of the individual, of the need to search within themselves for the mainsprings of the wisdom that makes suffering and sorrow a source of strength, of the love out of which, if it is great enough, is born a new man.

4

Textbooks: New Ideals and Responsibilities

One way to a better and friendlier world is the reform of textbooks which have in every country tended to reflect cultural attitude and political policy. But when an internationally representative group, animated by the greatest goodwill, sits down to discuss the problem of improving textbooks, the enterprise does not appear any easier than that of peace or disarmament. After the conclusion of the last war, as German education rose out of the ruins, Germany undertook a vast programme of textbook revision. But the task could not be accomplished by Germany alone; all the countries with which Germany had, or was likely to have, economic, political and cultural relations had to be satisfied that the German textbook not only reflected goodwill but also contained adequate knowledge about them. In 1954, Unesco adopted India's proposal to take up the mutual appreciation of Eastern and Western cultures as a project, and once taken up, the project inevitably became one of Unesco's major activities. That the realisation of this project depends largely, and for the growing generation almost entirely, on the production of textbooks and supplementary reading material inspired by the same aims as the project is too evident to require proof. Unesco, therefore, became closely interested in the improvement of textbooks, and began to encourage and sponsor meetings of international groups, hoping that every such meeting would yield good if not precisely definable results. The improved textbook is still in the making; no one can say how long its period of incubation is going to be. Pitfalls, barricades, stretches of mind terrain appear all of a sudden, a teacher who asks for more and better maps finds that he is in reality trying to involve publishers

---

From *Education and Traditional Values.*

in political conflicts, a book on Geography which states that Germany has been divided into three parts is cited as an example of capitalist war-mongering. The discreet reply to some questions with a diplomatic smile; those who wish to be both enthusiastic and safe reserve all the adjectives that can serve as safety valves for the particular system of textbook production operating in their own country and for the ineffectiveness of their National Commissions for Cooperation with Unesco. A French-man whom I have met at two international conferences habitually describes with scathing sarcasm the obscurity of Unesco in his city of Paris.

Much can be done, however, to improve the textbook without creating diplomatic and ideological complications. At the first conference for the improvement of textbooks, held in Paris in 1956, several countries submitted surprisingly frank appraisals of their history and world history textbooks, and it appeared that the most common defect was inadequacy of information in the West about the East and in the East about the West. No one, of course, could, make any commitment about the amount of information that could be included in textbooks; but it was said that even brief references could be very misleading, or form wrong attitudes unless the textbook writer possessed enough knowledge to form sound judgements or was provided with formed judgements about the country he was writing of by scholars of that country. There was a demand for a synopsis of world history in which the space to be allotted to the various civilisations was more justly apportioned; as the Indian member of the conference was asked to suggest significant topics on Indian history along with examples of how they should be treated. A German member of the same conference told me that he had asked for an Indian historian or a committee of historians to provide basic information about India which could be incorporated in German textbooks. His request went unheeded, with the result that an Indian with an undefined position in the Unesco Secretariat and without any standing as a scholar attended the seminar or conference that had been organised and provided the basic information about India. He was grossly ignorant of Indian Muslim history, and I had, much later, to submit a separate note which is now being utilised by textbook writers in Germany.

Most of the substantial improvement effected so far has been due to bilateral conferences of scholars for reviewing and amending textbooks. Germany has organised several such conferences, and now German and French parents, for instance, feel that the history their children learn, while providing full knowledge about their countries, will not incline them to continue the hostility from which their countries have suffered. India and Pakistan could follow the same policy and circumvent tendencies to foment discord and conflict in the minds of their growing generations. But sometimes improvements have been made without consultation also. I have seen a French book on world history in which several chapters had been devoted to Islam and the Muslims, but among the illustrations was a picture of the Prophet Muhammad. The picture was not the original contribution of the French publishers; it had been taken from an illuminated Persian manuscript. But since every visual representation of the Prophet is forbidden, one may be certain that every believing Muslim will object, and might even tear off the page, What was sincerely intended to promote knowledge and understanding could thus, because of the ignorance of Muslim susceptibilities, create suspicion, if not hostility. To understand and appreciate each other, we must, know that there are unreasonable limits to our reasonableness.

The conference at Paris in 1956 was followed by a second one at Tokyo in 1958, a third at Wellington, New Zealand, in 1960, and the fourth at Goslar. Each conference seems to have been treated independently by the bodies which nominated the representatives, and there has not been sufficient continuity. Each conference has, therefore, had to devote to introductions and to study of temperaments time which could have been more usefully devoted to carrying the work one stage further. But there has been progress. The conferences at Tokyo and Wellington could recognise as an existing fact the reviewing in one country of textbooks prepared by another and sent for review; they, therefore, laid down criteria for the assessment of textbooks, so that all reviewers could follow one standard. They could also discuss in an uninhibited way the value of the systems established in different countries for the preparation, approval and utilisation of textbooks and supplementary reading material and recommend the setting up of national and regional centres for textbook research. This recommendation has been implemented by Unesco and some member states, the greatest need being the chief factor in determining what specific activities a regional or national centre should devote itself to. The conference at Goslar was attended by representatives of publishers from Germany, Sweden, Denmark and Great Britain and the liaison officer between the largest teacher organisation and the educational publishers of the United States.

It is still not easy to keep a conference which is international in theory genuinely international in practice. The like-minded gravitate towards each other, two groups are formed and the discussion inevitably becomes political. The law of ideological gravitation offers a unique chance to those countries which know the minds of other countries (though not their own) to safeguard the rights of relevance objectivity. This chance could be considerably reduced if the Soviet representative arrived in time. But at the Paris conference was late by about four days, so that it was possible to elect the president and the vice-presidents and treat the Russian as an honoured guest rather than an active member. He was allowed to make his set speech on the universalism of Soviet culture and the perfection of Russian textbooks; but unfortunately he had brought a series of textbooks on world history along with him, and this provided a delegate who was mischievously inclined the opportunity to put some embarrassing questions. At the Goslar conference this year the Russian delegate arrived late; he came also as the guest of the German National Commission. But it was known that he had attended the conference at Tokyo and would not miss any opportunity for raising objections; a neutral had, therefore, to be appointed president, and a Czech to be one of the vice-presidents. No secret was made of the reason why a neutral had to be appointed, and since I was the unfortunate neutral in this case, I had to keep my fingers on the pulse of likely patients to forestall the need for sedatives. Happily, most of the delegates turned out to be like-minded, and the Russian delegate seemed to have only a watching brief. The need for sedatives did not arise.

The recommendations of the Goslar conference are very comprehensive; they even include three lists of suggested topics of world history, one for the benefit of Western textbook writers who wish to know what the eastern half of the world considers most significant in its cultural and political record, the second for similar enlightenment of eastern textbook writers, and a third, meant to assist all who write on world history by specifying movements and events which were spheres and occasions of contact between East and West. In fact, the recommendations of the conference were so many and so diverse that they had to be grouped under separate heads: recommendations to Unesco, to the National Commissions, to National Governments. to Educational Publishers, to Teacher Organisations and to all those interested in the improvement of textbooks.

The recommendations to Unesco express the dissatisfaction which all the delegates felt at the absence of adequate information in regard to what had been done towards the implementation of the East West Major Project by the member states, the improvement of textbooks by the member states and the discovery of the educational agencies in the various member states which were in the best position to further the Major Project at the class-room level. Unesco was asked to secure the support of teachers' organisations in publicising its activities and making known what services, existing and potential, it could offer to the ordinary teachers; to arrange, through the National Commissions, to put authors and publishers of one country in touch with those of another and, where necessary, to arrange for translation; to make available the results of scholarly study or discussion on difficult and controversial questions by historians of different countries and viewpoints; and to ensure that member states had the basic resources for implementing programmes under the Major Project by providing the necessary material and technical assistance. Two important recommendations were made in regard to policy. Improvement of textbooks was essential and indispensable, but as this could take place only slowly, Unesco was advised to recommend to member states the adoption of the following priorities: (1) background booklets for teachers, (2) supplementary reading material about different peoples, (3) more and better audio-visual materials, and (4) improved textbooks. As the agencies for producing the first three requirements could be different, the change in the order of priorities would not delay the improvement of textbooks, but rather prepare the ground for them. The other important policy recommendation was that member states should be advised to emphasise as much as possible the content of teacher training programmes for practising teachers, as it was obvious that a teacher who does not himself know enough cannot utilise material which is provided for him.

The conference realised that the National Commissions and the National Governments of the member states were the arbiters of the fate of all projects and ideas. It recommended—though here 'besought' or 'begged' would be more appropriate words—that the National Governments should see whether they were giving enough financial support to their National Commissions, and whether these Commissions had direct contacts with the official bodies which could help them in their work. Only National Governments, by adopting a policy of peace and goodwill, can induce the cultivation of sentiments which counteract self-centredness, and release education from the hold which narrow syllabuses, both of public examinations and in general school courses, sometimes still have in concentrating study on the nation, specially on its political and military history. National Governments were urged to take this bold step.

National Commissions were requested (1) to set up committees including representatives of publishers to organise the machinery for the improvement of textbooks, (2) to find out which bodies or agencies were best suited for promoting the Major Project, provide them with necessary information and examine from time to time how the recommendations in regard to this Project were being implemented, (3) to remove any dissatisfaction that exists regarding prescribed syllabuses, but always aim at influencing such syllabuses before they are published and textbooks printed in accordance with them, (4) to examine carefully their relationship with educational publishers and teachers' organisations in order to ensure close and continuous cooperation, (5) to try to coordinate the various interest groups working in the field of international understanding, and (6) to adapt, where necessary, Unesoc information material to the particular needs of their own country.

Among the general recommendations is one suggesting that university departments or institutes should provide courses for teachers and lecturers on subjects connected with the Major Project for mutual appreciation and understanding between East and West. Another recommendation is that teachers or boards of education should draw up lists of books, booklets, pamphlets, etc. which they consider suitable or good for reading—instead of lists of' undesirable reading material, as has sometimes been done. And, finally, it has been recommended that agencies for education should create an awareness of the different ways in which prejudices establish themselves in the mind and influence thought and conduct, so that misuse of the media of mass communication does not nullify efforts that are made to promote international understanding.

When the recommendations were being discussed, the Russian delegate reminded the Conference again and again that it was not an executive body and had no powers whatsoever; he even insisted that its recommendations should be called "suggestions". But none of the aims which brought the Conference together can be achieved through executive action. Only those persons and organisations who are willing to act on their own initiative can really help in the task of improving textbooks till they become a means of conveying knowledge and strengthening goodwill.

5

Education and Traditional Values

I must confess to a feeling of dissatisfaction at the title of this Symposium*—Education and Traditional Values. It implies a pre-judgement in regard to the nature of values; it implies that education can dispose of values, maintaining or discarding them as appears fit to those who determine the content of education, as if man's belief and conduct were entirely a matter of choice. There was, indeed, what might be called our traditional pattern of life. This was shattered by the political and economic changes that took place. But has our nature also undergone a similar revolution? Are our actions now determined by moral and psychological forces that did not exist before? Do we not throw doubt on the existence of the values themselves if we classify them as traditional and modern?

'Traditional' might be comprehended in a definition, but what does 'modern' mean? I remember a time when it meant arrogantly opposed to every habit, belief and practice that was not of British origin; dressing and behaving like a European; anxious to be regarded as eligible for English society; reluctant to buy and use anything not made in Great Britain or Germany; showing off knowledge of English and treating Indian languages with indifference or contempt. Now 'modern' seems to mean sophisticated; considering all values to be utterly relative; impatient of any tendency to insist upon accord between belief an practice; suffering from dizziness because of the stupendous technological development in the West; passionately desirous of reproducing in India all the ideas and educational practices of all countries that provide travel and maintenance grants; able to make eloquent

---

* Organised by the Ministry of Education in 1962,
From *Education and Traditional Values*

reference to the possibility of the annihilation of mankind through nuclear warfare. The use of the word 'modern' gives all our thinking a wrong direction. It confuses truth with the novelty or the general prevalence or the market value of ideas. Certainly it cannot be regarded as synonymous with 'wise', 'appropriate' or 'reasonable'. Let us freely use the word 'modern' with reference to time, as meaning our own days or the recent past, and scrupulously avoid it in all discussions of value.

The present system of education was gradually established in the nineteenth century and we are still suffering from the after-effects of the spirit and the manner in which the new replaced the old. It was like the young generation in a family turning an old relative, under whose guidance and care it had been brought up, out of the house with kicks and curses. Nothing in the old system appeared worth retaining because it was based on Sanskrit or Arabic and Persian, because it imparted knowledge the was extremely limited and out of date and insisted on the virtue of accepting the beliefs and practices that had remained almost unchanged for centuries. The knowledge which the new education provided was limited too, and because the knowledge came through the medium of a foreign tongue, there was hardly any question of Indians making material contributions to its advancement. The beliefs and practices, adherence to which was all-important according to the old system, were a mass of superstition, rituals and taboos. The new education fostered a feeling of intellectual superiority, the educated looked down upon the ignorant and superstitious, and thought it a blessing that they could do so. But there were obvious advantages in the Hindu continuing to call himself a Hindu and the Muslim a Muslim. Religion was gradually converted into what we now call communalism; and the impatient among us regard it as the cause of most of our tensions. The new education taught us to exploit religion without being religious, to be free thinkers without being thoughtful. It also transformed the loyalties which, in India, derived mainly from religion and were unconditional into formal and contractual relationships. It reduced life to a combination of colours which, no matter from which angle one looks at it, does no appear to be a picture.

Let me, before I proceed further, indicate my views about the character of the old system of education. It was not a system in our sense of the term. There were no schools and colleges and universities as we know them, no graduated courses of studies. But it was known which books should be studied, and in which order. These books were classics or commentaries on classics, and attention was concentrated on them. Their knowledge content was limited, but they were not merely books. They became powerful formative influences, moulding men into the patterns approved by society. The teacher, mainly because of personal contact with his pupils, also became a formative influence. Book, teacher and the environment together instilled into the young mind the fundamental importance of belief and of the achievement of excellence.

There is hardly anything to be said in justification of the beliefs themselves. But even if the insistence on things that were, according to our standards, patently erroneous or unjust, was almost fanatical, the underlying principle was a complete dedication of thought and action to what was believed to be true or beautiful. Let us try and visualise what this meant. Life was conceived as subject to unalterable laws; it was the duty of the individual to obey them. He had to regard his material, intellectual and spiritual resources as property held in trust, for which there would be a strict accounting. He had to cultivate an attitude of understanding and reverence, to grant to others the right to act according to their belief. Hindu and Muslim theologies were known to reject each other; this rejection was neutralised and converted into a means of looking beyond prevalent customs and habits to what was human and universal. As religion was not only a matter of doctrines but also of conduct, cultural forms acquired the force of religious injunctions, and the whole of life came to be governed by rules and precedents. Of course, the rules were disregarded by some people, as laws today also are, but the cultured man was he who abided by them. The difference between the old rules and modern laws is that while modern laws are essentially negative in character and concern themselves mainly with the prevention of wrong-doing, the old rules were positive prescriptions of doing the right thing. There were precedents for doing the right things, and doing them in the right way, an these precedents derived their validity from concepts that were both aesthetic and moral. It is true that they made relationships of all kinds and the routine of daily life into an elaborate ritual. They subjected the expression of opinion to a severe discipline; agreement and disagreement, love and hate, pleasure and pain could not urge intensity or necessity as an excuse for not appearing in the cultural form prescribed for them. But whoever the person and whatever the occasion, one had to aim at excellence. This ideal of excellence is reflected in the products of the period, in the textiles, the pottery, the jewellery; it is reflected in the literature; till abut fifty years ago, it could be observed in the speech and manners of the scions of old families. We gave up patronage of our arts and crafts, preferring products of western machines to the products of our culture. We have convinced ourselves that we have no time to be courteous and polite, that the writer does not need to bother about idiom if he thinks he has something to say, that refinement in behaviour can be subordinated to considerations of personal pleasure or profit. We regard the anarchy that has resulted from this attitude as a phenomenon of transition, which means that we are indifferent towards it and not anxious about what will follow.

But problems which have arisen in education are already warning us that the principle of *laissez-faire* cannot be applied any further. Committees on moral and religious education and on emotional and national integration are admissions of the need to take possible action.

The Roman Catholic Church is an example of institutional religion challenging and defeating tendencies subversive of belief. Communism has provided examples of indoctrination. But for obvious reasons these examples do not help us. Institutional religion, as we had it is India, cannot justify its claim to restoration, and revivalist movements have generally given evidence of narrowness and irrelevance to the real needs of the time. We have kept religion—but not communalism as far away as we could from our educational institutions. But now we have to ask ourselves whether organised, healthy life is possible without any commonly shared beliefs, whether the ideals embodied in our Constitution can be realised if we believe in them as tepidly as we believe in the value of truth and honesty, whether the socialist pattern of society can be established just through legislation and the rule of a particular political party. Of course, an optimistic reply can be given to any question, but even an optimist will have to give serious thought to the present situation if he does not wish to appear evasive or flippant.

A discussion of what education can do in respect of values associated with religion and ethics cannot be fruitful unless we recognise the significance of the greatest change that has taken place in our country—the establishment of an independent nation state, a state which is entitled to effective loyalty, competent service and that idealisation of civic duty which is essential for the cooperation of the citizens among themselves and of the citizens and the administration.

It will be obvious to anyone who is unwilling to be deceived by slogans and platitudes that we have as yet only a very vague conception of loyalty to the state. Political loyalty is not one of our traditional virtues. The Hindu and the Muslim states whose record constitutes our political history were governments by minorities in their own interest. This is true of governments all over the world till the discovery of democracy, and it cannot be said of all democracies even now that they are not governments of the majority by minorities which are able to prove that they represent the common and the genuine interest of the people. But in the Western democracies the sentiment of loyalty has become so deep-seated that in spite of differences of opinion the solidarity of the people is maintained. In India, unfortunately, that very system of education which should have created and fostered the sentiment of loyalty has been made a means of undermining it. The British Government, which introduced the new education, needed subordinate officers who knew English. The expansion of the administration and the relaxation of discriminatory rules and conventions in recruitment and promotion enabled Indians in the administrative services to push their way up.... But they were not responsible to the people and they could not become full members of the ruling class. From the beginning of the present century, loyalty gradually become a term of political abuse, because it meant attachment to the interests of a foreign power. The few years preceding 1947 during which it became apparent that India would become an independent, sovereign state were quite insufficient for the revolutionary change in attitude that was necessary. The swiftness of the change was not the only difficulty. The new education has brought with it a new interpretation of India into Hindus and Muslims and Sikhs and Christians in such a way as to rouse feelings of hatred, fear and vindictiveness, and effectively prevent the development of a loyalty which embraced the whole Indian people and not only one particular part.

The first task which education must accomplish if it is at all to reinterpret values and thereby justify itself is to establish by all means possible the belief in India being one country and Indian being one people. Unity and integration are words that are on everybody's lips, but a cross-examination of most of the people who talk of unity and integration will at best lead us to the conclusion that we are just keeping alive a very necessary illusion. If we are historical and realistic, we will understand that to mention a few persons like Ashoka and Akbar and a few incidents from the upheaval of 1857 is no proof of unity and integration. We have to realise that the intellectual and religious isolation of small and large communities, the conflicts of states and religions has been almost continuous. We can become united only if we create within ourselves individually and in consonance with our dispositions and our taste an overriding passion for a unity which can bear the moral burden of the wrongs we have committed and the mistakes we have made. This is the first step—the repentance from sin. We shall be aware of the nature of virtue only if our repentance is sincere.

The acceptance of this approach to unity will be a spiritual effort and can succeed only if it receives sustenance and power from the traditions of religiousness which are a part of our history. The state by declaring itself secular has thrown out a challenge to each and every citizen to show that he can enrich civic life by drawing inspiration from the institutional religion which he professes. Secularism is a challenge to education to give tangible form to the view—or hope, or dream—that all religions are fundamentally the same. The resources of the state cannot be utilised to teach religion; but they can be utilised to impress upon young minds the qualities of belief which make it indispensable in our life.

It would not have been necessary to mention religion, or belief amounting to what is understood by religion, so explicitly in this context if it were psychologically possible to provide a moral observation point apart from the affiliation or identification with the ethical teachings of particular religions. It is the gravity of historical associations that enables us to stand on our feet. Otherwise human beings float without any sense of direction from one hastily adopted view-point to another. If education can inculcate thoughtfulness an reverence and demonstrate the need to believe, it will have fulfilled the real objects of religious and moral instruction.

The second traditional value I have mentioned which it was the function of the old system of education to maintain was excellence, excellence in speech, in behaviour, in the cultivation and enrichment of personal relationships. We cannot restore the old not only because it has been destroyed, but because merely to seek revival of what once existed is a form of imitativeness and makes men into social anomalies. Our new concept of excellence must seek to derive inspiration from the beautiful wherever it is found, in the past or in the present, and to give the idea of the beautiful the necessary functional value.

If education undertakes the twin tasks of promoting thoughtfulness through search for personally satisfying and socially stimulative beliefs and of realising ideals of excellence in the performance of duty and in the creation and maintenance of relationships it will remain within its proper sphere of search, discovery and appraisal, but it will also enlarge its sphere to include essential features of life and conduct which it has so far ignored. It will not lose its value in terms of employment, and will contribute to the making of Indian citizens.

6

Culture

People who have everything else assume that they possess culture also, and people who have nothing else are proud of their sole possession—culture. The artist whose only topic of conversation is his own self, the writer who looks down upon world from his ground-floor window, the critic who vents his spleen on everybody and everything not up to his standard, the society lady looking for puppets—be they human beings or ideas—which she can play with, all claim to be creators of culture. In India today, culture means the fine arts and literature, and even more than these, the gatherings where they are talked about. People with no recognizable pattern of living, with no taste and no refinement belch out claims to being heirs to culture that has endured for thousands of years. The person who has impressed me most with her culture was a Hindu lady I met over twenty years ago. She was hunchbacked, with hardly any interests beyond her household work and her family. But everything she said and did seemed to me the expression of culture. It is true that, with my particular associations, I should take Hakim Ajmal Khan, Dr. Ansari and Dr. Zakir Husain as examples and proceed to a definition of culture. But such examples would, I fear, only increase my difficulties. Culture is not talent, however versatile it may be. It is not achievement, for too often culture is the price paid for achievement. We cannot isolate culture by any process of elimination, or give perceptible form to it by adding up the good qualities that appeal to us most. Culture seems to exist in its own right, independently of appearance, aptitude and the circumstances of living. It is either there or it is not there.

From *Education and Traditional Values.*

Does this mean that culture cannot be inherited or acquired? There are too many instances proving and disproving this statement for any conclusion to be drawn. But to say that culture cannot be communicated or acquired would be to deny the possibility of education in every sense of the term, and that would be frivolous. There is no human quality that is not acquired or inherited in some manner or in some sense. There would be no continuity in society and civilization without breeding and education. But the same breeding and the same education would not make a generation of people equally cultured. Culture seems to have the quality of an accident that may or may not occur.

How does this accident occur and what forms does it take? I believe we must put away most of our books on sociology and psychology and forget what we have learnt from them before we can answer these questions. Next to God—for those who believe in God—man is the least known and the least knowable. I am not thinking here of the mass-produced creatures crowded together in the big cities, who can be studied and analysed as if they were objects. I am thinking of those who have the will and the power to stand apart, if not alone, to watch the game of life even as they play it, who can judge themselves and others, and whom such judgements often lead to decisions. In other words, I am thinking of originals, not of copies of standardised products, whether they be the products of a technological civilisation surprised at itself or of a caste or other social system which has been dominant long enough to efface the individuality of all individuals. The accident of culture would occur least when here is stability without hope (or fear) of change or change without the desire for stability.

Stability implies belief in the permanence of certain moral and social values, the observance of certain imperatives. Change, in the context of culture, would mean recognition of the individual's right to select, order, harmonise accepted values, to give them an individual expression. Man cannot have culture if there are no values which he can reverence and preserve by giving them expression in his own personality, in his own life. He was culture when, because of heredity or education, he selects those values which his nature can best express, and succeeds in assimilating them to a degree that makes their expression spontaneous. Change in culture means novelty in the self-expression of those who, in assimilating existing values, also decide what should and what should not change.

If we do not confuse culture with accomplishment or talent, it will be clear that culture has really only one form, and that one form is given to it by faith. We have to distinguish, of course, between genuine, deep-rooted faith and fanaticism, dogmatism, addiction to custom, and prejudices engendered by the desire for self-preservation. Genuine faith has all the qualities of culture, and culture is living proof of the genuineness of faith. Its hallmark is a natural dignity, which is the product of self-confidence, and is the quality which strikes one first. The cultured man is free from fear, he is therefore free from all those psychological inhibitions which prevent us from showing regard for the welfare, wishes and interests of others. He has understanding, he has objectivity, and he never loses hope. His enjoyment of life lies in his way of looking after the world.

Can heredity and education bring about the happy accident of culture often enough for us to say that culture is possible? Serious people have maintained that culture and cultural values can be hereditary, and have looked to the aristocracy for both security and survival. Oswald Spengler, after his remarkable study of the rise and fall of civilisations, came to the conclusion that, so far as Germany was concerned, the hierarchical grading of society, with responsibilities increasing in proportion with status, was the only guarantee of survival. Most of us, almost unconsciously, associate culture with aristocratic birth and breeding. It is true that good family and wealth can contribute much to creating the kind of self-confidence which we find in all men of culture, but in any society the rot also begins with the aristocracy. As leaders of opinion, aristocrats take the lead in perversion of standards more often than they do in maintaining them. Education is almost ineffective by itself. As best, it can reinforce existing standards of conduct; it cannot create them or even raise them. For even if people are influenced by what they are told or what they read, they are affected far more deeply by the attitude of society towards moral and social values and the conduct of persons who are recognised as 'successful'. Education is organised by society for its own ends. It can only bring into relief patterns that exist; it cannot create patterns.

Whichever way we look at it, culture remains an accident. It is a form of what the Christians call 'grace' and the Muslims '*tawfiq*'.

But grace has degrees, and so, while none of us has grace bestowed in fullness, most of us, in some way or at some time receive enough of it to make a little difference in our life. It may not be given to anyone of us to be a type of the cultured person, but most of us are cultured in some way or at some times. And we can discuss what culture is, and perhaps understand what it means.

7

Conscience

God in His mercy has given us friends and neighbours endowed with an infinite capacity for gossip and with the sensitiveness that makes them so indignant at falsehood, hypocrisy, bad faith, selfishness, conceit, that we always know what is wrong with us. To some people, however, this earthly gossip does not appear to be enough of a directive principle or a deterrent. They believe that the angels in heaven are also engaged all the time in gossiping, eavesdropping, peeping through keyholes and gatecrashing at all intimate parties where two or more people are likely to enjoy themselves. Of course, you should not expect me to explain how angels can be in heaven and on the earth at the same time if the two are geographically apart, and if the two are not apart, why we so seldom have the feeling of heaven being in and around us. In fact, I would advise you to believe without thinking, because otherwise it might occur to you that God's omniscience does not need to be supplemented by the gossip of angels or His memory to be refreshed day in and day out and finally on the Day of Judgement by records kept by the angels, which are anyway purely subjective impressions. But even if you believe in God and the angels and have, for that reason, to keep your thoughts in leash, you would feel less constricted than those who believe that the process of recording our thoughts and actions is a part of the law of existence, and unless you get rid of existence itself, there is nothing you can do about this recording or its consequences. For instance, if you see a face so made up that it hurts your eyes or a form so scantily clad that your imagination feels like a skirt being blown up by the wind, you have just got to clench your teeth and assure yourself that nothing really

---

From *Education and Traditional Values.*

exists, otherwise, there is the risk that when the automatic record is played back, you might find yourself having to perform a belly-dance in some night club.

I know I am being flippant. You can put the case differently if you like. But what I mean is that with friends and neighbours, with angels and God's omniscience and omnipotence, with a law of cause and effect which cannot be evaded even by the lovely and the wise, we do not really need to have a watch-dog or an inquisitor or an internal auditor sitting right inside us, constantly reminding us of what we have done already when we want to do so much more. So it is quite natural that most of us allow things to happen because of us or to us, hoping that ultimately there will be such a mess that no one will want to clear it up. And we well able to say, with pride or stubbornness or indifference, that we have lived our life.

But it is also quite obvious that flippancy and cynicism and a happy-go-lucky attitude can only make good conversation or enable those gifted and persistent enough to produce readable novels or collections of essays. Anything but the truth is a make-believe, a subterfuge, and ultimately becomes tiresome and repellent. We cannot stop at being intellectual and sophisticated, epigrammatic and paradoxical. There is nothing here if there is nothing beyond. Let us not be cocksure and grim and forbidding when we talk of truth, or right and wrong. Let us not fall into the error of thinking that our conscience is conscience only if we inflict our virtuousness on other people. If we have to choose, let us prefer to be unassuming and say that truth and justice are so difficult to attain that all our efforts to realise them are ridiculously inadequate. Then we can be intellectual and laugh at ourselves without undermining our moral nature, and perhaps serve truth and justice in a way that might be indirect or roundabout but can be quite effective.

I wish this were the end of the matter, and I could tell you without fear of contradiction that man has a moral nature, and innate, ineradicable sense of right and wrong, that with knowledge and culture this sense can grow stronger and stronger, and that the aim and purpose of human existence is to make truth and justice objective realities. But no, I cannot say this. It would be unscientific, it would show that I am utterly ignorant of modern psychology, and of those experiments, which have established that there is nothing moral or immoral about man's nature, that what we call conscience is the individualised form of accumulated social experience. We are all creatures of our environment, ideas of right and wrong are like particles floating in this environment, and the amount we inhale and the manner in which we assimilate them is all purely accidental. This scientific approach has been reinforced by literature. There is hardly a novel, a play or a poem which critics will recommend you to read unless it contributes in some measure to the intensification of moral chaos. Life, according to generally approved literature, is an enormous abstract painting, and you would be taking just the wrong line if you tried to look for the intelligible in its pattern.

This scientific apocalypse make me hug my conscience, or my belief that I have a conscience. Imaging what I would be doing if I had abdicated my moral sense for the sake of a scientific approach. The conflict with China would not be a moral issue at all. I would be engrossed in analysing the minds and motives of those who think the national emergency a proper occasion for making themselves and their resources into national assets. I would dismiss as expressions of antiquated sentiment any idealisation of the widow's gift to the National Defence Fund of all that she had saved for her old age, and the dedication of the old and tottering Sikh warrior and his wife who came to offer as homage to the Prime Minister a long tradition of service in the Indian armed forces, kept alive today by their sons at the front. I would even have hesitated to mention the light I have seen in the eyes of my students, because in the thousands of years of human history this light has shone and been extinguished many times. I might have been more active if I had no conscience, but only a scientific approach, because science is based on observation and observation demands activity. But whatever I might have done would have been as barren, as immoral, I would even say, as my attitude.

Does this mean that the scientific spirit is to be excluded from political life, that there should be no impartial studies of polities and politicians, no exposure of mistakes and fallacies, no ridicule of marionette and pantomime shows improvised for the limelight? This and many questions of the same kind could be reasonably asked. But here I am really concerned with something else, and whether this is an answer to the many hypothetical questions and situations or not, I would say that the mainstay of genuine and enduring democracy is the conscience of the individual citizens, his sense of right and wrong, and the compulsion he feels to do the right. I have said this to myself in another context also. I believe I am not the only one who has felt during the past two months that our Government was thinking and wishing and legislating, but not giving orders, not requiring the regimentation now necessary to meet the known and unknown needs of the time. I realised, however, that I was thinking of government, not of democracy, and certainly not of a democracy which has thrown the whole responsibility for order and development and security on the people themselves. Such a democracy cannot deny its own nature because of an emergency, and if there is to be a swiftness of action, a tightening of controls, a regimentation, it must come as the demand of the people's own conscience, and find expression in their own individual and cooperative action. It will then be something significant, historic, and not merely a gearing of the machinery of government to a new situation. And so, along with some inevitable fretting due to bad nerves, those who thought like me and I have inhaled freedom and gained new vigour.

Conscience, being the moral sense of right and wrong, has been commonly associated with religion. But religion, like politics, can have its own interest. There are reasons of religion, as there are reasons of state; religion is no more absolutely subject to moral law than the state. Conscience stands above both, helping, guiding admonishing. This may sound like a heresy, and I suppose it is. But the heretic, though he may completely misrepresent himself by being aggressive, foolish and fanatical, stands out as the symbol of the human conscience, of the human mind demanding its freedom to express the moral laws in its own way in word and deed. For me, too, there is only one conscience. And it is my conscience that tells me not be too serious about myself. There are friends and neighbours around and gossiping angels in heaven.

8

When the World is Too Much with Us

A very long time ago I read what could be called an essay by Gorky on Man's Behaviour. When Alone. He relates among other stories how once, on a moonlit night, he was standing on a bridge. Hew saw a woman coming from the opposite side. All at once she stopped walking, looked around and, feeling sure she was alone, put out her tongue at the moon. Then she went on, as if she had done what she came for. On another occasion, Gorky saw Chekhov all along in a garden. It was a bright morning and Chekhov was trying to catch the sunlight in his hat and put it on his head. There were other examples also of the curious things people do when they imagine they are alone. This proves nothing. The woman who said, 'Sometimes I sits and thinks, sometimes I only sits' may have made a statement applicable to many besides herself, but that also proves nothing. Recently I told some of my colleagues that desire for company and conversation was a sign of weakness; one should aim at being self-sufficient and enjoy being alone. That was a rejoinder to their complaint that I did not meet them often enough. It does not represent a confirmed opinion. But the idea that a man can get away from the world and be all by himself has a long tradition behind it, a traditions of making a scapegoat of civilisation. I believe there is as little substance in this tradition as in the dream of a poetic fish to live on dry land.

It might seem prosaic, but I have found that the best way of arriving at the truth is to begin with elementary questions. After all, even the most fastidious interior decorator has to know the dimensions and the disposition of the rooms before he begins to exercise his imagination. He may, later, create what illusions he

---

From *Education and Traditional Values.*

likes, but he must have the basic facts to begin with. So we, too, must make elementary realities our starting point. That will give our adventure some sort of a direction, whether ultimately we end up floating on some flimsy cloud or slumping down exhausted because the mind fails to discover anything beyond the elementary reality which can stand the test of objective analysis.

The elementary reality, as I see it, consists of two factors—man's biological urge to live and perpetuate his kind, and the resources provided by nature which enable him to do so. Out of these man has created all the values of civilisation. But he has also felt exasperated because of the elusive quality and oppressive quantity of all that he has created, cities, workshops, smoke, noise, insatiable wants. He has developed the capacity to endure the consequences of his own ceaseless activity. He can work in factories and mines, he can move about unconcerned in petrol fumes, he can survive the merciless employment of instruments of destruction devised by himself; he can hold on to truth while propagating falsehood, and love in spite of becoming the embodiment of hate. We, today, like hundreds of generations before us, keep on adding to the expanse and intensifying the penetrative power of the world we live in. Some of us attempt, now and then, to take stock of the situation, most of us keep their noses to the grindstone. To satisfy our vanity, we distinguish between things we do because we must, such as earning our livelihood and performing our civic duties, and things we do because we want to do them, because they are a means of asserting our personal freedom, our right to have preferences. But, you will see, in either case we are doing something, and what is called the world may be even more with us when we are exercising the right to approve and reject, to make our independent contribution to the idea of the good life. One who is employed in an office or a factory lives, during his working hours, in a smaller world, a world with which he is basically less concerned than when he, in his moments of leisure, devotes himself to his hobby of collecting stamps or growing roses or reading poetry or being one with nature. All these inevitably enlarge his knowledge, his sensitiveness or his vision. The world, the same man-made world of smoke and noise and bustle, is not less with him because of his cultivating interests that take him beyond his surrounding. The idea that we can extricate ourselves from the world or even turn our backs on it, is a poetic fallacy. Even nature can be enjoyed only because of a sensibility which is one of the finer products of culture. Those who desire to be something by themselves and not just units of a mass, who realise that they cannot get away from the world but are determined none the less to exercise their right to accept and reject, to live by their own idea of culture and freedom can, I think, do so only if they suppress every tendency to make a bargain and, like Rousseau's citizen, surrender everything to the general will.

I remember I was once buying fruit from a vendor outside the Fatehpuri mosque. The vendor's small son was attending to me. I accepted all the prices he quoted. But before I had purchased anything, I heard the vendor shout at his son from behind, 'You rascal, don't you see the gentleman is not bargaining. Whey do you demand more than the real price?' And then I got the same fruit at much lower prices than I had agreed to pay. I would not say that all who do not bargain get things at the right price. What I would say, however, is that if you consider the prices as fixed, you know what you can afford to buy and what you cannot. Otherwise you get involved in measuring the intensity of your desire for a thing, the capacity of your purse, the honesty of the salesman, the time and energy required to go from shop to shop making a greedy search. I have never been forced to reflect on my own shortcomings because of the success of those whom I know to have made good bargains. But I wish philosophers and religious persons had not appropriated the concept of detachment and made it impossible for the unpretentious man to show that it is the commonsense way of looking at life and achieving happiness. I have experienced many forms and degrees of detachment that had nothing spiritual about them, and yet they were very effective. In fact, they enabled me to live in two worlds at the same time, one made by mankind and another equally human but entirely my own creation.

I have not made a secret of my basic disagreement with the poet who wanted us to realise that the world was too much with us. But I do look for variety and relief. I know what it means to return from the office and take up my woodwork. I have felt as keenly as anyone else the difference between drudgery and joyful occupation. But somehow I cannot identify peace with inactivity or accept the view that a man who is all alone with his feelings has got away from the world. Peace within should be a normal condition, not an accident or a target achieved according to some plan, and solitude should not take man away from the world, but only from one aspect of it to another. Civilisation is man's past and present, the expression of his being, not to be bargained with or, even for a moment, denied.

9

Secularism

The future of India seems to depend on secularism. We may be able to practise it without giving it a precise definition or define it to our satisfaction without being able to practise it. Whatever success we achieve in practice or definition, secularism will have fulfilled its main function by imposing on us the freedom to think. We are suffering from beliefs that are just sanctified habits, and secularism should help us to attain to belief that derives from personal intuition, thought and experience, and is strong enough to face the challenge of ever-changing circumstances. Our destiny will be moulded by the character of such faith.

It is already apparent that the organised institutional religions in India are not opposed to a secular state. Most of the dangers arise from the activities of the pessimists, the frustrated, the hypocritical, the highbrows, whose numbers are large though their strength is small and who nibble continuously at any solid intellectual food that can nourish the people.

The pessimist is of course always right. He knows of too many examples in history and contemporary life of the emptiness of dreams, the inevitable ultimate foundering of hopes, however many the storms, they may have weathered and however often they may have basked in the sunshine of fulfilment, The pessimist is as right as the man who says that the end of all life is death. We can agree with him cheerfully, for however we define secularism, we will not give it an eternal, changeless form. The frustrated are more dangerous than the pessimists. They do not discourse on the vanity of life, which is a healthy background for all concepts of progress, but on personal shortcomings and failures, on matters

---

From *Education and Traditional Values.*

of yesterday and today, on trains being late and clerks being slow, on the rich being greedy and the politicians being dishonest, on slogans being false and enthusiasms being faked. The pessimists do not want answers, the frustrated want too many; the pessimists can stand aloof, the frustrated are always looking for company and conversation. Secularism demands just that sturdy commonsense, that confidence in human nature which despises mental and moral anaemia too naturally and wholeheartedly to offer appropriate treatment. It is only the frustrated who have regard for their kind. They have soft and sighing ways of discovering each other, they mate and breed. As secularism gathers strength they dilate upon the invincible nature of its enemies, ignorance, superstition, conservatism, hypocrisy, the frivolousness of the 'moderns' and the snobbish frowns of the intellectuals. We must listen now and then to what they say, if we can do so without feeling frustrated and joining the wrong company.

Ignorance and secularism cannot, of course, go together. Because they cannot, we must think, as the frustrated want us to, of India's illiterate masses. The facts are distressing enough. While one process of multiplication is increasing the number of the literate, another, fatally swift, is increasing the number of those whom education fails to reach. But the masses do possess that commonsense which is the soul of secularism. There fanaticism and frenzy, wherever it becomes evident, is generally the result of their intimidation or indoctrination by the educated, not of their ignorance. For the propagation of secularism we must consider the educated as first needing our attention. Their maladies are must more complicated; and among the educated are those who teach as well as those who learn.

No knowledge or skill worth possessing can be acquired from a man without character, character being that peculiar grouping of qualities around a central theme which transforms persons into personalities. This central theme is always something to which a person dedicates himself. It may be as unexciting as punctuality or as lofty as self-realisation, but character is determined by the degree of dedication. Our education has ignored this, and knowledge has become a confusion of uncoordinated pieces of information, undisciplined desires, vague aims and vagabond thoughts. Such education, offered in schools and colleges that did not identify themselves with any traditional expression of spiritual and moral values, could not inculcate a spirit of dedication. Most of those who developed character, who became positive personalities, did so in spite of education. Very few of our teachers today have the type of character that imprints itself on the mind of the pupil because it attracts who are uninspiring because they are uninspired have taken refuge just behind those negations of which secularism can be all too easily believed to consist. It is non-religious, non-spiritual; in asserting the values of this world it has to negate the values of the next, in concentrating on man and his happiness it has to turn its back on the metaphysical and the divine. So the teacher who should inculcate secularism can assume that he has nothing to do except teach the rejection of certain things. He creates a void, and education is in many ways reduced to the cultivation of the illusion that intellectual activity and moral stability are possible within this void.

No wonder that hypocrites are found mainly and highbrows of course entirely among the educated. Some hypocrites talk after the manner of secularists but nurse ancient superstitions in their hearts and adhere to irrational rituals by giving them national status or anointing them with the fragrant oils of art and culture, others profess to be modern and defend superstition and ritual with all the weapons of secular knowledge. Eating meat and drinking whisky outside and being rigidly vegetarian and prohibitionist at home is a fairly common practice among the educated in north India; and such people generally know how the irrational elements of their religions, which they ostentatiously reject as moderns can be most easily and effectively preserved. I would not have believed that the services of *sadhus* could be utilised to popularise the Five-Year Plan if I had not myself been invited to a meeting where this proposal was to be discussed, and though the Five-Year Plan derived no benefit, the sadhus succeeded in infiltrating into high places. Astrology has established itself firmly in Uttar Pradesh and it is commonly known that Prime Minister Jawaharlal Nehru was chided by a Chief Minister for not paying heed to the warnings of astrologers about the imminent catastrophe. Celebration of Holi is a religious rite that has become a national obligation. There is, of course, a difference between hypocrisy and inconsistency, but in India they often appear to be animals of the same species and inhabit the same den.

Many would have been saved from inconsistency at least, but for the intellectual highbrows who cannot bear to hear any mention of religion. They have spread terror from the earliest days of English education. Long ago the poet Akbar of Allahabad wrote:

> Friends have reported to the police, so violent is their rage.
> That Akbar dares to mention God in this our modern age,

and belief has had the choice of living as a mouse in a hole, scampering away at the approach of every intellectual, or of turning political and criminal.

If secularism is intended to be an antidote to religion, there is grave danger of its being appropriated by the highbrow as a part of his make-up, of its becoming a fashion instead of a second nature, an aggravation instead of a solace. The *Oxford Dictionary* in an way condemns secularism by defining it as something fundamentally negative. Historically this definition is true; and its is necessary to remember this because for centuries organised religion and churches have exacted service of religious values for their own benefit. But it is no longer necessary for secularism to be militant. It can find a place for itself in the ordering of values without having to jostle and push; from being an adversary of religion it can become its helpmate and friend.

For ages people all over the world have suffered from the illusion that the flesh is the enemy of the spirit. Flesh and spirit are hackneyed terms, but the illusion is a chronic disease and does not deserve literary ornament. In India particularly, where piety is always imagined and portrayed in the nude, it is necessary to use a blunt weapon to dispose of the illusion which hypocrisy of the spirit as well as of the flesh has fostered for ages. The worldly have been forced to propitiate the spiritual with reverence and gifts; the spiritual have established their title to reverence and gifts by proving with unassailable logic that nothing could be attained without giving up the world. Between the obligatory humility of the worldly man and the cold logic of those who were wise enough not to be seduced by the world, the human personality was lost sight of. Man could not stand up on his two feet and look at destiny straight in the eyes, he could only fall on one side or the other, because he was made to believe that there was no such thing as balance. But now the West, by committing all the conceivable sins—

the most genial statement of which, however, I have found in India's Ghalib.

I have man's nature, I am born of man
And proud that I commit the sins I can —

has asserted man's right to postulate and discover the balance. In state policy, this is represented by secularism which, as we conceive it, does not imply negation or rejection of values associated with religion and the spirit, but only a limitation of the state's interest to what it can and should do as a state. I have seen people touching the feet of a minister; I have also been asked to wait till a minister finished his devotions at a time which I count among my working hours. But ministers are not policies or principles, and secularism is an assurance that ministerial idiosyncrasy or presumption will not extend to the vital question of what constitutes the real welfare of the citizen. It lays down that this welfare is physical and material, and measurable in terms of economic prosperity, health and happiness. The Indian citizen cannot be asked to choose between the goods of this world and the next. He must be given his due share here and now.

Secularism has been accepted by those concerned with their own institutional religion because it imposes an attitude and a policy of impartiality on the state. But that is the least reliable aspect of secularism. I suggested to a conference of Muslims, convened for the purpose of organising religious education, that secularism should be considered as a challenge to the religious to prove that they were interested in human welfare and not only in dogma, to make as large a contribution as possible to the moral development of the country by offering examples of how the true believer could rise above considerations of caste, creed, personal and even communal benefit. This interpretation is no doubt idealistic, but not much more than is necessary to put in the scales against vague fears and suspicions. And it was not unwelcome to the particular audience. But ultimately the policies of organisations representing institutional religion will be moulded by the reaction of those individuals who profess the various religions to all that is irrational and harmful, and it is here that the acceptance or rejection of secularism will prove most decisive.

It is a commonplace of political thinking and conversation to attribute all dissensions and conflicts to religion and religious organisations, and the slow change in attitudes to religiousness and superstition. The accusation is not unjustified. But the remedy does not lie in negation and rejection, in the creation of a void. Secularism must be inculcated wisely and patiently through positive concepts: the human being as the end product of evolution, the striving for physical and material welfare as the expression of true religiousness, personal fulfilment as the achievement of perfect harmony between material and spiritual values. Many of the superstitions which are proving hindrances to economic development are survivals of animism, and animism is the stage of belief in which man stood in terror of nature, and was willing to offer unquestioning reverence and worship to stones, trees and animals in the desperate hope that it would ensure his survival. Animistic superstitions will be cast off like worn garments as man becomes aware and proud of his dignity. To maintain this dignity he must cooperate with his fellowmen, and the only visible, tangible aim of such cooperation can be the material welfare of all. But man will be denying the fullness of his own nature if he sees nothing beyond the physical and material, for there *is* something beyond to which he himself bears witness in literature, art, scientific and philosophical speculation. Material welfare must be inspired with and governed by aesthetic, moral and spiritual ends. These should not be prescribed. No organisation, no institution, not even the state itself should possess authority to dictate what man should do in the privacy of his own being. Secularism asserts and guarantees the right to this privacy and ensures that nothing should stop the well-spring of man's action or divert the clear waters into barren lands.

10

Sufism in India

When one is dealing with people whose survival and influence depended on making the search for truth a solemn and exciting adventure of the spirit, one must begin by talking in their style, the style which offends commonsense and provokes the mind, so that one must sit up and listen. So I begin with the first paradox that occurs to me: If laws could not be broken, they would not have been made.

If human beings could live together in peace and happiness, respecting or at least making full allowances for each other's needs and desires, laws would not only be irrelevant; it would be an offence to think of making them. But human history begins with Cain murdering his brother Abel, and almost succeeding in concealing his crime. That may be only the Jewish version of beginning of history, and of why God made it a habit to meddle with human affairs, but it is symbolic of what must have happened, wherever and whenever human history had its beginning. And again, according to the Jewish version, which is most intimate and revealing, when God found His motives being persistently misunderstood and even His presence being ignored. He gave increasingly precise and emphatic expression to what He had in mind. Ultimately, He had to inscribe His laws on the hearts of the pious and on the tongues of the preachers. This is all symbolic, of course, but the fact is that when the first Muslim mystics, or sufis, as they are called, looked around at life and began their search for truth, they were appalled by the amount of law-making that had been, and was still being, perpetrated. People said, there must be, there is, law to cover every aspect, every minute detail of human

---

From *Islamic Influence on Indian Society.*

affairs; man must be yoked heart and soul to the law, for it is the law which represents truth, which ensures salvation. Knowing that man, wittingly, or unwittingly, is constantly guilty of transgression, God had, in His Mercy, enabled him to construct a system of law that was complete in all respects and would endure for all time.

But, the sufi asked, can this be absolutely true? Is it God's will that man should never rise above the level of thought and action fixed in the law-books? Was man to be guided in his relations with God by regal precedents and technicalities? Surely, God is not an angry and jealous autocrat, sitting eternally in judgement upon his won creatures. He is the God of Mercy and Solicitude, the Father who expects and exhorts His children to live up to the ideal He has set before them. His will cannot be confined within ass-loads of books. If He made laws, it must be His will that they should be broken, so that higher laws, which are closer to His will, might come into operation.

So we arrive at an entirely different interpretation of the paradox that laws would not have been made if they could not be broken. The paradox becomes a challenge. One must abhor the evil intentions that make laws and their enforcement necessary, one must despise the attitude which reduces man, in the words of a French writer, to a 'bourgeois compromise'. One must break laws so as to rise above them, to become one's own lawgiver, and look to God not for punishment and reward but for exalted guidance. This point of view loses its stimulating character unless it is expressed with a measure of extravagance. It was better to follow the example of Mansur Hallaj, to declare, 'I am the Truth', and suffer the consequences, than to preach and practise tranquility. But, of course, each sufi had his own disposition, his own way of breaking the law to demonstrate that the letter must be sacrificed to the spirit. Some broke the law in regard to the five daily prayers and thirty days of fast by praying and fasting most of their time, some by not praying and fasting at all. Ain al-Quzzat of Humadan declared that all worship performed as a matter of habit is idolatry; only that worship is real which releases the mind from the thralldom of habit. The sufis did not criticise and reject each other's view. They created instead the fiction that sufis were of two types, the sober and the intoxicated, that is, those who were careful because of the effect their words and actions might have on the generality of the Muslims and those who threw caution to the winds in a drunken ecstasy, and could not be called to account for anything they did or said. This makes it difficult to define sufism; it also makes the sufi infinitely more attractive.

Till about the middle of the eleventh century, there was no system of *shaikh* and *murid,* teacher and disciple. Those who believed in the higher life decided for themselves what they would do about it, and they sought each other out, travelling sometimes hundreds of miles, for comparing methods and experiences. Then many of them became sedentary, living in a *khanqah* or *tekieh* with their disciples and practising their particular form of spiritual discipline. But the number of those who did not accept the obligations of community life and a fixed routine was always large and influential in many inconsistent ways. And even when sufism came to be widely recognised as a system of life and thought, and books began to be written for study, the daring aphorism, the challenging paradox, remained the symbol of self-expression.

From about the eleventh century, poetry also became a medium for the sufi. Orthodox Muslim should, if they are strict enough, hold the same views about poets and poetry as Plato. But Jalaluddin Rumi went to the other extreme. The poet, he said is in part a prophet; only an ass would say that poetry is forbidden. Muslim culture has reconciled the two attitudes by regarding love, beloved, union, wine and song, Islam and *kufr,* Kaaba and temple, as symbols, and the poet who used these symbols strikingly enough was recognised as a mystic who desired to show the way to exaltation and ecstasy, to annihilation in God. So not only have collections of verses been attributed to almost every great sufi, but all the great poets have been given the status of sufis. Poetry can never be profane, if it is good poetry. In other words, aesthetics, if genuinely and successfully cultivated, becomes ethics and religion and spirituality.

Whatever other cultural offspring the marriage of sufism and poetry may have had, it generated in man a boldness which brought him into intimate converse with God. God was the judge who was sure to embrace the sinner brought before Him with a forgiving smile, the Friend and Beloved who placed a halter round the neck of His lover, and dragged him where He listed, the embodiment of all Beauty and Charm who nevertheless flashed angry looks around to wound most grievously those who adored Him most, the Omniscient and Omnipotent Being wearied by his labour, whom man could invite to come and rest in his bosom. One begins to wonder whether God made the poet or the poet created God. Either interpretation seems to be correct and neither seems to matter. What does seem to matter is the intensity of spiritual experience, the occurrence of the moment when man realises that he is the whole of existence.

11

Indo-Iranian Synthesis in Literature

I do not know when the first Iranian nightingale poured forth its passion for the rose in full-throated song. But this is an instance where time and circumstance do not matter; the nightingale and the rose have become poetic images which are an eternal symbol of the heart inspired to lyrical eloquence by the vision of beauty. All over the world there has been the ardour of love, and at all times beauty has had its moment of glory. Everywhere imagination has brought the two together, to make them timeless and to give life perhaps its only meaning. But I do not think there is, in any literature except the Persian, an image that is, to the same degree, daily bread and heavenly sustenance for the poet, and commonplace fact and exquisite novelty for the lover of literature. Persian poetry has other images also, as typical as the nightingale's adoration of the rose: cup, cup-bearer, wine, intoxication and, the source and origin of them all, the beloved. They can be ways of saying things; they can be the things themselves. But there is always an intensity about them that carries conviction and makes all questioning irrelevant.

Iran is not a land of birds and flowers. Except in some parts, the barren waste is a striking, sometimes an overpowering contrast, to the green of the pasture, the orchard and the field. The number of men who cherish the cup is not larger than elsewhere, and perhaps the number of those who can fill it full and drink it empty is smaller. The slender, silver-footed cup-bearer of Omar Khayyam, whom every poet has conceived in different forms and different moods, is perhaps entirely a poetic fiction. The place where lovers assemble to drink, where their thirst and longing evokes the fascinating

From *Education and Traditional Values.*

illusion of the cup-bearer, warm-hearted and generous, or gay and mischievous, clad in the garment of dazzling mystery, or just too humanly attractive, this place, called the *maikhana,* would in reality have been as ungainly as the English translation of its name, the wine-house. Why, then, has there been such a concentration of the poetic fancy on these things, why has the custom of drinking, common to almost all the peoples of the world, become so rich and meaningful an allegory, the fountainhead of a vast world of thought and feeling, of aesthetic achievement and spiritual endeavour?

One reason, not particularly Muslim or Iranian or Indian, is the inevitable reaction of human nature, in its search for balance and harmony, against the tediousness and legalistic stiffness of orthodoxy. The human spirit, when a new message has brought it deliverance, seeks freedom, space, opportunity. The creative force of a new idea drives it to establish new empires, worldly and spiritual. But when this initial force is spent, the need for consolidation is felt, the virtues of intellectual and social discipline are cultivated, and the best laws are made with the best intentions. The spiritual and worldly home thus created is them lived in, wisdom becomes an inheritance and not a personal acquisition, peace an security are not only desired but imposed, and punishment for any form of deviation, for any disposition of intellectual adventure, is considered necessary. This is the age of orthodoxy. It is the age also of repression and revolt, in which the human spirit attempts in different ways to shake off the fetter which its own logic has forged. It does not succeed always or entirely, but the form which its development takes, if it is not affected too much by political or social accidents, is mysticism. In Muslim history these four phases can be clearly distinguished. They can be distinguished in the history of other religions also. But, of course, we should not imagine that these developments in spiritual thought followed a precise pattern, or that the response to a new faith, the expansion and consolidation of its particular way of life, the establishment of its orthodoxy, the expression of its mysticism followed an evolutionary logic unaffected by the vagaries of human nature and earthly circumstances. The poetic religion of the *Rig Veda* leads to the expansion of the Aryans, the Aryan way of life is solidified in Brahmanic orthodoxy, which has to face the challenge of Upanishadic mysticism and a host of men adventuring into unknown lands of spiritual experience. From these Buddhism emerges as a creative force, with a momentum that takes its message far and wide across seas and mountains. Orthodoxy could not take a common Buddhist form in this vast expanse of territory. Buddhist orthodoxy was the orthodoxy of sects, but it was rigid enough to generate a reaction that took the form of a mystic adoration of the Buddha, of the sensuous images of Bharhut, Sanchi, Amaravati and Ajanta, and of the poetry of Ashvaghosha. Busddhism was brought dangerously close to Brahmanism by the development of its own religious thought, and by its mystic acceptance of all creations of human spirit, which meant acceptance of all the people's religions. We see then a revival that takes many forms, one of which is mystic devotion to a particular deity. This was about the time Islam found is way into India as the religion of Arab traders, of Arab warriors and, after a time, of Turkish conquerors.

There can be no doubt that these Turkish conquerors were the representatives of Muslim orthodoxy. If they had not succeeded, the orthodox might have sat in judgement upon them. But their success was spectacular; what was more, it provided for the Muslims of Khorasan and Iran, harassed by tribal migrations from Central Asia, both a spiritual consolation and a refuge. The orthodox did, indeed, occasionally admonish a king now and then. But the bread-winner had the last word. The Delhi Sultanate, the provincial dynasties, in spite of the irreligiousness of most of the rulers and their disregard of religious law for what appeared to them reasons of state, had the blessings of orthodoxy and the support of the vast majority of their Muslim subjects. But their orthodox state could not exist in a political and intellectual vacuum. It had to win the active support of its Hindu subjects. It must have succeeded in this, otherwise it would not have survived. But there have been, ever since Islam came to India, those for whom political success had no value, those who wished to erase, in as many forms as possible, the dividing line between communities and cultures. It was only in this way that they could establish an orthodoxy of spiritual values, a way of life that led people towards each other, in love and prayer and ecstasy. So they became the creators of a literary synthesis that was universal as an idea and is now an inspiring memory.

It was they who brought to India the story of the nightingale and the rose, the imagery of the cup, the cup bearer and the wine.

They were not only subtle and elusive enemies of orthodoxy, professing an adherence to the law more sincere and deep-rooted than the thinly veiled hypocrisy of the doctor of theology. They did not only expose the worldliness, the hunger for the joys of life crudely concealed by the grim visage of those who sought to terrify men into righteous living. They asserted the right of each man to be himself, to know God in his own way. From the abject creature whose only function was to learn the law that he might obey it, to suppress not only his body but his soul that he might escape punishment on the Day of Judgement, they raised man to the dignity of a free agent by divine grace, cooling his face in the breezes of eternity, looking beyond sin and sorrow, beyond innocence and guilt, a lover, a friend of God. In the language of European humanism, they made man the measure of all things. In the poetic images of their own language, they made intensity of feeling and beauty of expression the measure of man.

The synthesis that was the result of the fusion of Iranian and Indian cultures was not an imposed solution. Rose and nightingale, cup and cup-bearer, do not force themselves into Indian literature. They become a challenge, and the consequence of the challenge is the search for a new language, a new imagery and, what is most important, a new audience. Like the Muslim *sufi*, the Hindu reformer and saint addresses himself to the people; like the Muslim poet, the Hindu poet aspires to intensity of feeling, to imagery that will enchant the listener, to a vision of man conscious of himself and making his act of worship an event of eternal significance. Beginning with Amir Khusro, who was proud of his Persian and delighted himself and others with his command over Hindi, we have poets and writers of eminence who follow the Persian tradition, also poets belonging to this tradition who reject it and take up the spoken language as a medium having greater appeal. We have, on the other hand, those who meet effectively the challenge of Persian eloquence and imagery, poets like Sur Das, Kabir Saheb, Goswami Tulsi Das. A synthesis takes place by degrees, and is seen at its best in Urdu philologically. Its range is from the popular song where Persian words occur but rarely to almost pure Persian. And it should have been so. A cultural synthesis is an invitation to live and feel in a larger world, to see in love suffering, beauty and indifference, grace and elusiveness a universalism that resents and rejects the bondage of time and space.

12

The Perso-Arabic Script

'My pen works miracles' wrote Mir Ali, a calligraphist of Jahangir's court, 'and rightly enough is the *form* of my words proud of its superiority over *meaning*. *To* each of the curves of my letters the vault of heaven acknowledges its bondage, and the value of each of my strokes is eternity itself.' On the face of it, this is fantastic self-praise. But the calligraphist was admired as much the poet, the painter, the architect, and ranked high among the creators of the most cherished forms of beauty. He was definitely superior to others because his profession was recognised by law and religion as one of the most worthy. Copying out the Quran was almost as meritorious as teaching and reciting it, and anyone who wrote out the Holy Book in a beautiful hand was deemed to have performed a most acceptable act of worship. Calligraphy was also an art which had absorbed in itself the aesthetics of composition, line and movement, and cultured persons were expected to derive from it the exquisite pleasure of poetry. There was little reason, therefore, for the master of calligraphy to be modest.

Writing was not raised to the level of an art for the first time by the Muslims. The Iranians and particularly the Manichaeans had cultivated it, and they acquired a taste for it from the peoples of Central Asia, who were most probably influenced by the artists and calligraphists of the Han and T'ang dynasties. From the purely materialistic point of view, the cultivation of calligraphy can be traced to the manufacture of paper and the use of pen and ink. This again takes us to China, where paper was first made, and where the first book was printed around 600 AD. Calligraphy

---

From *Education and Traditional Values.*

became significant and widely practised as a profession among Muslims because books were much in demand. Copies of the Quran were needed by the hundred thousand. It was obligatory for every Muslim to read the Holy Book, which meant at least that there would be a copy of the Quran in every house. The calligraphist had to know his art well because it would have been irreverent to write the Holy Book without an honest effort to make the script look attractive. The evolution of a concept of beauty in script is in itself an interesting aspect of history.

Pre-Islamic Arabia had a language of which the Arabs were proud, but writing was not common. The earliest extant document we have of Islamic days is almost a scrawl compared with the later refined script. Contacts with Syrians and Iranians created the idea of a standardised script with an aesthetic appeal, and thus appeared the different styles of what is known as the Kufi script. There are copies of the Quran in this script, but the Quran has to be read correctly, and the Kufi script, though capable of being given highly artistic ornamental forms, could not ensure correct reading. So the script known as the Naskh was evolved. In this the letters were clearly distinguished, diacritical marks could be used, and it could be written with much greater ease and speed. Both the Kufi and the Naskh scripts were adapted by Muslims of different countries to suit their own tastes. But when painting began to be practised as an art from the 13th century onwards, the calligraphists felt that the Naskh script did not offer opportunities for realising the full value of the line and the curve, and so a third style of writing was developed, known as the Nasta'liq. This brought calligraphy much closer to line drawing, and the illuminated manuscript became a synthesis of literature, painting and ornamentation,

We have in India specimens of all styles of writing. In the tomb of Iltutmish in Delhi, we find inscriptions in the Kufi style as fine as anywhere else in the world and here and there are copies of Quran in imposing but almost illegible Kufic. The Naskh has been widely used, both in its decorative and utilitarian forms. But the style for which Persian and Urdu knowing Indians have opted most wholeheartedly is the Nasta'liq, and its shorthand form, known as the Shikast. Apart from books in Arabic, all the others have been written and are now being printed in Nasta'liq. It was the style used in official correspondence, in *farmans* and legal documents; it is now the style used for Urdu. Its shorthand form, the Shikast, was used for taking notes in the royal courts and later in the courts of law, for correspondence and private records. For the Urdu speaking Indian, basic literacy has consisted in the ability to read and write Nasta'liq and Shikast.

One of the things for which I personally feel grateful is the punishment I got for bad writing when I was being taught the Urdu alphabet. I feel now that I was punished not for carelessness or ineptitude only but for lack of respect for culture. A person's handwriting is also a form of self-expression, and till early in this century it was assumed, I think quite reasonably, by those using the Perso-Arabic script that indifference to handwriting indicated indifference to culture as a synthesis of the various types of excellence. Everyone who could write had to be something of a calligraphist, to know to give a proper point to a reed pen, to mix his own ink, and to make his writing conform to the standards of elegance that had been achieved in the forms of address and methods of expression. The Perso-Arabic script is not only a way of writing with a long history behind it, not only a heritage of great aesthetic value but a symbol of the essential unity of culture and art and an urge to the achievement of excellence in everything that is done.

We are living, however, in a scientific, technological and necessarily utilitarian age. Many questions have to be answered before the full contemporary value of Perso-Arabic as well as of other Indian scripts can be assessed. How long does it take to learn reading and writing the script? Can it be used without unnecessary cost and inconvenience in all the processes of correct and good printing? Can it meet all the demands of education in science and technology? How does it compare in legibility with the Roman script? The answers to these questions that are habitually given in India by the advocates of different scripts are based more on sentiment and political policy than objective reason. Following the general practice, I could say that the Nasta'liq form of the Perso-Arabic script is as good as any other. On the basis of experiments made it has been found that adults of less than average intelligence can learn to write it in 35 half-hour or 17 full-hour lessons, and those who speak Urdu or some form of Hindustani but cannot write it could learn to do so in ten days. The number of spelling mistakes made by those learning Urdu is certainly not more than students make in English. If the lithographic process is adopted, printing of the Perso-Arabic script can be cheaper and almost as quick as in type. Correct printing, as we all know, is a matter of luck. But the most ardent lover of the Perso-Arabic script will hesitate to maintain that the ordinary lithographic process could be used for printing scientific or technological works. As regards legibility, it could be said in defence of the Perso-Arabic script, that judgements on this point are liable to be subjective. I for one would not, however, let it go at that. The Perso-Arabic script cannot be reduced below a certain point without becoming illegible. It may not be inferior to Hindi in this respect, but it cannot, by any means, compare with the Roman.

Would it be advisable, in the interest of the survival of Urdu, which means of the adaptability of Urdu as a language to all the modern requirements of scientific education and the preparation of scientific and technological literature, to discard the Perso-Arabic script? The answer to this is that if by the Perso-Arabic script we mean the Naskh script, which is used in all the Arabic speaking countries and Iran, the question of a change in script does not arise. But in India a very large minority, if not the majority of those who speak Urdu and are keenly interested in its survival are non-Muslim. They regard the Nasta'liq script, which is now used, as Indian, and the Naskh as Islamic. Urdu being an Indian language, its script should also be Indian. They are not interested in the historical origins of Urdu or of the scripts in which it could be written, and if they had to choose between Urdu in the Naskh or the Roman script, they might choose the Roman. Muslims who desire the survival of Urdu should consider this matter with all seriousness. They are themselves not used to the Naskh script, and apart from some rare examples, books and journals printed in Naskh type have not been popular. Nasta'liq type cannot be made without destroying all the beauty of the script, and even if its beauty is sacrificed, the technical difficulties in using this type are formidable. The Perso-Arabic scripts are creations of great beauty, but the Urdu language is more precious than the script in which it is written. Its survival is not threatened by other languages, nor is the Perso-Arabic script endangered, by other Indian scripts. The real risk, lies in the possibility of the script isolating the Urdu language from the modern world of science and technology, and delaying the attainment through Urdu of the knowledge which moves the wheels of life.

13

Amir Khusrau

All that historians want to tell us about Amir Khusrau seems to me irrelevant. He was born in 1253. He called himself an Indian and was proud of it. Historians insist that he came of a Turkish family that had been driven from its home by the Mongols. His father had a fairly successful career as an officer, but he died when Khusrau was still a boy. Another relative became Khusrau's guardian. As soon as he was old enough, Khusrau, according to the common practice of the day, looked for patrons among the noblemen. He had not wanted to be educated. His teachers first tried to fit him into the usual pattern, then helped him to cultivate his extraordinary natural aptitude for versification. It was as a poet that he found welcome in the courts of the noblemen, and ultimately of kings. And for the historian it is of great interest that Khusrau composed in verse chronicles celebrating the achievements of his patrons. They are contemporary sources, and therefore of great value.

As poetic compositions, however, they are pedantic, ornate, heavy. I would say they are unreadable. But in between accounts of insignificant events which Khusrau has forced his skill to exalt, there are scattered lyrics of great beauty. To Khusrau they must have provided relief from tiresome artificiality. They must also have lightened the load on his conscience, because the chronicles were written solely for the purpose of earning rich rewards. And in a way they misrepresent him and his times. He had, against his nature, to assume the coarse political attitude of conquerors, to give to wars and warriors a religious and cultural character which they did not possess, to magnify little men and little things beyond

---

From *Education and Traditional Values.*

all reasonable measure, to indulge in partiality without regard for truth and justice. It is undeniable that the kings, the nobles and the armies Khusrau glorified in his chronicles could destroy life, happiness, property; they could inflict great suffering. This was not something that impressed Khusrau or appealed to his imagination. It was necessity, the moralist would say, necessity created by not a little greed, that made Khusrau the eulogist of noblemen and kings. Really he belonged somewhere else; to another court, to another people.

What history tells us about is the political and military activity of the Turks who established their rule in India. I would distrust any computation that would place their number above 20,000 families. Not all of these Turks were professional soldiers, and those who were would have realised, far more clearly than historians would have us believe, that they were a small minority in a vast country. I do not wish to belittle their ideas and their achievements. I only wish to emphasise that these ideas and achievements had a social background, and with this our historians have not yet learnt to concern themselves. They forget that the whole country was not involved in political rivalries, that it did not participate in campaigns. There was peace, goodwill, understanding, reinforced by powerful spiritual tendencies.

Perhaps the most important single factor in the social background of India of those days was the influence of the sufis, the mystics, particularly of the Chishti order. We are now inclined to question their social value, because they had no plan, no programme of any kind of philanthropic activity. They had no concrete aims. They just sat somewhere, prayed, talked to people; they gave spiritual advice, and sometimes indirect practical guidance to those who asked for it; they had no political ideas or interests; and if wrongs were openly committed, they prayed for a change of heart. We cannot now realise the effectiveness of this apparent inactivity. The sufi began to be called *Shah* or king. His seat became a throne, and at the times when people came to visit him, the etiquette of the court was observed. A king could kill a thousand innocent persons; that would be an evil fate. But he risked his throne if he took action of any kind against a sufi.

Amir Khusrau belonged to the intimate circle of the great sufi, Shaikh Nizamuddin of Delhi, whose influence, once established, was far greater than that of the most powerful kings. And this remarkable and enduring influence was always exerted to promote fellow-feeling, tolerance, reverence for all beliefs sincerely and steadfastly held. The example of the saint opened out to Amir Khusrau a vast field for the exercise of his intellectual and artistic powers. Nothing was alien to him, nothing without meaning and interest. He seems to have been completely at home in the village, to have seen how men and women lived and felt and behaved. He seems to have studied several languages, and there are still extant scores of couplets where he plays charmingly with words. His teacher had forgiven him his worldliness. He smiled at the liberties Khusrau took with ideas and beliefs, at all his poetic images, even when they inclined to be erotic. In Khusrau's lyrics, the saint figure everywhere and in all aspects, as the proud hero, as a woman of loveliness beyond description; as the master of the wine-house, dispensing spiritual intoxication in the form of the supremely handsome, and cruelly indifferent Turk. The saint did not mind. He must have been really pleased when Khusrau abandoned the current literary language and its style, and explored the possibilities of a new medium, which he calls Hindi. The mystics believed in cultivating the spoken language, and were the first to make the people's speech the means of expressing lofty spiritual ideas. Khusrau took over from folk poetry the from of depicting the woman as the lover, and nothing that has come down to us from that period is more delightful than the mixed Persian and Hindi lyrics of Amir Khusrau. But, judging from quantity alone, these expressions of love in Indian style would seem to be literary excursions. The achievements of Amir Khusrau which have made his name endure are lyrics that he wrote for singing at gatherings where music and poetry were used as stimulants to religious fervour, to spiritual ecstasy. Many of these lyrics express beliefs that are, from the orthodox Muslim point of view, heretical. But this heresy has the full support of a sufistic tradition of humanism, of an interpretation of religion which, while it intensified religiousness, also released the believer from the bonds of orthodoxy. It gave to the Muslim poet complete freedom as well as a peculiar spiritual status. It made the blending of intimacy and reverence, or beauty and sorrow, of poetic adventure and deep spirituality an outstanding feature of Muslim culture. The genius of Khusrau represents this quality of Muslim culture almost at its best. Khusrau has become a legend. He was called the Indian songster by his contemporaries, who thought his Persian compositions rivalled the best poetry of Persia. He was master of Indian music, the originator of particular styles of singing. He was supposed to have frolicked with village women, to have amused and confounded them with his riddles and his wit, to have so mixed up Persian and Hindi in his speech as to make people laugh and feel at one with each other. A song that is sung when the bride is leaving her home, something entirely and utterly Indian, is said to have been composed by him. A glossary of Hindi and Persian words and phrases, a masterpiece of scholarly frivolity, is believed to be a literary exercise of his. Whether one wishes to laugh or to make love, to study philology or folklore, to sing or to induce spiritual exaltation, Khusrau is there as the archetype. With him tradition becomes suddenly rich, versatile, exquisite. For centuries he was looked upon as the creator of Indo-Muslim culture. And even now we have to recognise him as the source of much that we cherish.

14

Ghalib: The Poetic Tradition

The poetic tradition which Ghalib represents was more than literature, more than culture. It expressed, vigorously and coherently, the response of human nature to the problem of human existence. It was a fusion of elements that were philosophical, mystical and aesthetic, also elements that were essentially trivial and ephemeral. The fusion took place in man, and could not take place outside him, in a system of philosophy or mysticism or aesthetics, certainly not in religious dogma. This poetry was, therefore, a means of human self-revelation and self-assertion. Its fault lay in its isolation of the individual, its indifference to social aims, its disregard of such basic institutions as the family and the emotional needs for the fulfilment of which it is maintained, its elevation of experience to pure idea.

This poetry grew as a form and as an outlook on life within the non-Arab Muslim world and may be considered a contribution of the Persian genius and of those who, like the Turks in the west and the Indian Muslims in the east, came under its influence. Its origins can be traced to several sources:

(a) The acceptance of human nature as the basis of both the spiritual and the worldly life in the teachings of Islam,
(b) The establishment in Islam of a direct relationship between man and his Creator, without any intermediary, such as a church or a separate organisation of those dedicated to the religious life,
(c) The inevitable conflict between the legalistic and the approach to religion,

---

From *Ghalib.*

(d) The aesthetic sense inherent in man, and
(e) The failure to create social and political institutions that could command the loyalty of the intellectually sensitive.

Human nature asserts itself, whatever the prevailing system of belief may be, but as a matter of history, poetry and the fine arts have flourished most in periods when human thought was man-centred. In ancient Greece, in Europe during the Renaissance and the centuries following, poetry as well as all the other fine arts were more and more widely cultivated. Among Muslims, though the religion itself was man-centred, the legalists succeeded in restraining the development of arts which depended on the presentation of living forms by carrying social opinion with them, and the seclusion of women, also based on a legalistic interpretation of Islamic dogma, created a still greater obstacle. Poetry mid architecture were the two main arts in which the aesthetic urge of the Muslim could find free expression, and for obvious reasons poetry provided opportunities to a far larger number of persons. It is in the poetry of the tradition with which we are concerned that the implications of Islam as a man-centred religion come into view most prominently and impressively.

The liberty to accept, modify or reject dogma on the basis of their own spiritual experience was demanded and exercised by the Sufis and has a history of its own. We can regard it as a resultant of the attempts of the legalists to give comprehensiveness and precision to Muslim religious law, the intellectualist attack on certain theological concepts in the ninth century, the defeat of the intellectualists by an alliance between the upholders of theology and the state, the oppressiveness of despotic rule, the denial by the established theological and political systems of the individual's right to think and judge for himself and, what is perhaps most important, the urge of the spiritually sensitive to find their own way to the Absolute. The Sufis were at first suspected and persecuted, but they established themselves through their appeal to the masses, and from the twelfth century onwards the Sufi *tariqah* and the orthodox *shariah* became two recognised ways the Muslim could follow, with the option of crossing over from one to the other as and when he liked.

The *shariah* had the support of the state, but in attempting to accommodate within Muslim law an institution as repugnant to

Islam as despotic, personal government, the representatives of the *shariah,* the official *ulama* completely undermined their own moral position. The Muslim was asked to obey the ruler, the ruler was asked to look to his is subjects, but neither was asked to cooperate with the other habitually and in accordance with the ethical precepts of Islam. The consequence of this failure to integrate the interests of rulers and subjects on a continuing and moral basis left the sensivity individual no choice but to withdraw within himself, to create a world of his own in which society was ignored, and to carry this world on his shoulders.

The mystic-poetic tradition also prescribed that the truly religious man must rise above distinctions of religion. In its philosophical form this prescription appears in the doctrine of the Unity of Existence—*wahdah al-wujud*—and, there is a fairly clear trace of continuous conflict between the believers in this Unity and those who upheld the orthodox, transcendentalist point of view. The poet could bow down in reverence before God and the Prophet, and if he was a Shiah, also before the Imams. There were poets like Mir Anis and Dabir who wrote *marthias,* or accounts of the martyrdom of Imam Husain and his family, and little else. Rejection of religion because of atheistic 'inclinations is completely absent. But it seems to have been regarded as essential for the poet's intellectual dignity to repudiate orthodoxy, its insistence on externals and its indifference to aesthetic values. In this way Urdu poetry, which represents the grafting of the Persian tradition on an indigenous base, brought together all those whom historical circumstances, social laws, ritualistic restraints and traditional beliefs kept apart, stimulating them to realise unity at a high intellectual and aesthetic level. And Ghalib may well claim to be the culminating point of an intellectual, aesthetic and ideologically integrative development which is of great significance in the cultural history of India.

Because of its character and history, the poetic tradition evolved its own symbols. The most basic of these was love.

The subject of love is universal. The unique feature of Persian poetry is the organic assimilation of sacred and profane love in a wealth of symbols where the sacred is seen through the profane as light through a prism, and the profane is seen through the sacred as God's light in the nature of man.

Like God, love is essence and attributes, and commands absolute obedience. It is power that creates and destroys, judges and condemns, punishes and purifies, and rewards those who have passed through its ordeals with unutterable bliss. It has many facets. It inspires a wisdom that makes acquired knowledge irrelevant, it liberates the spirit from all external forms of obedience, from all obligations inconsistent with its demands, from the opposites of piety and sinfulness, from concepts of reward and punishment, heaven and hell. It can also take the form of love for a person, and express itself as a passion, a madness, a total surrender of the self. Sacred and profane love can also become one and the same thing, the human beloved can acquire the nature of the Absolute, the Absolute can embody itself in the person of the human beloved. It is all within the power of love. Finally, love can also become a quality of the lover, a self-perpetuating fire within the heart, an end and purpose in itself, transfiguring the lover into absolute Man.

This makes the lover, the poet, essential for the manifestation of love. His urge for self-realisation opens his being to the influence of love, and he may or may not need the symbol of a beloved. Two archetypes of lovers are frequently alluded to in Persian and Urdu poetry, the Arab Majnun and the Persian Farhad. Majnun is surrounded with the imagery of the desert, pining to death for Laila; Farhad typifies the striving lover, who will demolish rocky mountains with his pick-axe for the sake of his beloved Shirin. Laila is quite indifferent to Majnun and his fate; Shirin can be won only if Farhad performs an impossible task, and the Emperor who prescribes this task has planned to cheat him of his reward even if he succeeds. But Majnun and Farhad are both mere symbols, which every poet has felt free to interpret as he liked, and not historical figures to be presented in their proper context.

In boyhood I picked up a stone to throw
At Majnun, but it struck me then
That I, too, had a vulnerable head,

says Ghalib. Majnun has become a common noun, meaning anyone who behaves in an abnormal way for romantic reasons.

The image of the beloved is extremely variable in form and meaning, and may be taken to change with the mood of the poet. Here also sacred and profane love dissolve into each other, and the poet who is asked why he conceives his beloved now as a lovely or wily woman, now as a spiritual guide, now as God himself can very well reply that he is not to blame, it is the beloved who takes on different forms. The poet Khusrau saw one morning that his spiritual preceptor, Shaikh Nizamuddin's eyes were red from lack of sleep. He knew that the Shaikh had been praying all night, but following the poetic fashion he asked, 'In whose arms did you spend the night?" as a jealous and suspicions lover would have asked a fickle woman whom he loved. The poet and mystic Sarmad, condemned to death, saw the executioner approach with a drawn sword. He smiled and said, 'Come, come, in whatever form. Thou appearest, I know Thee!' Ghalib says,

I do not fear the hangman or with the preacher quarrel,
Whatever the disguise may be, I know
who comes disguised.

On the other hand, when the poet Naziri says,

From head to foot wherever I look, a miracle
Tugs at my heart and says, Behold, I'm here!

he is referring to a human body, and to nothing beyond it.

An example of the transition from the physical to the spiritual image is the following couplet of an unknown poet:

Last night the image of a wanton ringlet
Entwined itself around my heart—and faded.
A light, bright as the very face of God,
Flashed lightning-like within my breast—and faded.

The mystics transformed the heart into one of their basic symbols. Spiritual experiences were 'occurrences of the heart', and naturally the poets took over the symbol of the heart with all its meanings. It was the seat of love, of the sovereignty of the will; it was the mystery of mysteries; it was the cause of all misery; it was the active element in man's nature, holding within itself all dynamic power, all power to create, change and destroy.

The Muslim has been told to avoid drinking, and theological and public opinion has for centuries made a virtue out of this particular form of prescribed abstinence. The question whether those who drink in spite of this prohibition commit a sin does not need to be discussed here; the poets have branded as hypocrites those who made a virtue of abstinence from wine. In Persian poetry, the *saqi* who poured out wine to the assembled guests, wine itself, and the *mai-khana,* or tavern, were elevated into lofty spiritual symbols. These symbols have been retained in Urdu poetry. Mosque and tavern have been contrasted as representing two opposite paths. Kaaba and the temple, the shaikh (here meaning not the Sufi shaikh, but the learned man, the man of external piety, the sermonizer) and the Brahman are other forms of this same contrast.

The frequency of executions and violent deaths could not fail to affect the minds of the poets or the generality of the people. Mansur Hallaj, the Sufi who was hanged or crucified for saying, 'I am the Truth' or, in other words, 'I am God', became the symbol of spiritual self-assertion, and 'gallows' (*dar*) and 'halter' (*rasan*) symbolic of what a man should expect for fearless utterance of the truth. Sword, dagger, bow and arrow inevitably crept in as poetic images. Their use is some times distasteful to us, but even in Ghalib's time these weapons were too much in evidence for references to them to be considered incongruous. The term executioner (*qatil*) for the beloved also continues to be used, but it is, like *kafir,* mainly a term of endearment.

Ghalib imbibed the whole poetic tradition and its symbolism as a part of his education and felt no desire for aesthetic or literary adventures that would take him away from it. Did he, for this reason, lose his identity and deprive himself of the opportunity to be original? Experiments in new forms in contemporary Urdu poetry have undoubtedly enriched it, but except for some diehard innovators the general tendency has been to revert to the ghazal of Ghalib's days, dipping and dyeing the themes, as it were, in a more varied if not richer experience. It was, however, primarily against the ghazal that modernist-innovators had revolted, and the reasons for the reversion to the old form in a new spirit will enable us to understand to what extent Ghalib could maintain his identity and claim originality even while scrupulously following the inherited patterns.

The ghazal, roughly defined, consists of couplets in the same metre, the second line ending in words that rhyme according to certain rules. The number of couplets in a ghazal can vary; the general practice has been to make each couplet self-sufficient, and there could be eight different themes in a ghazal of eight couplets. The aim was concentrated, epigrammatic and, of course, striking expression. The objection to the ghazal as a form has been that it forced the poet to look for words that rhymed together rather than for ideas worthy of expression. What was equally bad, ideas or sentiments had to be fitted within a given framework of expression, form was not moulded by substance, but substance by form. Both these objections are valid. But the typical ghazal has the charm of music as well as beauty of language; its appeal is immediate and difficult to resist. 'What its critics in fact resented was the popularity of the ghazal. This has not only survived their objections but has transformed the genuine poets among them into masters of the ghazal style.

15

Ghalib as Poet

Ghalib has made varying statements about the age at which he began to compose verses; the earliest is ten and the latest fifteen. His education was not systematic, and his experiments in versification must have begun before his literary attainment was anywhere near adequate. He took to poetry at the same time as he began to indulge in what he calls 'frivolities' and 'wickedness and immorality' that is, with adolescence. This was about the time he was married and became entitled, because of marriage, to associate with somewhat older persons, who would also have combined composition of verses with 'wickedness and immorality'. We are left to conjecture who, if anyone, gave him encouragement and guidance, and inspired him with the confidence necessary to cross his first literary hurdles and disregard his failures. We cannot trace his development as a poet because none of his earlier compositions can be dated. Besides, whenever a poet's ghazals were collected, they were always arranged alphabetically according to the last letter of the rhyming words, so that a ghazal written earlier could be placed much later in a collection. Finally, Ghalib made the first selection of his ghazals himself, now found in what is called the Bhopal Mss., and what he did not include in this selection has been lost for ever.

Till 1822, when he was twenty-five years old, Ghalib wrote in Urdu. Then he took to writing in Persian, a language for which he had great affection and admiration, and which he thought offered him better opportunity for self-expression than Urdu. By this time he had made a thorough study of all the masters who were held in

---

From *Ghalib*.

general esteem, but it was typical of him that to establish his claim to authoritative knowledge of Persian idiom, he first invented and later denied the story of a mysterious Iranian who came and stayed at his house in Agra for two years and taught him the language. The phase of writing almost exclusively in Persian lasted till 1850, when Ghalib began to be invited to the court and had to write in the language of thc court, Urdu, but he did not give up Persian. The seven years that followed are regarded as the mature phase of his Urdu poetry.

There are qualities common to the earlier and the later phase of Ghalib's Urdu poetry, which began from 1850. The lyrical element is more prominent in the later phase, but Ghalib maintained to the end his habit of drawing a few strokes and leaving it to the comprehension of his listeners or readers to complete the image. There are plenty of his verses in the apparently simple language of the second phase about the meaning of which critics are in doubt. Ghalib also did not surrender his individualism or his intellectuality, but in the court, and as a poet recognised by the court, he had to take his place among those whose poetry represented entirely different and much lower values. The compromise Ghalib made with the spoken idiom and the prevailing taste, though at some sacrifice of his independent genius, endeared him to the lovers of Urdu poetry. He was no longer the peak with its snow mountain-side also, with its forests, its breezes, its rivulets of snow changing into streams as they descended to the valley below.

It was natural for Ghalib to be influenced by other poets, specially those who were admired by his contemporaries. He has acknowledged Bedil as his master with an astonishing frankness and sincerity.

> My admiration is so passionate, I cannot portray
> The majesty of Bedil's genius; how can a drop
> Reveal the ecstasies the vast ocean bears?

Bedil wrote in Persian, in a style extremely erudite and involved, and Ghalib's early compositions are an obvious attempt to write in the same style in Urdu. A learned critic has given numerous examples to show the influence of other poets, Persian and Urdu, on Ghalib. The practice of holding mushairas, for which the metre and rhyme were announced in advance, tended to establish a uniformity by making the audience into judges of the merit of a composition through straightforward or oblique approbation or silence. It would also stimulate the urge to excel but the prevailing taste would be the decisive factor. For us the question would inevitably arise whether a ghazal, for which the occasion as well as the rhyme and metre were prescribed, could be a spontaneous and genuine poetic composition. But connoisseurs would know at once whether a poet was just offering a literary exercise in one of the approved and admired styles or had an individuality of his own. Traditional criticism distinguished between 'what comes' to the poet's mind as inspiration and 'what is brought in' by him as it were to fill in a blank, between the spontaneous and the forced elements of a ghazal. There is no doubt that, with all the symbols ready, to hand and the general tendency to admire dexterous manipulation of the spoken idiom, much that was mere versification could pass off as poetry.

Ghalib was a poet by nature. He was extremely sensitive to public opinion, but determined at all costs to avoid the commonplace. His first audiences, whether elders or friends of about the same age, few or many, must have been taken aback by his not saying what they expected him to say, even though he did not break with the poetic tradition, and using an idiom of his own to say what he did. He did not offer them the known pleasures of poetry, but a challenge to discover the meaning he had created. They could not ignore him; that would imply inability to understand; it would be confession of defeat. Besides, there was the majestic rhythm of his verse, the startling combination of words, never before attempted in Urdu, to convey shades of meaning which the same words did not express when used in the conventional way. There was the condensation of thought, which went far beyond the neat, epigrammatic phrases of those who excelled in skilful handling of the spoken idiom. It is true that words and meanings were sometimes stretched to the breaking point, and Ghalib got lost in intricate landscapes of words instead of giving striking form to an idea. There is a story that an elderly admirer of his youthful genius once strung together imposing words in an utterly meaningless combination and recited the verse as something remarkable that had come to his notice. In response to Ghalib's blank stare he admitted at once that the verse made no sense, but this could be the case with other verses also if the poet forgot that good poetry had to be intelligible.

Many examples could be given to show that in his earlier period Ghalib delighted in involved expression, following the style of Bedil and some other poets. But if poetry was to be the creation of new meaning in the old symbols, an addition of fresh intellectual and aesthetic experience to the traditional content of poetry, Ghalib felt that a new vocabulary would have to be assembled to serve as the medium. He fashioned this new medium for himself by a fusion of the vocabulary of both Persian and Urdu, exercising a freedom that was not inhibited by the idiom of either language. He achieved something unique. Even where the sequence of ideas is difficult to establish, the language holds the reader enthralled.

What was the new meaning Ghalib attempted to create, the fresh intellectual and aesthetic experience he desired to transmit? Let us take as an illustration a verse from his earlier phase.

> Purposeless travail all endeavour
> To make this life fit prelude to the next;
> Walk the exalted path of love, distress of spirit
> Is just a passing thought of weariness and rest.

A translation does not suffice. We must paraphrase, we must expand the concentrated expression to convey all that is implied. 'We are told,' Ghalib says, 'that man must bring his life on earth into accord with the life hereafter, to coordinate the immediate with the ultimate. This is tedious and unavailing. If we accept it, we ignore life's real purpose, which is to give free rein to our natural, aesthetic urge, to love, to the ardour of passion, to all that is essentially human in us. Let us be fully, richly human, let us make life into a ceaseless movement, and if ever we feel weary, let us assume that it is because we have wanted to rest, and not because the way is long. The weariness will pass as soon as we have started on our journey again.'

Some will observe at once that this is an instigation to moral anarchy, some will want an analysis and elucidation of love and ardour and passion and the ceaseless movement they create, most, let us admit, will just not understand. It is not difficult to see why. Those who believe in moral order do not realise that order is not an end in itself, it must lead to something. Those who demand clarity of ideas tend to be satisfied with 'clarity. Those who do not understand imagine that the function of the poet is to express romantic sentiments in a charming way; they want the poet to feel and speak at their own level, so that they can be pleased and mildly excited. They want to avoid, as far as possible, the strain of thinking; they have accepted what is, they do not wish to turn their backs on everything in the contemplation of what could be, of what must be, if man is to be man and life to be really man's discovery of himself. Ghalib cannot tell us what he has discovered, he can only stimulate the urge to make discoveries. It is not the poet's function to satisfy, but to create a dissatisfaction so deep, a restlessness so unabating that we are forced to think about life's possibilities—a thinking that makes living a significant experience.

Or let us take another example:

The lightning flash of beauty has consumed my sight,
Only the eye-lashes remain, like smouldering twigs,
Impudent relics of a burnt-out flame.

I have so strained my eyes in the endeavour
To see the vision again, that tears have washed away
All but my self-centredness; there's nothing left
Except the glance, clear as the dew-drop's sparkle.
The garden of desire has fallen victim
To autumn's withering hand, and spring again
Will come, as pale and bloodless as my sighs.

The wonder of the saqi's eyes is gone, no more
The festive cup goes round, and glum vicissitude
Is all the company I have.

This can be construed, of course, as a mood of utter pessimism, a repetition, in a different and complicated form, of what other poets have said with greater lucidity. But if we examine the verses closely, we will find almost a precise description of the stages by which the mood changes. The poet has beheld beauty, like a sudden flash of lightning it has struck him blind, consumed his sight, leaving only a few smouldering eyelashes, and it seems impudent that they should show a trace of the fire when there is really nothing left. But the eye was made to see, it will not give up being what it is. However, all that its self-assertion produces is the glance, like the sparkling dewdrop. It is pure, no doubt, but only a dew-drop. Or, to put it differently, the bloom of the garden is gone; it had to go, because autumn is inevitable, inexorable, and all that the passion to recreate the flowers of the garden will produce is a pale, colourless spring, as satisfying as the relief one gets from a deep sigh. Or, Corning down to the images of daily life, one cannot look into the saqi's eyes and be filled with wonder, one cannot drain the cup and ask that it be refilled, one has to live with time, with meaningless change.

If in saying this, Ghalib claimed to have created a new meaning, he was justified.

Traditional methods of criticism have been applied to the final and popular edition of Ghalib's ghazals; his earlier phase has been almost completely ignored. Critics of the traditional type have been ignorant of any literature other than Urdu and Persian, and incapable of isolating any new meaning apart from showing how concepts of the beloved, the rival, jealousy, etc., had been given a novel and individual expression. Critics of the modem type, who have had the opportunity—seldom utilised—of a comparative study of literatures and literary movements have been so obsessed by canons of Marxist criticism that their historical and literary perspective has been distorted, and the idea of a free, creative human personality is incomprehensible to them. Those not so obsessed are themselves lacking in the experience and sensitivity necessary to appreciate the working of the creative human mind. In the only study of the poetry of Ghalib's earliest phase it does not appear that Ghalib had any knowledge of the existence of women, or that his image of the beloved was in any sense a reflection of women he had loved. Ghalib is thus by implication accused of that artificiality of sentiment which the use of stylised symbols suggests, and also of that isolation from the realities of physical and social life which literary convention required, but which it was impossible for a person so full-blooded as Ghalib to accept.

For the understanding of Ghalib it is necessary to emphasise that poetry represented for him above all a form of aesthetic and intellectual self-assertion. Where self-assertion is the urge to attain self-realisation in and through some system of thought or belief, the results are different. We are concerned here with the self-assertion of the poet (and only of the Persian and Urdu poet) as an end in itself, as a striving for release from all that fetters the mind and the heart, as a search for the ultimate freedom. This self-assertion implies a negation of everything except the poetic mood and the poetic image. Every mood has to be taken by itself, as complete and self-sufficient, and the change of mood has to be accepted as inevitable, because existence itself is a process of continuous change. Further, if the change of mood is to be brought home, it must be abrupt, not gradual. The ghazal exhibits in an exaggerated form the poet's right as well as his ability to change his mood. Any attempt at a synthesis of moods for the purpose of determining a poet's ideas or beliefs could be a repetition of Khwaja Nasiruddin's experiment of cutting off the legs and the neck of the stork to make it look like other birds. All that the critic can do without encroaching on the poet's freedom is to look for the most prevalent moods, or those which appear most in keeping with the poet's real nature, when all his powers are fused together in the creation of the poetic image.

Ghalib's most usual mood could be described as one of negation, expressing itself in his discontent, disillusionment, restlessness, pain, grief, and leading on to a denial of the value of physical existence because of its many limitations. This is both a logical and natural consequence of his urge for self-assertion, which brings him into continuous conflict with physical reality, a struggle in which the living spirit is always defeated and always return to the fray. The mood of negation has its own symbols—wilderness, desert, lightning flash, chains, wounds, and the corresponding conditions are madness, despondency, tears, sighs, lamentation, pain of unfulfilled desires. The evils and afflictions of life are the necessary consequence of physical existence; Ghalib sometimes blames it all on awareness, both of what is and of what could be, now taking the form of madness and rejecting the world of ordered living in favour of the desert, now demanding of God something more worthy of man than the heaven and earth he has created. But this mood of negation, however often we may come across it in Ghalib, is not an obsession. It overflows into other moods and is in its turn softened by them. And however intense and absolute the negation may be, it is not final, for man remains.

Ghalib's religious mood, which can be called religious only in a nominal sense, is not a primary but a secondary mood. He had studied the literature of Sufism and took for granted the doctrine of the Unity of Existence. But the company of the pious was odious to him, even as an idea, and he was too intellectual, too self-centred, too headstrong in his freedom for that absorption in the world of the spirit which is basic to the mystical experience. He could not aspire to the bliss of annihilation in God; annihilation was not possible because life, 'madness' pervaded every particle of the universe. And when God's mercy embraced even those who did not ask for it by falling into error and sin, when, as Spring, it came to intercede for the lovers of wine, Ghalib could address God almost as a court favourite would talk to his sovereign lord, light-hearted, flippant, apologetic but never serious about his own offences of omission and commission. And he could not ask for anything, because nothing was worth having except a heart that had no desires.

Ghalib's mood of love is too intellectual to have a deeply emotional quality. He has more the nature of a rebel than of a person seeking to surrender his self to the beloved, and while he recognises the power of beauty and is sometimes overwhelmed by it, be cannot forget or deny his nature. In the later phase, his images of the lover and beloved and the sorrows of love often become conventional and to that degree a lapse from his own aesthetic standards, though even where he is conventional his individuality is striking. In one of his ghazals where the mood is continuous, he is more concerned with himself than with the beloved, who appears as a figure on the roof with dark tresses scattered on her face, or as sitting opposite, the daggers of her eyelashes sharpened with collyrium, or as a youthful countenance flushed with wine. These are passing fancies, conventional, unreal; he ends with the desire to remain in perpetual contemplation of the beloved, the beloved as such, an ineffable creation of the aesthetic mood. Ghalib's aspiration was the pure aesthetic experience, a glory that is known neither to the lover nor to the beloved, but encompasses both.

Nature did not inspire any of Ghalib's moods. He had an urban mind, and he could regard nature only as a background to human life. The supreme poetic image, the creator as well as the creation of Ghalib's poetry, is man himself, and Ghalib's loftiest and fairly constant mood is contemplation of his humanity. No matter how far an intellectual or a romantic quest might take him, he returns to himself, to man. Man is the garden with its flowers, the desert waste, the lover seeking union with the beloved, the pawn in the game of being and non-being, the agonising awareness of reality, the rebel, the creature crushed to dust by fate, the detached spectator, ironical, flippant, the beautiful sin that captivates mercy, the madness that would reduce creation to chaos. Ghalib did not discover man, but he invested him with a new insight into his own nature and the nature of life, with a passion for intellectual adventure and a courage to reject, with a confident, meaningful smile, or sheer disgust, conditions of existence which encroached upon his freedom and dignity.

16

Iqbal

Most Muslim poets got themselves involved in sinfulness just to the degree that assured them against the risk of being taken for teachers and philosophers, and provided them with a springboard for those exalted flights when vision apprehends as much of absolute truth as is possible for the human mind to assimilate. Iqbal (1873-1938) began extremely well, breaking through conventions and artificialities that clouded the aesthetic atmosphere as he rose towards the heavens. But then something happened. Instead of steadily looking up, he began to look down; instead of attaining the pure nudity of the poet, he wrapped himself in the gray cloak of the preacher; instead of getting lost in truth, he became a reformer. Some fervently believe this to be the natural and inevitable unfolding of his personality; most do not think consequently enough to draw any conclusions. There are a few who, like me, regard this as a tragedy. Iqbal lived at a time when he could have made a large number of Muslims sober, enlightened and creative men; by becoming a reformer he invested his invaluable resources in mass-producing them according to the old, orthodox pattern, using moulds that had long ago lost the cementing power of commonsense and utility. Now anyone who writes of him must beware of offending against the dignity of a prophet. The critic's only protection is the tradition which has regarded poetry as a part of prophecy. He can appraise and admire Iqbal the poet, and let Iqbal the prophet take the consequences.

Iqbal received the right kind of education—a thorough grounding in the traditional sciences and systematic instruction in the new—and was appointed a lecturer in the Government

---

From *Islamic Influence on Indian Society*

College, Lahore. He came into prominence early in life because of his poetic gifts, and was much in demand at conferences and meetings held to bemoan the sad plight of the Muslims and exhort them to bestir themselves. His is not the only instance of poetry being asked to serve as the handmaid of reform, nor is it the only instance in which a poet, through forced contemplation of the circumstances of the Indian Muslims, lost sight of humanity. The seeds of specialised if not exclusive thinking and writing about Islam and the Muslims had already been sown in his mind when Iqbal went to Europe for further study in 1905, and he was in the mood to discover that European science and philosophy was showing humanity the road towards Islam. This, according to my own firm belief, is a perfectly tenable position. But it would be disastrous to imply that the Muslims of today could stand proudly where they were now or had been five hundred years ago, and expect modern knowledge to come to them and make grateful acknowledgement of their superiority. However, political policies and events—European imperialism and general cultural aggressiveness, the Italian invasion of Tripoli, the wars of the Balkan States against Turkey, the world war and its aftermath—did not create an atmosphere conducive to a purely human outlook. Iqbal was forced to adopt the tactics of self-defence, not only against the hostile and destructive elements in western civilisation, but against the forces liberated by human progress—creative nationalism, democracy, liberalism, freedom of women. In his passionate love of the Muslims he overlooked the deep inconsistency of preaching to them, on the one hand, that they should, like the eminent personalities of their history, laugh at suffering and death and develop within themselves the firmness of the rock-hewn fortress and, on the other, advocating political separation from the Hindus because otherwise they would be crushed and their religion and culture obliterated by the economically and educationally more advanced Hindu community. There is no continuity between one poetic moment and another, and the poet is not concerned with those who hear or read his verses. But the preacher has to see that one sermon does not contradict another, and religion does not go down because love of God is stultified by fear of the devil.

Iqbal could create poetic values in the most time-saddened sentiments; what was new in him was fresh as the dawn. Let it suffice that his turning a preacher is a matter of regret. He was beyond doubt a great poet and a most lovable man.

Urdu was naturally Iqbal's medium when he first began to write poetry. After his return from Europe he affected a preference for Persian. It is idle to discuss which medium gave better opportunity for the expression of his genius; he was at home in both, and he did not give up either. His *Mansnavi Asrar-o-Rumuz* is his most didactic and perhaps weakest work; the *Bang-i-Dira* contains his freshest, the *Bal-i-Jibril* his maturest compositions. His *Payami-Mashriq* is a poetic response to Goethe's *West-Ostlicher Diwan,* and reflects more than any other work the wide range of his vision and the catholicity of his ideas. The *Jawid-Namah,* following the tradition of Ibn Arabi's *Futuhat-i-Makkiya* and Dante's *Divine Comedy, is* a book of judgements. In his *Reconstruction of Religious Thought in Islam,* Iqbal began boldly and ended timidly, sometimes disowning the conclusions that followed from his own arguments. The attempt to identify the whole of western science and philosophy with extracts from thinkers and writers selected for special reasons by himself also does not carry conviction.

Iqbal rejected Muslim mysticism in principle as something promoting passiveness and quietism, but he was deeply imbued with it. He rejected western humanism as a spiritual blind alley, but his poetry is steeped in humanism.

> Come, nestle in many bosom for a while,
> 'Tis such a weariness being God and Father.

It is something that would occur most easily to a mystic contemplating the self-inflicted sorrows of mankind and God's pathetic omnipotence. His humanism appears most clearly in his identification of Satan with man's determination to learn for himself. Some of Iqbal's poems and many of his verses indicate that he could move far away enough from orthodoxy to be able to view traditional beliefs objectively and critically that when he spoke of man's responsibility as God's representative on earth he was not repeating a theological cliche but asserting the essential freedom of man's will. Iqbal's mysticism and humanism—the blending of which is a unique feature of Persian and Indian Muslim poetry—is a flower that grew on the stem of orthodox belief. There can be no flowers without trees; and need the tree ask to be forgiven because the flowers are rare and lovely?

Iqbal was knighted because he was an outstanding Muslim: in politics be was never a force to be reckoned with, but be participated in important political discussions and was invited to attend the Round Table Conference in London. The distinction he attained did not affect the simplicity of his nature. He never had enough of money and often less than enough. He lived in a shapeless sort of house and was most of the time to be seen in a corner of its front verandah or an adjoining terrace. Anyone could visit him for any purpose at any time, but the particular hours for visitors were from about four in the afternoon till late at night. He sat on his bed and smoked his hookah and talked. He did not show preference for any type of visitors or any variety of topics. Nothing restrained the flow of his conversation, which possessed an inexhaustible charm and reflected the amazing versatility of his mind. At home he was dressed invariably in a shirt and a shalwar: his outdoor dress was the typical Punjabi combination of a coat, a necktie and a shirt hanging loose over a capacious shalwar. He did not seem to care for anything, least of all for the time spent in aimless conversation with aimless persons. But he was lively and lovable, and even idle questioning would quickly reveal how intensely concerned he was with the political and spiritual fate not only of the Indian Muslims but of all mankind.

17

Umrao Jan Ada

Over twenty-five years ago I read a review of Mirza Ruswa's novel, *Umrao Jan Ada,* in a literary magazine. I felt curious. The novel is the biography of a courtesan. But what really roused my curiosity was the praise lavished on it by the reviewer, a scholar of uncompromising orthodoxy and notorious puritanism. I made haste to buy the book and read it. And I understood why the scholar had lost his hold on orthodoxy and why puritanism had lost its grip on him. *Umrao Jan Ada* was the kind the person whose company and conversation would make thing look entirely different.

Her life was not in any way remarkable. In the disorder and decadence characteristic of the middle nineteenth century Indian states, it was nothing uncommon for a girl to be kidnapped and sold for whatever her face and figure would fetch. Such girls were bought by people who wanted domestic servants or courtesans who kept brothels or trained singer and dancers. Umrao Jan was bought by a courtesan with a good head for business, taught to read and write, and trained as a singer. She made use of her opportunities better than other girls did. She learnt Urdu, Persian and Arabic. Composing verses was almost an essential accomplishment for anyone who claimed to be literate, and Umrao Jan cultivated her natural gifts with remarkable success. When she was forced by the influence of her environment to adopt her mistress's professions, she distinguished herself by her qualities as a singer and even more by her wit and conversation. Her life was perhaps less eventful than that of any other girl brought up with her. She met peple whom she liked and suffered many whom she disliked. Some awakened

From *Education and Traditional Values.*

in her the faculty of dreaming, but passed all too quickly out of her life. She eloped with a man who turned out to be a robber, she was betrayed by one who should have been loyal, and protected and helped by another who was himself a scoundrel. Sometimes it seems as if a pleasant accident has really been invented to give substance to the story, but Umrao Jan lived in a world that was socially and geographically very small indeed, the world of courtesans and their friends and admirers, of nawabs and their hangers-on, of adventurers, thieves and robbers, of lovers of music and poetry, all within the petty state of Oudh, deemed to have lost its right to independence in 1856. There is nothing far-fetched in the story, not even the prudence with which Umrao Jan saved as well as spent, and the shrewdness because of which she retired before the indifference of men told her it was time to do so.

We meet her in the novel when she has already retired. She gets herself invited to join a group of amateur poets who assemble occasionally in a house next to her own, and beginning with the recitation of her poems, we are led, on to an account of her life, given by herself with a sweet but transparent diffidence. As she tells her story, Umrao Jan also gives her views on things and passes judgement of herself and others. Her judgements are always fair and balanced but there is nothing original or profound in her reflections on life. Every system of living evolves a philosophy of its own, spontaneously and as a matter of course, and the first prize for wisdom goes to those who are able most convincingly to affirm the truth the illustrate the justice of the principles underlying this philosophy. Umrao Jan does not aspire to anything beyond this wisdom. She does not exaggerate her sorrows, or make any claim to the possession of knowledge, conscience or virtue. All the time she is just herself, and we are so fascinated by her being herself that no doubts or conflicts are raised within us.

We begin to wonder only when the last incidents have been related and the last verses aptly quoted, when we are left with a woman past middle age who has told us all about herself and now looks at us with a challenging smile. Do we understand her? Has she asked for understanding? Does she need sympathy or forgiveness, or only an intense appreciation of her many gifts, of her ability to rise above all situations, to live without regret? She has been so frank and open, she has invited us so often to condemn her for being what she is, she has been anxious, so ingenuously, to prevent our lifting the veil which she has obviously thrown over all the ugliness in her life, that it would be rude, almost vulgar, to attempt any form of moral judgement. But then we have to explain to ourselves the deep impression she makes on us of dignity, of innate virtue, of a detachment that not only helped her through the vicissitudes of life but seems to possess a deep spiritual quality.

It is quite clear that Umrao Jan is not the Anglo-Saxon heroine waiting for the chivalrous knight, and longing for fulfilment through love and lover. She has grown far beyond this. No surrender is possible for her; she knows too well that two persons do not become one by any process of spiritual melting or smelting. And if they could, she would not submit to it; she can exist only as an independent entity. But what of the great risks involved? What about personal security, social standing, the flagellation of a conscience worried by age and stung to action by unsatisfied desires? What about the emptiness of life, lived for oneself and alone? These are common fears, not real in themselves, perhaps, but so constantly communicated from one to another that they become a disease which none can escape and against which immunity can be developed only through sacrifice of many of the finer qualities. Umrao Jan seems to be well protected, first by her strength, secondly, be her culture.

What is her strength due to? I think it is a commonsense acceptance of the inevitable. This is not the same thing as belief in fate, of which the peoples of the east, specially Muslims, are so often and so lightly accused. There are, no doubt, many among us who talk of fate, but even a cursory examination makes it apparent that this talk is just a cloak for ignorance, laziness or obstinate refusal to do the right thing. Umrao Jan accepts the inevitable cheerfully and deliberately, making a limited study of life and men go a long way in guiding her safely across the dangerous and unsparing quicksands in which she is placed. She will have nothing to do with romance, with the uncertain quantities of human emotion, the unknown factors that govern human behaviour. She would rather be the innocent victim of circumstances than offer herself as a sacrifice on the altar of love and marriage. She would rather plead guilty with charm and get a verdict of innocence out of a fascinated jury than condemn herself with passion and lead a crusade of those whom she knows to be unjust against an injustice that is almost self-inflicted.

In fact, she is far too cultured to take all the usual talk about morality with more than a passing seriousness. What matters to her is company and conversation. She would delight in planning for days and nights the strategy and tactics of an intellectual skirmish that might last for five minutes or even less. What she asks of men is not admiration or love. She suspects both and will not take them at their face value or even as current coin unless she has proved to herself that they are supported by an intelligence, a discernment and a power of cultured expression equal to her own. She does not find her match and does not look for one, but is willing to give a try to such as desire it. In the end she convinces us that she has won, that of the many definitions of culture at least one is valid, an that is her definition. Culture consists in the mind moving freely upon a world in which virtue is the kept mistress of temptation, and understanding waits upon sin.

18

What Shakespeare Means to Me

The question what Shakespeare means to me could be framed in another way: What do I owe to Shakespeare? I owe to him my first experience of articulation, of association between language and feeling, of the value of the apt word, the striking phrase. Does this not mean everything.

My education began with learning to read the *Quran,* and I was charmed by its magnificent rhetoric. But I did not understand it at all. I then went on to Persian and the *Gulistan* of Sa'di, one of the world's classics, but beyond the comprehension of a child of six or seven years. I also learnt Urdu. *St. Mark* in the Authorised Version was my first real acquaintance with English, and I felt compelled to learn it by heart. A *Midsummer Night's Dream* and *King Lear* were my texts in the Senior Cambridge, but I knew most of *Julius Caesar* and *The Merchant of Venice* by heart from the books of the senior boys before Shakespeare's plays became a part of my course. I must have made many mistakes in my English exercises, and I do not remember having every been fluent of speech, but Shakespeare gave me a thrill that took me beyond correct English and beyond fluency to the music of words, the cadence of sentences, the sheer emotional delight of dramatic expression. English became my language in a far more intimate and exciting sense than the 'mother-tongue' of the educational theoretician.

The Russian master, most of all Tchehov and Dostoevsky, first made me aware of human character, of human beings who were basically amorphous and of those who struggled to attain meaningful form. This experience had nothing to do with language and was different from what I had learnt from Shakespeare. Then

---

From *Education and Traditional Values.*

I wandered into what I could call the world of Jalaluddin Rumi, in which the poet claims to be something of a prophet, and poetry to be something of revelation, a world of intense expression and enigmatic confusion of symbol and reality. This is the world of Persian and Urdu poetry, and this is where, for most of the time, and find myself now.

Am I more satisfied than I was in Shakespeare's world? One cannot compare one's first moments of exaltation with those that follow; the occasions and the responses are somehow so different. But after passing through more and more of real situations, the created situation, however, near to reality, appear created, or rather as reality qualified with an 'if'. When one has looked for years for the purpose of one's own life, and had just a bare glimpse of it, or not even that, imaginary identification with characters who live within the enclosure of a known purpose, which is their emotional and mental horizon, or lesser fry whose world is a still narrower circle of hope and desires, becomes a strain on the mind. But I would be misrepresenting myself if I emphasised this too much. I have not moved away from the Renaissance or the aesthetic concepts of Greece, which modern writers and artists have broken through as a limitation on their freedom. And I feel there would be many reasons why, if I had to choose, I would prefer to abide with Shakespeare rather than the moderns.

What of the world of Jalaluddin Rumi, where I find myself now? Is it God-centred or man-centred, is it a world where one cultivates the pleasures of self-denial, where one turns away, even if without disgust, from man and human interests? It is, no doubt, a masculine world, in which love is real but woman non-existent, or just a faint or vague suggestion. Here Nature appears in few symbols—spring, rose, poppy, valley, mountain, shore, wave, stream, sun, moon, light, shade, darkness, thorn, wasteland. There are archetypes of lover and beloved, mythical figures whose resemblance to man is purely nominal. Three are typified emotions, typified situations. The wine, the wine-house, the intoxication, the hangover, all are hypothetical.

This fruit, you will say, has no flesh and no juice. How can it have nay relish? I do not think this is a problem for the philosopher. There are no philosophers or prudent, knowledgeable men in Jalaluddin Rumi's world; they cannot survive in its atmosphere. Those who confuse desire with physical desire, those who aim at happiness derived from worldly goods, peace, success are regarded as carriers of the disease of vanity. In this world there is only intensity, the intensity of the aesthetic moment which expands into a universe of thought and feeling. It is sight, not the eye, mind, not the object apprehended, heart, not body.

That is why its most striking quality, in terms of literature, is epigrammatic expression. That is why though characterisation is quite foreign to it, it gives the must comprehensive rendering of the human personality. It is man-centred, in a larger, freer sense, than the world of antiquity or of the Renaissance; it is not world of problems but of solutions, the solutions arising from within man in quite as real a sense as problems in the Greek drama. It is a world of experience in which the trivial and the commonplace also acquire aesthetic value, in which the divine and the human, truth and falsehood, piety and sinfulness are taken to pieces and man is judged and honoured ad understood in the background of the immediate as well as the ultimate reality.

I know that those who are not intimately acquainted with Persian and Urdu poetry will find it difficult to accept these statements. I cannot substantiate them, because the best translation would be a disfigurement of the original. But I shall admit that, though anyone who finds himself in this world after having passed through the labyrinth of thoughts and emotions which is the world of Shakespeare, might feel that he had entered the open spaces, the very expanse of these spaces tends to convert them into an abstraction where one is not certain of being able to live and breathe, to retain one's identity. There is an inevitable inclination to set up a dividing line between imaginative experience and physical existence, to seek refuge in compartmentalisation. That is a relapse, an admission of defeat in the ordering of values. It is the realisation of this risk for those who attempt to establish permanent domicile in the world of Jalaluddin Rumi that takes me back to Shakespeare, to the images of man, to sheer earthly fun, to passion and conflict, to life and, let me admit this also, the despair of ever being able to see beyond life.

19

Glories of Indian Art

The oldest known examples of art are the oldest expressions of belief; the creative artist was perhaps the first articulate human being. The oldest Indian representation of a deity, a figurine known to archaeologists as the 'dancing god of Harappa', is the statement of a view of life that has not changed basically for five thousand years. This figuring is imbued with a vital, dynamic quality; it suggests a movement that is at once rhythmic and powerful; and there is that spontaneous and complete identification of the artist with his work which expresses a belief that is inborn, that is the whole of man's nature and the whole of his universe.

Students of religion connect the dancing god of Harappa with the Hindu god, Siva. The relationship between the bulls on the amulets of the Indus Valley, the Rampurva bull and the Nandi bulls of later years is even more obvious. The presentation of the deity are necessarily abstract; but the animal world can be brought close to man in a concrete form, and help us to guess the quality and measure the depths of that feeling which bound man to the mysterious forces of nature that governed his life.

In course of time, religion acquired its own identity through metaphysical doctrines, rituals and ethics. Intellectually, man had associated himself with a group of concepts, he had realised the need to discriminate between his emotions and to discipline his nature. But the approach to metaphysics was something which the believer discovered for themselves. On the railings of Bharhut and the gateways of Sanchi, story upon story and scene after scene was carved upon stone where the primeval attitude of oneness with all creation is depicted with an exhilarating spontaneity. There

---

From *Education and Traditional Values.*

is no question here of a conception of sin or wrong, or sanctity and profanity, in fact of any divergence between moral command and natural urge. The wood nymph of the Sanchi geteway is a symbol of joy, an assertion, both innocent and intense, of 'I am what I am'.

The art which represents this view of life has been called naturalistic. It reveals an inner awareness of nature, of the rhythm of cosmic movement, of the need to achieve harmony between symbol as compressed meaning and fact as the alphabet of expression. It could base itself ideally only on a doctrine of the unity of all art. In a book that could be called the artist's scripture, the principle is laid down that he who wishes to understand the theory and practice of art must begin with music and song, then go on to dance and then to painting and sculpture. He will then realise the inner unity of all art, which leads to the realisation of the absolute within one's own living body. This unity of all art was supported by a technique, by a symbolism in which posture, arms, gestures, the expression of the face all contributed to the exposition of a metaphysical idea. 'The likeness of man became merged', as a writer has said, 'into the presence of God.' The principle of unity of art has also a social significance, in that the craftsman, his patron and the public became magically one.

While this principle was taking shapes, there were revolutions in the political and social world. In the third century BC, the Emperor Ashoka imported Iranian stone-masons ad patterns. The Indian environment and the Indian genius transformed the styles to suit its own ideal of perfection. Some two centuries late, Greeks settled in the north-west of India introduced their own conceptions of art, and in their sculptures made the Buddha into a Greek god, if not Buddhism into a Greek religion. But in fact all that the Greeks achieved was the introduction of a new concept of proportion and symmetry and the general acceptance of the idea that making images of the Buddha was also a form or worship. The craft of image-making established itself at Mathura and then at Sarnath. At Mathura was made the statue of Buddha with transparent robes and sensuously moulded limbs, the grace of his form revealing the boundless grace of his spirit. At Mathura were also made female figures of a wondrous charm and lasciviousness, snaring other-worldly men with wicked smiles. They had to be made, and to be displayed in all sobriety, for was not the Buddha himself tempted, and is not temptation a part of the universal order? At Amravati the question is stated with almost a deliberately cultivated frankness, heavy anklets, and bangles tying the ethereal slenderness of limbs to the earth we know so well. The seated Buddha of Sarnath, is a vision of another world, the perfection of spirit embodied in perfection of form.

We have, unfortunately, very few examples left of painting, which must have developed side by side with sculpture. Prayer halls and living quarters for Buddhist monks began to be carved out of rock in the third century BC. But the world, with it stories and its colours, invaded or was led into the monastery. We have not much evidence of how it unfolded itself before the monks, apart from the frescoes of Ajanta and Bagh. But what we see of it passes understanding. Critics select a figure here and an episode there for discussion and comment, for the mind is staggered by the vastness of the panorama, the endless variety of experience, the exquisite beauty of every detail of form and feeling.

The ideal of unity within diversity and the plasticity of form found their consummation in temple architecture. However big the temple may have been, and the natural tendency was to make them more and more imposing, they symbolised the silence and the solitude of the cell where the individual soul could hold communion by itself with the world soul. We now look for other values. For us the Kailash temple at Ellora, carved out of one piece of rock by four generations of reverent craftsmen, ranks as one of the wonders of the world. At Konarak, in Orissa, standing by itself near the seashore, is the temple that represents the highwater-mark of design and sculpture, planned on a scale so magnificent as to have defied completion.

By the end of the fourteenth century, the naturalistic views of life and style of art had fulfilled themselves. Still, the formalism that the Muslims brought into India must be regarded as revolution. The Muslims had an entirely different view of life, of its significance and its meaning, an entirely different tradition of relationship with the divine. They had a religious law consisting of commands and prohibitions, a doctrine of community life in which the individual was just a fragment, and a concept of God based on the rejection of all material symbols. Image worship was condemned and representation of living things forbidden. Architecture, calligraphy and crafts were the only permitted means, if satisfying the craving for beauty, but to these the Muslims added the arts, sinful perhaps but not past forgiveness, of music and painting and poetry. They cultivated almost everything, in fact, except sculpture, which was too obvious a challenge to the iconoclast. When the Muslims came to India, they had acquired and given a distinct form to all the arts recognised by culture, except the presentation of the human form in wood or stone. They had evolved, besides, a philosophy of what they called Love, and developed a craving for the beautiful that could not satisfied. They believed also in the assertion of the human personality, in majesty in power, in domination over space and time.

The first Muslim work of art, the Qutub Minar, is a tower so named and so constructed as to present the typical Muslim values and aspirations. Its mass is cleverly concealed by variations in the surface of its several stories, by calligraphic and floral bands across its tapering length, by balconies supported on clusters of miniature arches; its slenderness creates an illusion of height, while the pyramidal distribution of weight gives it great stability. The arched screen of the mosque, of which the Qutub Minar formed a component, has not stood the test of time, but what remains is fascinating in grace and beauty of proportions. The inscriptions on the older arches constituting this screen are a unique mixture of Quranic verses and floral patterns, and create the feeling that the word of God is being whispered among leaves and flowers.

Beginning with the Qutub Minar, the Muslims experimented in architectural forms. The most characteristic structures were mosques and mausoleums. The mosque, as the house of prayer, represented the numbers, the strength, the aspirations, and the democratic character of the community as a congregation. The Atala mosque at Jaunpur and the Purana Qila mosque at Delhi are typical symbols of strength and stability, one expressing them in a primitive, the other in a refined and disciplined form. The mausoleum has a long history behind it. In Indian Muslim architecture it is not a reminder of death but the last and the most glorious message of life, for what else could be said of Humayun's Tomb, of Sikandra where Akber lies buried and of the Taj Mahal? Architecture collected around itself, with striking discrimination and tastefulness, the arts of calligraphy, of mosaic, of gardening. It explains to us the beauty and significance also of what is not there, of the craft of the jeweller, of the brass-worker, of the ivory-carver, above all of the textile worker, whose patterns, simple or elaborate, belong to the world of the minaret and the dome, of channelsand cascades, of birds and flowers. Like architecture, Indian Muslim or Mughal painting belongs to the category of formal art. But the rich illuminated manuscripts, the birds of Ustad Mansoor, the portraits, some of them most exquisite, reveal an inner unity of culture, vibrant with an intense longing for beauty, a beauty out of which we are born and to which we return.

20

The Red Fort

Nothing looks so dreary as a house that is not lived in but only visited. The dreariness of the palace that has become a monument—even a national monument—is is proportion to its erstwhile magnificence. Still we admire palaces, for even as monuments they impress the mind, and enable some of us to exercise our imagination and see them as they once were. But the Red Fort is a challenge which the most imaginative would not venture to accept. It has a moat and a high wall around it, but it is most unconvincing as a fort. The buildings supposed to have been once inhabited leave us wondering how even kings and queens cold have lived in them. We have either to tell ourselves that it is all make-believe or to accuse the Mughals of having sacrificed comfort to a hard and showy elegance.

In fact, there would have been nothing to perplex us if the civil and military officers of the British Government had not been afraid of ghosts. In 1858, the Mughal Empire was dead and the last Mughal Emperor a prisoner. There was no one even to haunt the Red Fort. Still it was thought necessary to convert it into a cantonment. It was only much later that the Fort was given the status of a monument, but only a small part of it, and that, too, overshadowed by ugly military barracks. The other buildings were pulled down, the orchards removed, in order to make the place look like a proper cantonment. Another reason for perplexity is that the Indian way of life has changed. We think, like the Europeans, that a house consists of rooms, and rooms are not rooms unless they have four walls. Even the verandah, which so far served as a relief from enclosed living, is fast disappearing. We now think

---

From *Education and Traditional Values.*

in terms of permanent fixtures, isolation, privacy. The ghosts of earlier centuries would prefer to haunt their own prisons rather than live in our houses.

The age of the Emperor Shah Jahan, the builder of the Red Fort, was an age of refinement, in which what are called the minor arts attained their highest level of excellence. Shah Jahan was the wealthiest of the Mughal Emperors, and he could build as grandly as he liked. He did not really need a palace, the one at Agra was commodious enough. But architecture seems to have been his principal means of self-expression and so he planned a new city at Delhi, to be named after him, Shahjahanbad, a new palace and a new mosque. The palace of the Mughal emperors was only the hard core of the imperial camp. But the royal palace was still only the hard core of the royal camp. It did not eliminate improvised outdoor living, the tent of the nomad, the exquisite carpets hung and spread, the flow of water, the blaze of colour and the bloom of flowers. The imperial palace was also the seat of the government. Its privacy was not the privacy of the householder sheltering himself from prying eyes, But the dazzling publicity and the baffling mystery of power.

Shah Jahan had the gift of making the solid look immaterial, the strong appear delicate. I said the Red Fort was most unconvincing as a fort. That is because there is nothing grim and forbidding about it. The wall and the moat could really protect, but the gateway of the Fort is more an invitation to loyal subjects to come and pay respects to their sovereign than a warning to actual or potential enemies. Those who entered the gate and passed the scrutiny of the chamberlains would proceed through the attendants, quarters to the Naubat Khana, where the time of the day or night was indicated by the music played. If a public audience was being held, they would be taken between serried ranks of soldiers to the Diwan-i-Am, the Hall of Public Audience. This is a pillared hall, its roof supported on broad graceful arches whose proportions have a striking harmony. Here the Emperor sat on a balcony, the entrance to which is from the back, from the interior of the palace. Below the balcony stood the Vizier, on a pedestal high enough for him to hand over and receive documents from the Emperor. On both sides of the royal balcony the nobles stood with folded arms, in strict accordance with their rank, and they stood stiff, silent and motionless till the audience was over.

This audience was really the second audience of the day. The first or informal audience, called the *darshan,* was about the time of the sunrise. The Emperor appeared on a balcony at the back of the palace, towards the river. Anyone who wanted could come and have a look at him, and some families in Delhi made it a tradition not to have breakfast before they had seen the Emperor. But those who had complaints or requests to make also came at this time, and they had the opportunity of presenting their papers directly. These were received and examined, and orders passed on them were communicated to the officer concerned at the Public Audience on one of the days following. It was a most serious event if the Emperor did not appear for the *darshan,* and usually people began to fear for peace and security and to pray for the Emperor's life.

The Public Audience was generally followed by another consultation, the most important of the day. This was held in the Hammam, the royal Bath, after the Emperor had refreshed himself. The royal Bath has now a very plain exterior. But inside, with the water-channel and the small fountain from which came a spray of scented water, it is almost the ideal place for the thoughtful mind. Subsequent generations associate with the Bath mysterious ways of heating the water and regulating its temperature as it flowed into the spacious pool, but even without this mystery one cannot but envy the luxury which the Emperor enjoyed of having so much water to himself.

The part of the palace which was meant to overawe the mind with the imperial splendour was the Diwan-i-Khas, the Hall of Private Audience. This was for the evening assemblies, when cradles were lighted and the Emperor and his courtiers appeared in full dress. This Hall is of marble, its ceiling is elaborately painted, and there is the presumptuous inscription that if Heaven is to be found anywhere on earth, it is here in this Hall. But architecturally this Hall seems gaudy and pretentious when compared with the simple elegance of the Diwan-i-Am. In this Hall stood the Peacock Throne, a marvel of the jewellers' craft. It was taken away by Nadir Shah as part of his booty in 1739, and was too valuable to have remained intact. But judging from its descriptions and the picture of what is left of it, it must have been a piece of artistic extravagance.

South of the Diwan-i-Khas there is a suite of rooms and a small hall. In one of the rooms one can still see the furnishing. Were these carpets, these cushions and pillows, this bed, all that the emperor had for himself? We hope not. But if this room is an indication of destitution in the midst of wealth, even what is left of the ladies' quarters sickens us with its contrast of abundance and deprivation. The Emperor had an abundance of ladies in the palace, the ladies having nothing except what the Emperor bestowed on them as a favour. The Rang Mahal, the Palace of Colour, must have been seething with humanity, filled with the noise almost of the country fair, and repellent to anyone not brought up in its atmosphere. The two buildings of the ladies' part of the palace that we see now are survivals of what must have been a township of females. The situation was really much worse than appears at first sight, and makes the household of the simple honest citizen a haven of contentment and peace.

Odd structures come up in every group of buildings that grows with time. Aurangzeb put a jewel of a mosque right in the midst of the worldly pomp of the Red Fort, as if to show that he could have communion with God while all around him worshipped pomp and power. The two pavilions, Sawan and Bhadon, Early Rain and Late Rain, with the water-channel and the pavilion in the lake between them were part of a large garden, the garden which ahs disappeared and in whose stead stand military barracks. We can give our imagination free play in reconstructing the architecture of the Red Fort, but the barracks remain where they are.

21

The Qutub Complex as a Social Document

The Memoirs and Reports and Lists of Delhi Monuments published by the Archaeological Survey of India contain complete and detailed information about the groups of buildings which constitute the Qutub complex and other related material which is beyond the scope of this paper. My purpose here is not to reproduce all that information in an abbreviated form. I have had to study Indian architecture for a book I wrote some eighteen years ago on ancient Indian culture and now for lectures on Indian Muslim architecture. I am not a specialist in any sense. I can only present certain methods of approach that have occurred to me in the attempt to make architecture intelligible and interesting to myself and to my students, and I have selected the Qutub Complex as the subject of this paper because it is particularly useful for this purpose.

The study of my specimen of architecture consists, I feel, in reading the architect's mind to discover how he adopted techniques and selected material for the construction of the building, the purpose of which was known to him. In reading the architect's mind we are moved by the same sentiments, we participate, as it were, in the planning, in the choice of ways and means, in the execution of the plan and in the assessment of the completed work. It may bring us no joy if we feel from the start that the architect was content to imitate or to follow a fashion, to use the prevalent techniques and the most easily available material, and to look forward to no appreciation beyond what is shown by the unimaginative for work which did not involve exercise of the imagination. We may, on the other hand, share the rapture of the artist who discovered the most perfect harmony between purpose

From *Islamic Influence on Indian Society.*

and design, and find that the plan, the techniques, the material and the proportions of the created work reduce themselves to a single moment of exaltation. It is this experience which assures us that the beauty of architecture is the beauty of poetry, music, painting and sculpture, and the great artist can enable us to overcome our imperfections and realise the underlying unity of all art.

Unfortunately, we tend to impose many limitations on ourselves. In Indian architecture, for instance, we consider first the categorisation—is the building Hindu or Muslim? Then we look at the size, the costliness of the material, the names and dates of the builder and the building. We also overlook certain basic facts of the history of architecture. The technique of corbelling, that is, projecting stones or bricks of the upper layer over the lower so as to make an arch or a ceiling, and the use of the beam and post, or the trabeate systern, are much older and more universal than Hinduism; the use of the arch and dome, or the arcuate system, was developed by the Romans and is much older than Islam, but we have labelled one system Hindu and the other Muslim. We look everywhere for borrowed elements. I do not mean that there are no differences between Hindu and Muslim architecture or that they should be ignored. The temple and the mosque represent two different concepts of worship, and cannot, therefore, be built in the same way. But if we begin, as we should, by understanding the purpose of the structure and then attempt to read the architect's mind, we shall appreciate the beauty of the created work without being misled by irrelevant considerations.

What we have to remember, I think, when studying Indian monuments, is the difference between architecture and sculpture. While trying to explain this difference to any class a definition of both these arts occurred to me, which my artist friends have since assured me is fairly apt and comprehensive. Architecture is creation with material; sculpture is creation out of material. The canvas of the architect is space; in space he creates a form putting together whatever material he builds with. The canvas of the sculptor is the material itself, out of which he makes a particular form emerge. A very small building can be a specimen of architecture; a very large building, or even a complex of buildings can be an example of sculpture. Not only the Kailash Temple of Ellora, which was in fact sculptured, but many other temples have been deliberately given an outline which creates the impression that they were not built with but hewn out of stone, and are sculptures on a gigantic scale. Between the definitely architectural and the definitely sculptural we can have variations of approach. The architecture of Gujarat is generally characterised by a sculptural approach, though there are also buildings, like the Jamé Masjid of Sarkhej, where the influence of sculptural standards is completely absent. We could say that up to a certain time in Indian history the aesthetics of sculpture dominated architecture. During Muslim rule sculpture may not have been patronised to any appreciable extent, but the stone-masons and sculptors certainly did not give up their profession, and they took their time to accept the aesthetics of architecture. It would be fairer and more precise not to make distinctions on the ground of religion when the real difference ties in the degree to which the standards and aesthetic principles of sculpture and architecture have been applied in the planning, the construction and the ornamentation of a building. If we bear this in mind, a study of the Qutub complex becomes an exciting intellectual and aesthetic adventure, and gives history another perspective.

I cannot here dilate upon the purely archaeological problems. We know that the Quwwat-al-Islam mosque grew with the Muslim population of Delhi. As constructed originally, in 1199, it would not have accommodated more than 2000 persons. Its final extension by Alauddin would have made it sufficient for ten or fifteen times that number, if not more. These extensions have been traced out without much difficulty by archaeologists, and fairly reasonable and convincing reconstructions have been made to show what the mosque looked like after its first extension by Iltutmish and second extension by Alauddin. Here I propose to consider only what is still standing, and can be seen and judged by those who do not have the imagination and the training of the archaeologist.

The Turks who occupied Delhi came from an area in which both brick and stone were used in building, but architecture in brick, such as we see in the oldest monuments of Bukhara, would have set the standard. Along with brick structures, the art of making tiles had been developed and was making continuous progress, both aesthetically and technically. On the other hand, sculpture and stone-masonry practised in the Greek colonies of Bacteria and Gedrosia would not have died out. Thanks to Alauddin Jahansoz, we cannot now say whether Ghazni was mainly a city of brick or of stone or of wooden structures. But we may be certain that those who thought of building a mosque and a *minar* at Delhi were thinking in terms of architecture and not sculpture. Construction in wood was ruled out; bricks were not available; they could only build in stone.

There is an inscription above the northern entrance to the Quwwat-al-Islam mosque stating that the material of 27 temples was utilised for its construction. If this was done after the people of Delhi had submitted, it was certainly against the *shari'ah,* but there would hardly have been any among the Turks occupying Delhi whose conscience would have troubled them on that account. We must, however, unequivocally condemn the action. Some of the temples would no doubt have been damaged and desecrated during the fighting, and they would have been abandoned for that reason. But the inscription indicates that these temples were deliberately dismantled, and it was not only a matter of utilising the material of temples destroyed as an act of war.

While the moral and legal issue is clear, however, the question of who carried out the dismantling has still to be answered. We can assume that Hindu stone-masons were forced to do it, or that Muslim masons were employed. In any case the work was done by stone-masons. If they had been Muslims brought over from the Punjab or beyond they would have known the technique of building true arches and we would have had corbelled arches in the screen of the Quwwat-al-Islam mosque. As it is, the true arch appears for the first time in the Alai Darwaza, built in 1311. We must assume, therefore, that the stone-masons were Hindus. And not only in this first instance. It appears from an inscription on the 5th story of the Qutub Minar that the repairs and additions in the reign of Firoz Tughlaq in 1368 were carried out under the supervision of a master-mason named Nana Salba, son of Chahada Dev Tala.

The stone-masons unproved for dismantling the temples and building the mosque would not all have been residents of Delhi. The city was not large enough to provide continuous employment for any considerable number of stone-masons, unless we assume that a good proportion of the 27 temples mentioned was in the process of construction. Family group or communities of stone-masons and sculptors generally migrated from one place of work to another, remaining settled for as long as was necessary to complete a particular project. Many such families and groups would have been collected in haste from near and far, for the mosque had to be built soon and the Minar was to follow.

What would have been the attitude of these stone-masons and sculptors to what they were asked to do? Would they have undertaken it for fear of losing their lives, with hatred seething within them? That would be the logical deduction, considering what had happened. But, then, would not their feelings have affected their work? Cunningham has pointed out some technical defects in the construction of one or two corbelled ceilings and their supports in the south-western corner of the mosque colonnade, and attributed them to haste. But the later extensions have not stood the test of time as well as the original mosque, and instead of any evidence of slipshod work we find unimpeachable examples of free, creative effort. The stone-masons were not submissive instruments. They must have asserted themselves as technicians, and also, exercised their imagination to appreciate and their skill to realise in practice the architectural values they were asked to express.

There are many mosques in India with colonnades around their courtyards, but none in which the eastern side has been so definitely emphasised. The gateway built by Iltutmish and the Alai Darwaza are on the southern side, because the city lay to the south. But the main gateway of the original mosque, like the entrance to a temple, is on the east, and the column on this side are four deep, while those on the north and south are only three deep. Does not this imply that the stone-masons, or their chief, feeling instinctively that the eastern colonnade must represent the vestibule of a temple, insisted that this should be emphasised, and had his way? The screen, which stands opposite, was probably the central feature, following a prevalent style in mosque construction which was further developed in different parts of India. It must have been higher than the domes of the covered area behind it. What remains of the screen now is the central arch and three of the four low arches which flanked it, two on each side. Originally, one would have looked through the central arch into a shadowy interior, and felt that passing through it one would enter the world of the spirit, of calm and quiet contemplation of the divine. Now one looks through it into space and feels that in isolation and decay its beauty has acquired another and far richer meaning. I remember taking the Russian artist Magda Nachmann to the Qutub over twenty years ago. Once she had seen this arch she would look at nothing else. She stood before it in rapturous silence and wept when it became dark and we had to return. And indeed, if we look at the arch and take in its beauty, we feel that it is something that can be translated into many forms and many moods, into the peace and tranquillity of the Buddha image, into the timeless contemplation of the Trimurti of the Elephanta Caves, the ecstasy of the *sufi*, the poet's dream of a loveliness that eludes the drapery of woods. It is something beyond architecture and beyond sculpture, a chiselling out of space that creates the framework for endless horizons of thought and feeling.

I referred earlier to reading the architect's mind in order to understand his work. Archaeologists have found inscribed, on a pillar of one of the arches of the screen, and again near the entrance to the Minar, the name of Fazl-bin-abi'l-Maali as superintendent of the works. He may have been an Arab or an Iranian or a Turk. He may have been a genius in the art of communication as well as of architecture, able to design beautiful and impressive monuments and to explain to masons who did not know his language how to build what he had designed. But if he were a Muslim from outside India, would he have designed corbelled arches, knowing that they could stand much less weight than true arches? We can be sure that he would not. It must have been the Hindu masons who insisted on building according to their traditional techniques, disclaiming all responsibility for the stability of the structure if any other technique was followed. And when this had been agreed to, they must have made their own calculations of the width and height and the massiveness of the supporting piers. This explains the exquisite proportions of the central arch, its quality of being eloquent and alive, its rising upward with a moving, natural grace, the two sides meeting not with a mathematical precision, but as it were by mutual attraction, with an upward tilt at the meeting point symbolic of the joy of union.

But this is only a part of the sculptors' contribution. I imagine that the suggestion of making the decorative reliefs sweep upward instead of running horizontally, as in temple decoration, must have appeared to the stone-masons as an exciting novelty, and their enthusiastic response is evident in their work. Among the decorative bands are verses from the Qur'an, inscribed in bold relief. The architect may have known of a mausoleum in Uzkund, built in 1187, where the Quranic inscription has a setting of flowers and foliage, and have proposed to do the same here. But while the oral setting in the Uzkund monument is stylised and repetitive, the setting in the Qutub screen is naturalistic, warm and vocal. The Hindu sculptor did not know anything about the doctrine of evelation, he knew only about nature, and instinctively he has represented the Qur'an as an utterance of nature, the voice of leaves and flowers, the whisper of the woods.

Some thirty years later, the mosque was enlarged, and the screen extended to maintain symmetry. The arches of this screen do not have the same proportions. In the relief work on their frontage there is stiffness and austerity; the exuberant naturalism of the earlier work has given place to something severely geometrical. An archaeological expert has expressed the view that this relief work is in the Saracenic style, and must have been executed by imported craftsmen. This is unlikely. The arches are still corbelled; there is still lack of faith in the strength of the true arch. As for the ornamentation, it is doubtful if a sufficient number of skilled stone-masons would have been found in the neighbouring Muslim principalities or would have been worth recruiting when so much skill was available in India. Besides, Persian and Central Asian ornamentation is of tiles or inlay, and depends for its effectiveness very largely on colour compositions. On the screen built by Iltutmish and on the inner walls of his tomb the patterns may be similar, but they have been executed on different material. They are neither plastic nor colourful and give the impression of overloading. The craftsmen must have been Hindus or Indian Muslims, but because more than a generation had passed since the construction of the first screen, they would be new men, less imbued with the sculptural traditions of their fathers. In any case, a change was bound to come, with architecture seeking independent self-expression.

In the context of this aesthetic struggle, the Qutub Minar stands midway between the first screen of the Quwwat-al-Islam mosque and its extension. It was built in two stages, the first story in 1199, and three stories by Iltutmish about 1230. Firoz Tughlaq repaired the Minar because it had been damaged by lightning, and very unwisely converted the fourth storey into two. He somewhat increased the height of the Minar, but also introduced incongruous elements. Apart from the alteration made by Firoz, the Minar would have been planned as a whole, Iltutmish completing what Qutubudidn Ibak had left undone. An inscription—the lower band on the second story—states that Iltutmish ordered the completion of the Minar.

What was the idea underlying the Minar? It, would have ratified the religious if it were called a mazna, a lofty tower from which the muezzin called the faithful to prayer. There are examples of such maznas in Muslim countries, but probably not as tall as even the first story of the Minar, which is 95 feet high. There are also examples of free-standing Minars which have an architectural significance of their own. The lower we now call the Qutub Minar has not been so called in the contemporary histories. It could have been used as a mazna. But its architectural qualities most probably derive from the fact that a small group, determined to occupy and rule for all time as much territory as it could, found it necessary to create a symbol for its confidence in itself, in the stability of its power and in its destiny, But great architecture, let us remember, is the instinctive self-assertion of man against time and death. It is the offspring of inspired moments. The purpose of a great monument cannot, therefore, be too precisely defined. It is almost always something beyond what the planners themselves could have stated in words.

The Minar has a Central Asian Turkish ancestry. There is a minar at Jar Qurgan, near Termez, built in 1108-9, which has the appearance of 16 round columns tied together, and there is a strong resemblance between it and the second storey of the Qutub, which has a pattern of rounded flutes in section. The Minar-i-Kalan, at Bukhara, built in 1127, has a round, arched clerestory at the top, supporting a cluster of arches, like three balconies of the Qutub. The Minar at Ghazni consists in part of a polygon with deeply indented angles, a form of which the wedge-shaped flanges of the third storey of the Qutub could be considered a variation. An almost contemporary structure was the minar at Wabkent, built in 1196-97. All these minars have a taper. But these were examples for the Muslim architects of the Qutub, Fazl bin abi'l Maali, whose name is inscribed near the entrance, and Muhammad Amir Koh under whom the minar was completed in the reign of Iltutmish, as appears from an inscription on the side of the doorway of the third story. One question of basic importance have been decided the way the Hindu craftsmen wanted it to be. These craftsmen, in accordance with their inherited notions, would have insisted that to ensure stability, horizontal pressures should be entirely eliminated. The minar has, therefore, a very pronounced taper. Its diameter is 46 feet at the base and, as it now stands, 10 feet at the top. As originally built, in four storeys, the top would have had a diameter of perhaps 12 to 15 feet. There are notations on the south face of the minar's plinth, which Cunningham believes refer to an adjustment of about an inch in the plumb-line of the building. In this respect, the Hindu master-masons would have left nothing to chance. The minar at Jar Qurgan has a fairly high plinth, the Minar-i-Kalan of Bukhara, a very low one, and there would not have been much discussion if the Hindu master-masons insisted that there should be no visible plinth. They were not used to the idea of the plinth as a distinct feature of a building. The rounded flutes and wedge-shaped flanges as we see them give the Minar an exquisite sculptural character, and it is my conjecture that this, too, is either entirely a contribution of the Hindu master-masons or their interpretation of the treatment of the facing shown in the plans or explained to them by word of mouth. The massing of inscriptional and ornamental bands and decorative mouldings below the balconies reminds us of the decorative treatment of temple walls, but the restraint shown in the spacing out of the other bands on the shafts of the three storeys of the minar is something on which the Muslim architect would have insisted. The balconies, which form one of the most attractive features of the Minar are an essentially Muslim idea, and so are the cluster of miniature alcoves, or vaulted arches, which support them. But, in a network that looks like honeycombing and in the cusped tracery reminiscent of temple ceilings, there is evident an attempt to disguise architectural forms with sculptural effects. The result of the technical and aesthetic cooperation of the Muslim architects and Hindu master-masons is one of the most striking monuments of the world. But in form as well as meaning it is not what it was probably meant to be. The Turks wanted to create a symbol of power and stability; with its upward surge, expressed in the taper and in the almost organic emergence of one storey from another, the Qutub Minar is such a symbol. But the Hindu sculptor has also put his stamp on it. You can have power, he seems to have said, but I shall so suffuse it with beauty that those who see it will know that beauty is the only power that endures.

Political conditions following upon the death of Iltutmish and up to the time Alauddin had ensured security from foreign invasion and established law and order in his dominions were not such as to stimulate architectural ambitions. At least, there is nothing in the Qutub complex that can be traced to this period. Stone-masons would have been employed in miscellaneous minor projects and by degrees lost touch with their sculptural traditions. Perhaps the need for employment forced them to accept the new styles, to learn the technique of building the true arch and to put trust in its strength. Some of them may have experimented in buildings that no longer exist, in various methods of assimilating sculpture and architecture. For the next monument that we see, the Alai Darwaza, is the work of practised hands and of minds thoroughly versed in the art of creating pleasing compositions of architecture and sculpture.

As originally planned, the Alai Darwaza consisted of a domed chamber with three entrances and a fourth archway leading into a portico, which was projected into the enclosure of the mosque. There were extensions also sideways, east and west, to combine the Darwaza with the enclosure wall in a harmonious fashion. The portico, which must have been built on the trabeate system, with a low roof, to be in keeping with the colonnade around the courtyard of the mosque, is no longer there, but the extensions still form visible parts of the existing structure. The architect of the Alai Darwaza was beyond doubt a Turk steeped in the Seljuq and earlier traditions of monumental architecturc. He must have had the good sense to seek out the best stone-masons and sculptors and to consider how their skill could best be utilised before he gave a final shape to his plans. In this process he must have had consultations and discussions, and his plans must have been endorsed by his master-masons before they were submitted for final approval. The idea of three entrances into a chamber and an entrance into the mosque across a portico would have been his and it would have appealed to his master-masons because of its resemblance to the structure of a temple. People would enter the mosque through what they thought was a gateway, but when leaving they would pass, like Hindu worshippers, from the *mandapa,* or the vestibule, into the *viman,* or shrine.

Structurally, the Alai Darwaza is a marvel of inspired simplicity. The arches of the three entrances are so exquisitely proportioned that they are equally beautiful whether seen from the outside or the inside, although the floor of the chamber is several feet above the ground level. The square of the chamber is converted almost imperceptibly into the circle of the dome, which rests on elegant squinches of a simple, sculptural pattern. From the outside, the dome is rather low. In fact, it is not a separate unit of the structure but the roofing of the vault, the height of which, when seen from the inside, is very impressive.

The plinth of the Alai Darwaza is indicated by means of a projection round the base, which could be used for sitting on, and of a cornice, but in a way, it has also been concealed in sculptural patterns, most of them of the traditional Indian style. This may be taken as an instance of the architect adapting a feature of temple architecture to suit his own purpose or as a contribution of the Hindu master-masons, who would have had considerably less opportunity to display their skill if the plinth had a straightforward architectural character. The superstructure of the Darwaza appears from the outside divided into two stories, the distinctive features of the lower storey being ornate arches, small replicas of the main arch, two on each side of it, and of the upper story rectangular panels formed by a judicious and pleasing juxtaposition of inscriptional bands of marble and red sandstone. The impression of height conveyed by the lofty entrance arch is toned down by the panels into a quiet dignity, and the eye could wander long and admiringly over the whole facade without any feeling of satiety or weariness. The three main entrance arches, with their white and red nook shafts, their intrados or inside surfaces alive with patterns of foliage in deep relief, their spearhead fringes and their marble frames have a beauty and a meaning all their own. If the central arch of the Quwwat-al-Islam mosque leads outwards into an uncharted world, the entrance arches of the Alai Darwaza leads inwards to a beauty distilled in lucid and harmonious detail, which holds the eye and mind in thrall.

And what of the two exactly similar arches, one of red sandstone and one of marble, on the fourth side, where one now enters the mosque enclosure, but which formerly led into the portico? These arches, with their delicately suggested trefoil, are something unique; they have no ancestry and no offspring, Indian or foreign. They obviously bear the impress of the ivory-worker who has undertaken an adventure into the dimensions of architecture, or let himself be lured by a dream. But the social and religious aspect of these arches is even more significant. For, quietly and unobtrusively, they tell the Muslim worshipper that as he enters his mosque he is also passing beneath the shadow of a temple, under an archway that was created for him by devotees of beauty who could see all facets and all forms of truth.

The Alai Darwaza is the parting kiss of architecture and sculpture. They meet in fruitful union in Gujarat, but the next monument of significance in Delhi, Ghiyasuddin Tughlaq's tomb, is pure architecture disdainful of any sculptural devices and interpretations. Even in Gujarat, though the ascendancy of architecture does not appear in any chronological sequence, architecture has the last word in the Jamé Masjid of Champaner. Arid so it is evident that, while in political and social life, in literature, music and dance the movement is towards unity, in architecture the tendency is in the opposite direction, the drapery and the aesthetics of sculpture being gradually discarded so as to achieve purely architectural expression. Akbar brought artisans together from all parts of India to build Fatehpur Sikri, but all that he could achieve was a harmonious assemblage of different styles. The sculptural beginnings of Indian Muslim architecture are an indication that we must revise our perspective. For while the written record of history shows the establishment of authority by force and bloodshed, we have in the architectural record unimpeachable evidence of understanding and cooperation, of joyful participation in creative work of the very highest quality. Should not this incline us to reconsider any views we may have formed of blind hostility between Muslims and Hindus in the first stages of the Turkish occupation of north India? War and destruction would have been inevitable in any case if ambitious men came from outside to displace the rulers of the country, but need we also assume that the people as a *whole,* Hindus as well as Muslims, were committed to *this* conflict, that there was no mutual appreciation and cooperation between the urban populations of north India, the Ghaznavi kingdom of the Punjab and lands beyond the Khyber Pass? Surely the actual builders of the Qutub complex must have known, if not admired, each other, for how else could they have achieved such perfect understanding? And if we assume that they knew and admired each other, we must exercise our imagination to correct impressions created by the rhetoric of the medieval historians and the political slogans of our own times.

22

The Status of the Individual Conscience in Islam

Every Muslim who talks or writes about Islam has the feeling of being a reformer. It appears to him that the judgements of Western scholars are prejudiced and disrespectful, while traditional presentations of Islam are mostly inadequate or irrelevant to our times. He has, therefore, to guide those willing to accept guidance, the *ulama* or the conservatives or the modernists or the indifferent, who are by far the largest number, towards a genuine understanding of Islam. I have no intention of becoming a reformer. My purpose is merely to attempt a re-examination of our approach to Islam, and I am doing this because such re-examination has to be a continuous process if we are to prevent belief and practice from becoming habits, and for that reason, sterile, if not lifeless. Sensitive Muslims, in particular the sufis, have always realised this. Long ago, Shaikh Ainul Quzzat Hamadani said, 'Worship of habit is idolatry, true worship is that which releases us from habit,' and Shaikh Nizamuddin Auliya referred to prayer and fasting and haji as things any old woman could do; manliness required us to get beyond them. During the last three hundred years, however, movement of revival have led away from the spirit to a stricter adherence to the letter. Some good has, beyond doubt, resulted. Superstitions have been given up, rights asserted, and in the matter of rights I think particularly of Syed Ahmad Shahid's successful insistence on the remarriage of widows. But in all such reforms, conscience was brought in to re-inforce theological argument. Religious thought in the real sense is absent, only a piety has been

---

From *Islamic Influence in Indian Society.*

aimed at that would derive consolation and strength from a more correct or thorough conformity with the law. The Muslim was called upon to think only that he might be more firm in his adherence, in *taqlid*.

Syed Ahmad khan was an intruder in the theological world, but his re-examination of beliefs is extremely significant, because he brought critical reason into religious discussion and challenged the principle of *taqlid* itself. Apart from what he considered the fundamentals of the faith, he took nothing for granted. We may think what we like of his effort to show that the Qur'an's teachings were in accord with scientific knowledge, that jinns and angels are not what they have been believed to be, his commentaries on the Qur'an and the Traditions represent the thoughtful Muslim's right to think for himself. But Syed Ahmad Khan's whole argument is vitiated by his criterion of progress. Of course, he believed that he was looking for the truth, but what he considered to be truth were only the scientific ideas and what might be called the reasonable materialism of his time.

Syed Ahmad Khan abjured religious discussion in order to establish an educational institution; Maulana Azad, who had perhaps much more to say and who was not inhibited by any concept of science or progress, thought it better to remain vague on such an important issue as to whether the Muslims ought or ought not to have become and remained a separate religious and political community. But he did suggest an attitude which, if sincerely adopted, would have revolutionised our life. The Muslim, as a believer in God who is the *rab*, the Providence nurturing, sustaining, guiding mankind, should regard it as his function to nurture, to sutain, to guide those among whom he lives. Maulana Azad could be regarded as having performed this function to the best of his ability, but it demands a degree and a quality of simultaneous involvement and detachment that is beyond normal comprehension, and his suggestion seems to have remained almost unnoticed. What needs to be clarified is not how a Muslim can be a good Muslim, but where he should act according to his conscience as a Muslim and not rely on theological support.

What is meant by conscience in the context of this discussion is that sense of right and wrong which governs our everyday conduct and the recognition of the obligation to do what is right. This sense is strong in some persons, generally it is weak, and depends on the example of others and the direction of social opinion. So it is only every rarely that we determine for ourselves what is right and what is wrong. Generally, we follow social practice. Muslims who felt bound as a matte of conscience to repudiate any aspect of such practice appeal ed to the highest authority, the Qur'an, but the right of appeal was itself circumscribed. Only those acknowledged as possessing the necessary knowledge could make use of this right of appeal, and they, in their turn, had to follow the system of interpretation adopted by some school of jurisprudence. This brings us back to the position that right and wrong in matters of religious belief and practice are determined by social opinion and established habits of thought. The conscience of the individual Muslim has had to find satisfaction in adherence to one of the accepted system of interpretation of the Qur'an and Tradition.

The Qur'an does not prescribe any such adherence. It recognises both the community of believers and the individual believer, and dos not ignore the possibility of the community being in the wrong as well as the individual member. "O believers, be you securers of justice, witnesses for God, even though it be against yourselves, or your parents and kinsmen, whether concerns rich or poor, for God is nearer to you than both. And do not follow caprice, so as to swerve (from the truth)."[1] The Prophet't example and his injunctions would serve as something to be adhered to only for those of his contemporaries who were able to observe is behaviour and to ask him questions. The Traditions, as they have come down to us, have already undergone an interpretation in terms of accepted ideas and practices, and though we may not agree with Syed Ahmad Khan's view that all the Traditions are just reports of statements made by the Prophet or of the things he did and, therefore, binding only if they appeal to our reason, we cannot ignore his view either. The methods for scrutinising. Traditions were laid down long ago just because all reports and reporters were not reliable.

This whole question of adherence can be considered also from another angle. Is belief to be regarded as something static or dynamics? This not the same as asking whether beliefs should or should not change with time and circumstances, but involves an inquiry as to whether there is something in the nature of belief itself which makes it an expanding and developing force. Is there anything, for instance, in our belief regarding the relationship between Muslims and non-Muslims that could make it a healthy, creative element in our present-day democratic life? Historical situations in which certain attitude were prescribed in the Qur'an, or the deductions made from these prescriptions are no longer relevant. The Indian Muslims have no opponents like the Quraish of Mecca, they do not have to deal with Jewish and Christian and other tribes, they have no opportunities for expansion such as the Muslim Arabs had in the seventh and eighth century, they are not a state that has to consider possibilities of peace and war with non-Muslim states. The categories of *darul-Islam* and *darul-harb* do not apply, and the neutral category of *darul-amn* would imply not only passive acceptance of the present situation but an abdication of the obligations and rights of citizenship. Are we, in this situation, to look for some theological authority to guide us, and to wait passively till this authority is found? Or are we to act according to our conscience and continuously remind ourselves that we must be 'securers of justice, witnesses for God,'[2] not only for ourselves but the whole political community of Muslims and non-Muslims to which we belong?

As a matter of history, the Muslim conscience has found ways and means to release the Muslim mind from confinement within the idea of a rigid division of beliefs into true and false and of a community regarding itself as the sole possessor and upholder of true belief. Ibn 'Arabi has become the symbol of the doctrine of the Unity of existence, *wahdahal-wujud,* but belief in immanence is found mush earlier. The Unity of Existence, as expounded by Ibn 'Arabi, is complicated and abstruse; it would not have caught the imagination as it did and would not have found such fervent expression in sufi thought and in poetry if there had not been among Muslims a subconscious urge to acknowledge all humanity as co-existing with the Muslim community and the right of non-Muslims to profess their own faith. It was the Muslim conscience which made sincerity and constancy and not allegiance to Islam the test of true belief, and which made Akbar ask the fundamental question: Have the beliefs of men no common ground?

In the politial field, however, the Muslim conscience failed to become operative. The Umayyad dynasty suppressed ideas and tendencies subversive of its authority. Even more fatal was the attempt of the Mu'tazila to enforce acceptance of their doctrines through the power of the state, as it led ultimately to an alliance between the orthodox *ulama* and the government, and established unfortunate precedents of interference which made freedom of thought and even scientific inquiry a matter of grave risks. We could excuse the orthodox *ulama,* perhaps, if they refused to give theological support to those who opposed the existing political and social order, but they went much further and did all they could identify the religious interests of the Muslim community with the interest of the ruler, placing him virtually beyond the judgement of his subjects. Equality before God remained, but it was more than neutralised by the forms of inequality created by the policies of the rulers. This meant complete domination by those in power who, though always a minority, posed as the representatives and upholders of the majority point of view in all matters, and it was logical that the majority opinion should prevail, specially in questions of belief and practice. Thus this hypothetical majority was regarded as equal to the whole community, which was identified with the existing political and social order; this, in turn, was identified with the best interests of the *ummah,* and, therefore, of Islam. *Taqlid* meant, in this situation, the abrogation of the individual Muslim's right to hold an independent opinion about right and wrong, in other words, elimination of his conscience. What a farce *taqlid* could degenerate into became very obvious in the second half of the 19th century, when Muslim and lost every vestige of political power and the religious-minded were forced to practise the type of casuistry which the poet Akbar ridiculed

You can wear these socks and shoes
And make love to Miss D'Souze,
If only you fast and pray
You can live and love as you choose.

During the same period, the creative potentialities of belief were reduced even more by apologetics, whose appeal to sentiment increased with time. The modern Muslim's listlessness, his lethargy, his disregard for his own welfare, his betrayal of a great religious and cultural heritage was contrasted in eloquent terms with the faith, the energy, the splendour of earlier times. The Muslim was so carried away by the eloquene of the apologists that the achievements and the glories of the past came to life again, and the experience was so vivid and intense that the present was merged in the past, and the most spineless subject of the British Raj transformed himself in imagination into a conquering world force. Apologetics also generated a pride which made the Muslim look down on others, and if forced to face reality, he excused or even justified his won degradation by arguing that others were worse. Another aspect of apologetics derived from the resentment created by the judgements on Islam by Western orientalists. The beliefs and practices embodies in the *shari'ah* of Islam were not studied more deeply to refute unfavourable criticism, only everything Islamic came to be admired with greater fervour. The facts of history were forgotten, incidents not very significant in themselves were magnified into permanent characteristics. For instance, if Muhammad Tughlaq once appeared before a qazi to explain his conduct, or Jahangir had a bell put up in his place which any person unjustly treated could come and ring, this was enough to characterise Muslim rulers as upright and just. I shall not multiply instances. Even a cursory examination will reveal that apologetics inculcated an approach to Islam and Muslim history that was completely unrealistic and distorted.

It is from this confusion of sentiments and ideas that the mind and the conscience of the individual Muslim has to be salvaged.

Where and how do we begin?

Where traditional answer to this question is that, as the matter concerns belief and practice, the *ulama* as a body, or the *imam* or leader must propose what should be done. The principle implied is that the community must change as a whole, otherwise there will be a mass of conflicting individual opinions with no authority behind them. On the other hand, the *ulama* have been insisting for centuries on the completeness and the perfection of the *shari'ah*. They cannot conceive of any amendment being necessary, because the circumstances of life or the demands of a particular situation are not recognised as a valid argument. Even the present position, of Muslims in India, to say nothing of the political, social and economic revolutions that have taken place in the world, cannot make them think of a re-examination of what they consider the injunctions of *shari'ah*. If driven into a corner and forced to admit the need of a re-examination, they will insist that anything done must be with the consent of the *ulama* as a whole. What authority they have for assuming this position of arbiter in matters of religious law is by no means certain, and even a cursory study of a book of *fiqh* will show that on many points there are differences of opinion, and the accepted view is only one that is to be preferred. It is clear, therefore, that the *ulama* as a whole have almost never been in greement, and if thoughtful Muslim had not been afraid of exercising their own judgement, the *ulama* would have possessed no status or authority at all.

The functions of the imam as a religious leader have not, to my knowledge, been laid down anywhere. In the law-books, *imam* and *amir* appear to be interchangeable terms, that is, the ruler could be called *imam,* as he could be called the *khalifa,* on the basis of the traditional appellations of the first heads of the Arab Muslim community—*khalifa, imam* and *amir al-mo'minin.* The *ulama* were, in practice, subject to the ruler, and that is why rebellion against the established ruler has been made theologically unjustifiable, except when he becomes a *kafir* and enforces *kufr.* Akbar raised an interesting point in regard to the status of the *sultan-i-'adil*; that, however, is something which could be discussed endlessly. For, while according to the ruler almost unlimited power as the possessor of political authority, the *ulama* were not willing to assign him any religious status.

It is more relevant for our purpose to consider whether anyone could be a leader, let us say, of the Sunnis in a religious sense, having authority, by virtue of his religious and spiritual pre-eminence, to exercise the right of *ijtehad,* of giving new interpretations or interpretations differing from those of the orthodox schools. There have been persons who have been called *imams* and *mujtahids* out of respect for their learning, and generally after their deaths. I do not think, however, that the possibility of such a leader has been contemplated. The concept of *ijtehad* has been made much of by apologists, as if it implied the right to think afresh and regard as obsolete and without force the thinking done and the opinions already expressed on any matter of law or religious practice. In fact, it seems to me, *ijtehad* had only a technical significance; it is the exercise of the right, by someone possessing the necessary prestige, to give an opinion, differing in some considerable degree from the opinion already expressed by theologians of prestige and regarded as more or less conclusive. Those who disregarded the authoritative texts would be considered innovators deserving of condemnation. Syed Ahmad Khan's ideas would not be regarded as an example of *ijtehad*; they were condemned as heresies and innovations. Maulana Abul Kalam Azad's contribution is also not *ijtehad*. Dr. Iqbal, when arguing in the style of an apologist, regarded *ijtehad*, as an adequate provision against outmoded thinking, but he was afraid even of liberalism. He was a great poet who made generations of Muslims crazy with self-admiration, but his contribution to religious thought, when objectively examined, contains nothing that could be called *ijtehad*.

Anyone who wished to exercise the right of *ijtehad* has had to show from where he derived his right. His awareness, his moral sense, his ideal of creating a better society, not being theological values, could not be regarded as giving him the right. In the second half of the 15th century, Syed Muhammad of Jaunpur, a person of extraordinary learning, spiritual insight and moral courage, was deeply moved by the irreligiosity and moral decadence of his time. He wished to transform the profession of Islam into an absolute commitment to the spiritual and social values embodied in the faith. We have no record of any of his discussions with the *ulama* of his days, but it seems they could never prevail against him. However, Syed Muhammad was forced, by the tactics of the *ulama*, the enthusiasm of his followers or his faith in his own mission, to declare that he was the *Mahdi*, the expected saviour of the world. This claim at once became the point of orthodox attack, and a theological pandemonium resulted in which the real teachings of Syed Muhammad became of secondary importance even for his followers, and no change came about in Muslim society and its way of life. In our own times, Mirza Ghulam Ahmad of Qadian attempted *ijtehad*; he, too, was forced into, or adopted a position similar to that of Syed Muhammad, claiming to be Christ returned to earth, and disputing the accepted interpretation of the Qur'anic verse which declares that the Prophet Muhammad was the last of the prophets. Mirza Ghulam Ahmad's life, if objectively examined, shows that he was aware of the perilous condition of theological Islam, of Islam as expressed in doctrines and as represented by the *ulama*, that he realised that Western civilisation was based on social and material values for which a proper place would have to be found in the Muslim mind and that, in spite of the decline of the Muslim peoples, Islam could spread as a religion among the nations of the West. I am not interested in the claims Mirza Ghulam

Ahmad made for himself, but I am interested in the reasons why he made the claim. Possibly it was because success is a heady wine which few can hold, and he felt that, having established his position as a reformer and a theological disputant, he could go to the limit and aspire to be a prophet. He had measured the theological and intellectual capacity of the *ulama* and might have felt that they would not be able to challenge him effectively. But supposing he had not made the claim to be a prophet, what would his position have been? A mere *'alim,* a theologian with novel ideas who would have many to applaud, but none to follow him, or a political leader with a religious bent of mind who would be considered a loyalist, a kind of Khan Bahadur under the special protection of the British government. He would have had no recognised form of authority, he would not have been able to lead and guide and command. His movement would, in any case, have aroused controversy, but it would have fizzled out as a mere controversy if he had been content to remain an *'alim* or a religious-minded political leader.

Muslims in general were so shocked by Mirza Ghulam Ahmad's claim to be a prophet that his genuine contribution was completely ignored. He had committed a theological crime which could not be forgiven. They gained nothing whatever by their opposition to him. He, on the other hand, became the founder of a religious community, a well-knit organisation able to look after itself and also after a liberal-minded group within it which became the spearhead of its missionary activity. But the sect of the Qudianis, in order to justify its existence, has had recourse to theological arguments, and narrowed rather than broadened the approach to Islam.

It seems, then, that neither the *ulama* nor the hypothetical leader can find a way out. The only possibility is that the conscience of the individual Muslim should be his guide, and should be recognised as the only guide.

There are statements in the Qur'an which indicate clearly that societies were punished collectively. This is a matter of history. In the Qur'anic dispensation itself, the responsibility for his actions, good and bad, is entirely on the individual. 'Upon that day when a man shall flee from his brother, his mother, his father, his consort, his sons, every man that day shall have business to suffice him.'[3] And it is also said, 'And whoever does a righteous deed, be it male or female, believing, we shall assuredly give him to live a godly life; and we shall recompense them their wages, according to the best of what they did.'[4] This is not, however, something new. It was revealed to the prophets Moses and Abraham also 'that no soul laden bears the load of another, and that a man shall have to his account only as he laboured, and that his labouring shall surely be seen and that he shall be recompensed for it with the fullest recompense.'[5] Where responsibility is thus placed squarely on the individual, he cannot go around asking for advice, or plead, when a reckoning takes place, that he was wrongly advised.

Having said what I have about theological argument, I realise that it is inconsistent for me to quote from the Qur'an to prove my point. In fact, I think it wrong and unfair to the Qur'an itself to take a verse and use it to fortify an argument. The Qur'an was meant to inspire, and not to be quoted from, and though many of its verses can be taken to represent the whole of its spirit, the contexts of its verses are not those that precede and those that follow; the real context of every verse is the whole of the Qur'an. Piety and habit and the instinct that makes us evade responsibilities we cannot bear have made the reading of the Qur'an a mechanical process. We do not read in order to contemplate; we read for spiritual merit. This we cannot show that we have attained, and the results of contemplation we miss altogether. We must look to the Qur'an for the stimulus to spiritual experience. It is only through such experience and not through clever interpretations that we can give it genuine contemporary significance; in other words, make it an operative force in our personal lives and, collectively in our society.

I have emphasised experience of the Qur'an rather than an academic study of it because its statements are, in the crucial matter of man's free will plainly contradictory. 'If God had willed, He would have made you one nation; but He lead astray whom He will, and guides whom He will, and you will surely be questioned about the things you wrought.'[6] There are many verses of the same tenor. If we attempt a logical explanation, we get confused. If we accept these verses as true, contemplate the nature of God's omnipotence and what flows from it, we shall find the contradiction resolved. Belief is not something which comes of itself, like hair on the head, it is an act of will. If we read the Qur'an for inspiration and guidance, it is an act of will. If it is not that, then what the Qur'an says of the hypocrites applies to us also. 'Do the people think that they will be left to say, We believe, and not be tried? We assuredly tried those that were before them, and assuredly, God knows those who speak truly and assuredly, He knows the liars.'[7] Man's free will is, in the Qur'an, assumed. It is God's omnipotence that has to be accepted, and to be accepted as an act of will. That we thereby also accept what is a reality is what the Qur'an wants us to understand, and that is why the Qur'an lays an abomination upon those who have no understanding.'[8] The Qur'an is, in a way, a dialogue between God and man, where man has spoken through his actions in history, and God expresses His judgement on the actions, asserting the all-comprehending nature of His power. Islam, as submission to God's will, is not passive acceptance of what happens and what does not happen (and thereby throwing the responsibility of all our inertia and purposeless living on God), but an active association of our will with His in the realisation of the highest of which human nature is capable. 'O believers, if you help God, He will help you and confirm your feet.'[9]

It is in this light that the status and function of the individual conscience has to be considered, and not with fear in our hearts of the possibilities of error. Error, as commonly conceived, is a theological concept, a deviation from the letter of the law, which those who believe in the letter and not in the spirit condemn because it endangers the system they have built up. The Qur'an takes a different view. 'Whoever struggles, struggles only to his own gain, surely God is All-sufficient nor needs any being. And those who believe and do righteous deeds, We shall surely acquit them of their evil deeds and shall recompense them to the best of what they were doing.'[10] In another verse it is said, 'If you avid the heinous sins that are forbidden you, We will acquit you of your evil deeds and admit you by the gate of honour.'[11] The heinous sins referred to here have to be deduced from other verses, and that is a task which theologians have performed with relish. But the reference here is to those who, of their own will and with fullest understanding become God's friends[12] and agents, in the spirit of the verses, 'Then We appointed you viceroys after them, that We might behold what you would do,'[13] and 'It is He who has appointed you viceroys in the earth and raised some of you in rank above others, that He might try you in what He has given you.'[14] It is with reference to men and women generally, and not only to members of the Muslim community, to all whose conscience is alive and alert, and who act according to their conscience in all matters of importance, but also inevitably commit mistakes. Fear of such mistakes, they are told, should not deter them; they should do the best they can.

What they should do is indicated only in general terms, such as good deeds and righteous deeds, "bidding to honour and forbiddin dishonour." It is the believer who determines specifically, in the light of his conscience and under the circumstances in which he lives, what a good and a righteous deed is and what 'honour' and 'dishonour' imply. But belief and good deeds are mentioned so often together that we must assume that they cannot be taken apart, that one is impossible without the other. The theologian will insist that belief comes first, and with belief all the forms of obedience, prayer, fasting, zaket, haji. But he must not be allowed to stop there. He must be equally specific about the particular forms of good and righteous deeds, and as insistent on their being performed as he is about prayer and fasting. He would have done this, perhaps, only we must understand that it is not his function. His field is law and precedent, the precise fulfilment of clearly defined duties. He cannot apply his standards in matters where the individual has to decide for himself. He has, therefore, been of the view that there are no such matters, that the *shari'ah* is all-comprehending and perfect. We must part company with him and with his rigid concept of the *shari'ah* if we are to act in accordance with our conscience for the fulfilment of the obligations that the Qur'an has laid on us, as an entirely individual and personal responsibility to God.

II

The first question every Muslim must ask himself today is whether he really regards Islam as a universal religion or only as the religion of those who call themselves Muslims. The theological statement, based on the authority of the Qur'an, is that the true faith has been revealed to all mankind through prophets, not all of whom have been mentioned in the Qur'an by name. But the people to whom the true faith was revealed have deviated from it, the deviations of the Jews and the Christians specially being commented upon in the Qur'an. The Muslim have believed that they are rightly guided, and some theologians have gone so far as to guarantee forgiveness and heaven to anyone who has recited the formula of the faith. But there are doubts also about certain sects, and about the mass of the ignorant who, for lack of guidance, hold theologically reprehensible beliefs, being really and truly Muslim. Theologians apart, Muslims in general, who are proud of their faith and sure of being rightly guided, forget the conditions that are almost always attached of sincere belief and performance of good works whenever anything is said in the Qur'an about believers and Muslims. It is also forgotten that the Qur'an mentions that there are believers also among the Ahl-i-kitab, the Jew and the Christians.[15] But the inclination of the theologian or the ordinary Muslim to exclude does not affect, in Muslim belief, the universalism of Islam. We may conclude that Islam is a universal faith revealed by God to all mankind, that the Qur'an is, as it says, 'an exposition for mankind and a guidance, and an admonition for such as are god-fearing[16], and the verse, 'We try you with good and evil for a testing, then unto Us you shall be returned'[17] is addressed to all humanity, Muslim and non-Muslim.

If Islam is a universal religion, and among mankind are those who believe, those who only profess to believe and those who do not believe at all in the one God and His guidance, all problems should be considered not in the light of Islamic theology and history only, but in the context of world history. We must know how the human conscience has operated among all the peoples of the world at all times, in the light of the status which the Qur'an assigns to man in creation, and of the directives it has given: 'O believers, be you securers of justice, witnesses for God'[18] and 'Let there be one nation of you, calling to good and bidding to honour and forbidding dishonour.'[19] We must study the history of all religions, their beliefs and practices, not to see how far they have deviated, for of that God alone is the judge, but how close they are in essence to the fundamental human faith. And we must not confine ourselves to religious beliefs and practices. We must study, for instance, the lives and thoughts of all those who, like Socrates, set examples of that examination of beliefs and actions which is implied in 'bidding dishonour,' that diagnosis which reveal ignorance and hypocrisy, that idealism which seeks to create a society based on justice and that determination to suffer all the physical consequences of struggling in the way of God which is the hallmark of true Muslims. We must look everywhere to discover when and how the Islamic values which we believe in have been realised in practice. And we must be willing to judge ourselves as we judge others, for unless we do that, our claim to believers will not stands impartial scrutiny. 'O believers' the Qur'an says, 'be you securers of justice, witnesses for God.' This part of the verse I have already quoted. But the Qur'an continues, 'Let not detestation for a people move you not to be equitable; be equitable, that is nearer to god-fearing.'[20] Muslims have had friendly and hostile relations with different peoples, and the judgements of contemporaries, both Muslim and non-Muslim, are liable to prejudice our own, to the extent even that we cease to look for the good in other people and see it only in ourselves. In India, Muslims have lived for centuries with the Hindus, and it would require a supreme effort of our conscience to arrive at an impartial and just assessment of the historical record. Christians and Muslims have fought against each other for centuries, events and circumstances have made feelings of hatred and hostility almost a permanent quality of their relationship, and though in the balance it might be shown that one party is more to blame than the other, the Muslims are under a definite obligation to be equitable in their judgement.

We must give the Western peoples, even if theologically they are not such Christians as they ought to be, full credit for having at last abolished slavery. We ourselves should have done it much earlier, but we preferred to impose on ourselves the social framework of seventh century Arabia, without any regard for the fact that the merit of freeing slaves was an obvious indication that we should grow out of this framework. These same Western peoples ultimately succeeded in establishing political democracy, as a matter of conscience and not religious belief, while we have, from the establishment of Umayyed rule onwards, suffered despotism to continue, with only individual protests on grounds of conscience, though such despotism is neither permitted nor contemplated in the Qur'an. Imam Ghazali advised the good Muslim to avoid spiritual contamination by keeping away from kings, courtiers and government officers, and good Muslims followed his advice. There would have been bloodshed and suffering if they had obeyed the Qur'an and attempted to fulfil their obligation of being securers of justice. But democracy and the ideals of political freedom and legal equality were not achieved in the West without bloodshed and suffering extending over centuries; the Muslim peoples did to act in the same way because their conscience was not assertive enough to break the fetters of theological opinion. That democracy should be the form of all Muslim government may not have been explicit enough in the Qur'an to prevent despots from bending theological opinion in their favour, but nothing could be more explicit than the responsibility of the administration to help the needy with the resources created by the collection of *zakat*. The first Khalifah levied *zakat* by force from Muslim tribes unwilling to pay it, the second Khalifah set instructive examples of personally helping the needy, even the non-Muslims. Then we have the instance of the Umayyad Khalifah, Umar bin Abdul Aziz, who ruled only for two years, and the obligation of using *zakat* for assistance and welfare ceases to be recognised, although some rich and pious persons console themselves with acts of philanthropy. The welfare state of today owes nothing to Muslim idealism or the exercise of the Muslim conscience. But it is nearer to the ideals of Islam than any Muslim system of administration after the first two Khalifahs.

There was much religious persecution among Christians in the Middle Ages and up to well within modern times. There are examples also of persecution of Muslims by Mulims, but the burning of heretics among Christians has no parallel in Muslim history. As against this we must set the ideals of service cultivated by the Christian monastic orders, ideals which continue to be acknowledged and served in different ways in our own times. There is nothing to compare with this in philanthropy as practised among Muslims. Then, there was the revolt against the domination of the Roman Catholic and later of the Protestant churches, an apparently intellectual but basically spiritual revolt. The result was cultivation of knowledge for its own sake and at all costs, leading to the advancement of learning and science which we see today. There was no church among the Muslims, only an alliance between the rulers and the orthodox *ulama.* Philosophers, scholars and scientists like Shaikh bu Ali Sina and al-Beruni were, however, constantly in fear for their lives. They would have felt safer, and hundreds of others would have been willing to take risks for the advancement of knowledge if the Muslim conscience had not been cowed down by theological opinion and betrayed the cause of intellectual and scientific inquiry. The surrender of conscience was so complete that religious knowledge suffered quite as much as any form of secular study. What we have done for the exposition of Islam during the last two hundred years is ridiculously insignificant in comparison with the contribution of non-Muslim scholars to Islamic studies. Perhaps they are lacking in reverence and sometimes obviously prejudiced. But their study of the sources is deeper and far more thorough than ours, and merely condemning their prejudice does not prove our being in the right.

If it is evident from world history that the principles of Islam can be realised in practice by non-Muslims, what considerations should, as a matter of conscience, govern our conduct under the present political and social conditions?

Nationalist Muslims have looked for theological authority to support their view that the Indian Muslims should form an integral part of the Indian nation. There is no such authority. An objective judgement of persons, ideas, movements is possible only through the exercise of an enlightened and sensitive conscience. If the individual conscience had been given the status that rightfully belongs to it, the argument of world history would have been more than enough. The Muslim could show that non-Muslims were not only capable of realising but had in fact put into practice the Islamic principles of equality and justice, and that it was the primary duty of the Muslim, as a matter of conscience, to cooperate with his non-Muslim fellow-countrymen for the attainment of freedom and the establishment of a democratic welfare-state. Unfortunately, the weight attached to theological authority gave those whose main consideration was self-interest the opportunity to propagate the ideas of an Islamic state. The explicit claim put forward was that the Muslims were a separate nation, the implicit claim was that the Muslim was a different type of human being, with moral and social responsibilities which the non-Muslim could not share with him.

The Muslim state is a well known historical and contemporary phenomenon; the Islamic state is a fiction created by the Indian Muslim mind. Muslim rulers have done their best to show that in their policies they served the interest of the Muslims and Islam, generally by exhibitions of intolerance and by waging wars against non-Muslims. The *Hidayah,* a thirteenth century compendium of religious law, considers all wars against non-Muslims as *jehad,* and the spoils of aggression could thus be acquired along with spiritual merit. But no Muslim ruler would have dared to risk an assessment of his administrative and political actions on the basis of Islamic doctrine. That would have made the nature of his irresponsible, despotic ruler far too obvious. But the Islamic state which the enthusiastic, or rather the hysterical Indian Muslims dreamed of was not a purified Muslim state. They believed that God's omnipotence could not be qualified or modified; therefore, no persons or even the Muslim community as a whole could be sovereign. There could be no legislation that was not certified by the *ulama* as being consistent with or at least not inconsistent with the injunctions of the Qur'an. An aspirant to spiritual and temporal leadership has gone so far as to declare that only men known for righteous living should be elected to the legislature or appointed to offices. This concept of the state and its functions reveals how disastrous has been the dissociation of the Indian Muslim mind and conscience from public affairs, even when the rulers were Muslims. There was personal loyalty to the ruler, but no personal involvement, no loyalty to the state as an institution. Everyone looked after himself and God looked after the state.

This was not, however, the attitude of the Muslims only. It has been the general Indian attitude throughout history. The national movement united us against the British government; since independence the absence of a personal and unqualified commitment to the state and the common interest has become distressingly clearer. The individual conscience has not been brought into play as a power controlling and directing actions and creating healthy patterns of social and civic behaviour, the general tendency is to sit back and expect others to do what should be done.

It is not my purpose here to give general guidance to Muslims as to what they should do. I am concerned with only one aspect of a vast and complex problem, and that is the status of the individual conscience. I consider this aspect not only important but crucial, as it is his conscience alone which can give the individual Muslim the awareness of his duty to exercise his initiative and the confidence that God wills that he should exercise it.

I do not wish to repeat what I have said already about the idea of an *imam* or a leader. It is our weakness and not our conscience which makes us look for him. The question of the solidarity of the

Muslims as a community is different. It has become apparent in many ways and at many times that there is an element in the majority community, we do not know how large or small, but we do know that it can be effective in its destructive measures, which will continue to reject us so long as we continue to remain a distinct community with its own beliefs, way of life and economic interests. We cannot, and we should not, for that reason give up our concept of a community. But I have already stated that the principle of adherence, as understood and insisted upon for several hundred years, can undermine spiritual and intellectual freedom. As a matter of history, I do not think the Muslim have had a common religious front after the Prophet, unless we identify Islam with the opinion and policies of the majority, whether Hanafis, or Shafi'is or Shi'as. Under the conditions prevailing today, the organisational difficulties of constituting a common religious, political or economic front would be insuperable. We would not, however, pin our hopes on a concentration of forces if we had faith enough in the individual Muslim conscience to rely on a dispersal of forces, each unit, however small, and each individual acting in accordance with his own conscience, and in the interest of truth, justice and generosity. The concept of an organised community, committed to the attainment primarily of what is good for itself, makes it necessary for its members to distinguish between themselves and the members of other communities, and this is being done in India by almost all communities, though only the Muslims are openly reproached because of it. If the function of Islam is to unite and not to divide, it must be left to the individual Muslim conscience to decide how far in particular situations the maintenance of distinction is necessary or advisable. And it is only for the individual Muslim conscience to determine in what ways it can serve the spiritual, moral and social ideals of Islam.

We must remember that, in spite of all that has been said to impress on our minds the significance of the community, Islam is in essence an individualistic religion. There is no church, there is no intermediary between the individual Muslim and God, to whom his responsibility is immediate and personal. Men and women have the same obligations, and are subject to the same judgement. Property, though a trust, is held by the individual, and marriage does not affect a woman's rights to hold property. The true Islamic spirit seems to be that the individual should uphold the community as an act of his own will, and not that the community should absorb the individual will into its own.

There are problems in which, it seems to me, the concept of community has been adhered to a controvertible extent, and in which we look to theology for guidance instead of reason and conscience.

When the Sarda Bill was being discussed in the Central Legislative Assembly, those Muslims who were aware of the practice of child marriage among Muslims and its unhealthy consequences preferred to keep quiet or were induced by the pressure of community opinion to oppose its application to the Muslims. The only argument for this was that an Assembly with a majority of non-Muslim members had no right to legislate for the Muslims in matters concerning their personal law. It seems to me that the more valid theological argument would have been to oppose the bill on the ground that the age of consent was too low, and marriage being a contract, it could not be entered into by a minor. If the age could not be raised, the girl should be given the right to repudiate the marriage, if she so desired, when she came of age. The argument against non-Muslims tampering with the *shari'ah* was weak, because judicial decisions had already tampered with it in the matter of a daughter's right to inheritance, and there was no consideration shown to the *shari'ah* in the penal code or any other branch of law under British rule. As it turned out, the Muslims in demanding exemption from the Sarda Bill lowered their prestige in the eyes of all thoughtful persons.

Islam was the first religion to convert marriage from a sacrament into a contract, from a ceremony essentially religious into a pubic and legal proceeding. Now, instead of trying to make their own socially more just conception of marriage generally accepted the Indian Muslims are allowing themselves to be regarded as defenders of polygamy, or conscientions objectors to monogamy, whichever might be worse. It should have been a matter of conscience for all thoughtful Muslims, and in particular the lawyers to come forward with contract form of marriage that would preclude bigamy; instead, they drift into the position that the consensus of the *'ulama* alone can permit changes in their personal law, knowing very well that there will be no such consensus, even if all the *'ulama* could be brought together. We shall only confirm the view that is already gaining ground that though we might be quite reasonable as individuals, as a community we are imprisoned, mentally and morally, within a completely static religious system.

I shall now again raise the question: Do we conceive of Islamic belief as something static or dynamic?

Islam means submission to God's will. God's will was reveasled in the Qur'an. But everything that happened before and after the Qur'an was revealed, also happened by the will of God, and we are supposed to see in everything that happens the working of God's will. We cannot disregard events; the Qur'an itself refer to those of the past and also to contemporary occurrences. A reference back to the Qur'an for what has happened, and in spite of what has happened since would mean that the working of God's will since the revelation of the Qur'an is to be disregarded. If it is to be disregarded, we must have clear authority for doing so, and I do not know of such authority. The Mu'tazrila believed that the Qur'an was created. Their view was not accepted, perhaps not even examined as it should have been, for reasons that were less theological than political, and the present orthodox view prevailed, that the Qur'an is eternal truth. But even that does not oblige us always to look backward for we do not go back directly to the Qur'an but to its interpretations and to semantics of the Arabic language.

As belief and practice, Islam was perfected in the Prophet's lifetime, but the development of jurisprudence itself shows that many questions had to be answered that arose because of the change of circumstances, change of the environment or the context in which Islam was being practised. Later, the acceptance of the principle of *taqlid,* whatever the reasons behind it, put a stop to the development of religious thought, and it was not events and occurrences but the old texts that were studied to discover the working of God's will. It is the great contribution of the sufis that they broke through the rigid framework of *taqlid,* claiming to establish a direct relationship between man and God through the guidance of the *shaikh.* This relationship, however, suffered from being too restricted. At its best it was spiritual experience and ecstasy, in its ordinary form it was just an escape from the world of events and occurrences, and from the study of God's will as revealed in them. But sufism stands out, none the less, as a symbol of the self-assertion of the Muslim conscience.

The question how we can submit to God's will unless we know how it is seeking and finding expression still remains unanswered. It is not enough to say that everything is predestined. God is omniscient, we are not. God's omnipotence and omniscience is emphasised in the Qur'an, but the individual is also held responsible for his beliefs and actions. We cannot, on the assumption that God has already willed what is going to happen, abstain from action which to reason, to human reason, appears beneficial or necessary. We have to understand for ourselves the attributes of omniscience and omnipotence, the necessity of belief, the necessity of submitting of God's will through good works, through 'bidding to honour and forbidding dishonour,' through the establishment of justice. This cannot be done in a vacuum, but only in this world of actions and events. It can only be done by individuals who are sensitive and intelligent, who are engaged in a constant endeavour to enlarge their awareness and whose conscience compels them to commit themselves to the cause of truth and justice. Islam is a dynamic faith demanding continuous involvement of mind and energy in the affairs fo the world for the fulfilment of the purpose for which man was created; there can be no complacency, no self-satisfaction. The conscience of the Muslim must ever repeat to itself and others: 'Nigh unto men has drawn their reckoning, while they in heedlessness are yet turning away.'[21]

NOTES

1. Qur'an, IV, 134.
2. Ibid., V, 11.
3. Ibid., LXXX, 34-37.
4. Ibid., XVI, 99.
5. Ibid., LIII, 39-42.
6. Ibid., XVI, 95.
7. Ibid., XXIX, 1.
8. Ibid., X, 99.
9. Ibid., XLVII, 9.
10. Ibid., XXIX, 5.
11. Ibid., IV, 35.
12. Ibid., X, 64.
13. Ibid., X. 15.
14. Ibid., VI, 165.
15. Qur'an II, 106.

16. Ibid., III, 132.
17. Ibid., XXI, 36.
18. Ibid., V, 11.
19. Ibid., III, 100.
20. Ibid., V, 11.
21. Ibid., XXI, 1,

23

Freedom and Obligation: The Islamic View

Freedom and obligation have legal implications for those who wish to avoid the embarrassment of thinking for themselves. It is enough for them to know what they must and what they must not do; and freedom consists in doing what the law permits. But even those who follow it without question believe the law has a spiritual basis, and expatiate on its underlying 'wisdom.' If we probe deeper, we discover that this 'wisdom' is in fact a way out of a controversy which agitated the minds of thoughtful Muslim for many generations, a controversy arising out of the question, whether in his acts of obedience or disobedience, man was really a free agent or, considering God's omnipotence and omniscience, *could* be a free agent when everything happened or was done by God's will alone. An attempt to answer this question, without placing limitation of any kind of the operation of God's will and without admitting the validity of any argument exonerating man from responsibility for his acts, led to considerable verbal quibbling.

There are four statements of Muslim authorities, embodied in a kind of catechism, which might be regarded as representing the orthodox or, to be more exact, the majority view on the question of free will and predestination, upon an answer to which the determination of the extent to which man is really free, depends. The first is found in the *Wasiya* or testament attributed to Abu Hanifa (d. 767), the founder of the Hanafi school of jurisprudence:

'We confess that works are of three kinds, viz., obligatory, meritorious, sinful. The obligatory are by Allah's command and in accordance with His will His linking, His good-pleasure, His decreeing, His predetermining, His creation, His judgement, His

---

From *Islamic Influence on Indian Society.*

knowledge, His help and His writng on the Preserved Tablet.[1] The meritorious are not by Allah's command—exalted by He—but are in accordance with His will, His linking, Hid good-pleasure, His decreeing, His predetermining, His writing on the Preserved Tablet. The sinful are not by Allah's command but are in accordance with His will, not in accordance with His liking but by His will, not in accordance with His liking but by His decreeing and His predetermining, by His creation but not by His help, in accordance with His abandoning and His knowledge, but not with His recognition, and in accordance with His writing on the Preserved Tablet'.

The second statements from the credo of al-Ash'ari (d. 935) evolved as a result of controversy with the philosophical school:

> Nothing exists upon earth, be it good or bad, but that which God wills; but all things are by God's will (*mashiya).* No one is able to do anything before God does it, neither is anyone independent of God, nor can he withdraw himself from God's knowledge. There is no Creator but God. The works (*a'mal*) of creatures are created and predestined by God, as He said (Qur. 37, 94): "and God has created you and what ye do." Man is able to create nothing; but they are created, as He has said, (Qur. 35, 31): "Is there any Creator except God?"

The third statement is that of Imam Ghazali (d. 1111):

> We witness that He is Willer of the things that are, a Director of the things that happen; there does not come about in the world, seen or unseen, little or much, small or great, good or evil, advantage or disadvantage, faith or unbelief, knowledge or ignorance, success or loss, increase or diminution, obedience or rebellion, except by His will. What He wills is, and what He wills not is not. Not a glance of one who looks, or a slip of one who thinks, is outside of His will: He is the Creator, the Bringer-back, the Doer of that which He wills. There is no opponent of his command and no repeater of his destiny and no refuge for a creature for disobeying Him, except by His help and His mercy, and no strength to a creature to obey Him except by His will. Even though mankind and the Jinn and the Angels and the Shaitaans were to untie to remove a

single grain in the world or to bring it to rest without His will, they would be too weak for that. His will subsists in His essence as one of His qualities; He has not ceased to be described through it as a Willer, in His infinity, of the existence of things at their appointed times which He has decreed. So they come into existence at their appointed times even as He has willed in His infinity without precedence or sequence. They happen according to the agreement of His knowledge and His will, without exchange or change in planning of things, nor with arranging of thoughts or awaiting of time, and therefore one thing does not distract Him from another.

The fourth statement is in the *'Aqaid* of al-Nasafi:

And God Most High is the Creator of all actions of His creature, whether of unbelief or belief, of obedience or of rebellion; all of them are by the will of God and His sentence and His conclusion and His decreeng.

And to His creatures belong actions of choice (*ikhtiyar*), for which they are rewarded or punished, and the good in these is by the good pleasure of God (*rida*) and the vile in them is not by His good pleasure.

And the ability to do the action (*istit'aa)* goes along with the action and is the essence of the power (*qudra)* by which the action takes place, and this word "ability" means the soundness of the causes and instruments, of limbs. And the validity of the imposition of task (*taklif*) is based upon this ability, and the creature has not a task imposed upon him that is not in his power.[2]

Sectarian views on this question, in particular the Shi'a creeds, are different. But it is clear in every case that there is difficulty in reconciling logically God's omnipotence with man's freedom of action, and God's justice with the punishment of evil-doers who could not have done what they did, and unbelievers who would not have rejected the true faith except by the will of God. It is not Muslims alone who have had to face this difficulty. It has existed and still exists for all who are aware of the subjection of individual human beings to forces outside their control. Their faults and offences raise the question as to how far they can be justly held responsible for their actions. Here we are concerned only with Islamic doctrines, but these, too, must be seen in the light of a common problem of all right-minded and thoughtful men.

The Qur'an is the basic document of Islam, and no statement about the faith can be valid unless supported by the authority of the Qur'an. The result, as seen in Muslim history, has been that the Qur'an has been quoted in support of the most diverse views. One of the earliest differences was on question of free will and predestination, the Qadaris emphasizing man's power (*qadar*) to choose without qualifying God's omnipotence and the Jabris[3] holding man responsible for his acitons while asserting that everything happens by the will of God. The Qad'ri point of view was developed by the Mu'tazila thinkers and the Shi'as, the Jabri standpoint had the wide support of those who firmly believed in God's omnipotence and did not wish to indulge in what they felt was unnecessary argument, and one that could lead to the weakening of their faith. But the reconciliation of free-will with predestination was not an isolated problem. Other issues, not strictly relevant, got involved. Most important was the question of the rightful ruler, a successor to the Prophet in political authority and, therefore, responsible for the maintenance of the true faith. This was not a matter for academic discussion. The rulers were naturally interested in maintaining their power, and those opposed to them in discovering reasons which made opposition to the rulers obligatory on religious grounds. Some verse or verses of the Qur'an were the starting-point and mainstay of all argument.

Islam was preached in the seventh century to a people with unpredictable potentialities. The situation was dynamic from the beginning, and change and development are evident in the Qur'an itself. However, only someone with personal experience of the spiritual occurrence which has been called revelation and with a complete knowledge of the relevant facts could claim the competence to understand the actual relationship between the series of revelations which comprise the Qur'an and their historical and circumstantial contexts. The Prophet's aim was to preach the faith and not to construct a philosophical system, and those who later on had to discover a system of thought in the Qur'an were forced to convert the living word into logical propositions. Their difficulties were enhanced by the changes in the connotation of words. The Arabic of the pre-Islamic period, the Arabic of the

Qru'an and the Arabic of non-Arab scholars of Islamic theology is substantially the same language, but anyone who, like Professor Izutsu, dives deep into the meaning of concepts, discovers shades and even varieties of meaning which baffle an average mind. And the possibility of a precise answer to the question as to which is true—the meaning which emerges from a philological discussion or the one that has been accepted for centuries—is as remote as ever.

The literary form of the Qur'an is generally that of a dialogue. The language is rhetorical and powerful, and there is considerable repetition for the sake of emphasis. Sometimes the revelation seems to be obviously related to a particular fact or situation and, therefore, different in type or character from that which has a general application. The Qur'an itself has made a distinction between what is clear and direct (*muhkam*) and what is ambiguous and not clear (*mutashabih*). The question has also arisen as to whether some revelations have not been abrogated by subsequent revelations bearing on the same matter. The Qur'an is not a systematic treatise; it is not a theological compendium. There was much that required explanation and exposition; there were blanks to be filled in. For this purpose, the saying of the Prophet had to be collected and studied, and criteria of criticism and evaluation to be evolved. This was done continuously for generations, and the result was a mass of what are called Traditions, which were regarded as supplementing the teachings of the Qur'an. These Traditions reflect changing need and circumstances and might contain ideas not found in the same form in the Qur'an. Those who interpreted the Qur'an and the Traditions were affected by the tensions within the Muslim community and by political and cultural tendencies. Defenders of the established order would have one approach, its opponents another. Christian, Hellenistic and Greek thought also influenced Muslim minds. If we regard Islam contradictory, they will form part of it. But they all base themselves on the authority of the Qur'an, and it is only by a study of the relevant statements of the Qur'an that we can estimate the relationship of these ideas and beliefs with the original source.

The teachings of Islam in regard to free will and predestination are governed by the concept of God. This is not defined or defined clearly enough in the Qur'an, and must be regarded as the sum total of His attributes. These, according to tradition, are expressed in the 'Most Beautiful Names', a term that has been used but not explained in the Qur'an. They are traditionally believed to be ninety-nine, but according to other calculations, they are five hundred to a thousand. In a recent study[4], it has been shown that names these have had a devotional purpose, and are not an enumeration of God's attributes. What the Qur'an stresses is God's omnipotence and omniscience; His knowledge, will, decrees or commands, His measuring and apportioning (*qadar* or *taqdir*) which control everything. It is from the manner in which, according to the Qur'an, God exercises his power that we can deduce the extent and nature of man's freedom of action.

The first point to note is that the Qur'an denounces a predestination interpretation of God's absolute power as an argument for not accepting His guidance.

> 'Those who associate others with Allah will say, 'Had (Allah) willed it, we would not have associated others with Allah, nor would have our fathers, nor would we have had any taboos.' So did their ancestors argue falsely, till they tasted of our strictness. Say to them, 'Have you any knowledge? If so, bring it forth to us. You only follow your fancy; you only tell lies.'
> Say to them. 'Allah's is the convincing proof, and if he had wished, He would have guided (i.e. He had the power to guide you will.' (6:149-50)
> When they are told, 'Fear that which is before you and that which is after you,[5] perhaps you may receive Mercy, (they turn back).'
> And so you cannot bring them a sign from the signs of your Lord from which they will not turn away.
> And when they are told, 'Spend out of that with which Allah has provided you,' the unbelievers say to the believers, 'Shall we feed him whom Allah would have fed, had He so willed? You are certainly in manifest error.' (36:45-47)

But if God has absolute knowledge and power, is not man helpless? The rhetorical style of the Qur'an very often leads one to think that God knows everything, and can do and does what He likes, but there are also obvious indications that God's absolute knowledge and power is asserted against those who are reluctant to believe, indifferent or defiant. According to Dr. Rehbar, there is no evidence in the Qur'an that God's knowledge predetermines human conduct, and the following verse (5:95) should be taken to represent the actual situation in the light of the statements of the Qur'an:

> 'O believers! God will try you...that *He may know* who fears him in secret.'

There are eight other passages of similar import, and at least five others containing phrases like 'God does not yet know the patient,' or 'God will eventually know the truthful.' For example:

> Do men then reckon that they will be left to themselves when the say, "We believe", ad not be tried?
> We did try those who were before them, and Allah will surely know who are truthful, and he will surely know the liars.' (29: 1-2)

The conclusion to be drawn from the verses asserting God's knowledge, and His seeing and hearing everything is, according to Dr. Rahbar, that God is to be known as a vigilant, well-informed and wise sovereign.[6]

How does God's will (*mashiya*), absolute power operate? The following typical passages, apparently indicating that believers and non-believers are what they are by God's will also indicate when the will is exercised:

> It is for Allah to show the path; from it some turn aside; Had He willed, He would have guided you one and all'—(16.9)
> For each one of you we have made a law and a pathway. And had Allah willed it, He would surely have made you one people, but He shall try you through that which he has given you.[7] Be, therefore, emulous in good deeds. To Allah is your return in any case, and He will let you know concerning that wherein you disagree. (5:52-53).
> He leads astray many and guides many, but He lead astray only the evil-doers. (2:24)
> Nor will Allah lead a people astray after He has guided them until that is made manifest to them which they have to fear. (9:116)

Although it is stated in may verses that God's will governs man's beliefs and actions, a large number of verses also show that God's will is not arbitrary, but works in guiding men's dispositions in accordance with their willingness to be guided and only those are led into error who stubbornly defy His ordinances.

> If you are ungrateful, behold, Allah has no need of you; and He finds no pleasure in the unbelief of his servants; but if you are grateful, He is pleased with you. No bearer of burdens shall bear the burden of another. To your Lord is your return, and He will inform you in regard to what you have done. (39:9)

Though God judges, and judges strictly, His concern is not to sit in judgement only. A study of the uses of the word *qaddara,* from which *taqdir* is derived, shows that it means that God has created everything according to a measure.[8] In his *Tarjuman al-Qur'an,* Maulana Azad argues that the meaning of *taqdir* is that the providence of God, the Father (rabb), embraces everything. His power is exercised to enable growth and fulfilment in accordance with His will and purpose, and Islam or Faith (*din*) is an enterprise in righteous, purposeful living in which man must participate.[9] Destiny, in the sense of an absolute determination beforehand of all that is to happen or to be done, is not the meaning of the term *taqdir* as used in the Qur'an, and no statement in the Qur'an can be quoted to prove that all human actions is by arbitrary decree of God.

There is reference in several passages of the Qur'an to a 'Perspicuous Book' or a 'Preserved Tablet', as for instance:

> No misfortune befalls the earth or yourselves, but it was in the Book before were let it befall.(57:22)
>
> There is no beast that walks upon the earth but its provision is made, and He knows its settlement and resting place. All is in a Perspicuous Book. (11:8)

The first verse implies that there is order in the universe. But as to everything being in a Book, there are two obvious questions: (a) how long is misfortune written down in advance, and (b) is it written down arbitrarily or with a righteous purpose? If we make allowance for the rhetoric, the verse means no more than that misfortunes and accidents are in God's control. It would be stretching the implication too far to make it mean what human actions or what happens to human beings is written down ineffaceably in a book. This idea has been introduced through Traditions whose validity is open to doubt. But the idea of a Book suggests the need of a macrocosmic view. This we shall discuss later.

As already stated, the Qur'an itself makes a distinction between those of its statements and commands that are clear and of established meaning (*muhkam*) and those that are not clear or ambiguous:

> He it is who has revealed the Book, of which there are some verses that are *Muhkamat*; they are the mother of the Book; and others are *mutashabihat*; but as for those in whose hearts is inclination to error, they follow what is *mutashabih* in the Book, and do crave for sedition, seeking their own interpretation of it; [but none knows the interpretations of it] save Allah. And those firm in knowledge say, 'We believe in it; it is all from our Lord.' But none will grasp it save those who possess understanding. (3:5)

The physician, mathematician and philosopher al-Razi, in his commentary on the Qur'an maintains that when there is some decisive argument showing that the outward meaning of an expression is not intended, it is not proper to try to interpret that expression at all, for he says, metaphorical meanings of an expression can always be many and preferences of one over the other is bound to be conjectural, as it is always based on linguistic arguments which should never be relied on in fundamental matters of religion.

In the following passage of his commentary, Razi gives some examples of the *Mutashabih* and the *muhkam* on one subject:

And an example of it (i.e. of the *mutashabih*) from Qur'an is the expression of the Exalted One:

> 'And when we desired to destroy a city we bade the opulent ones thereof; and they wrought abomination therein; and its due sentence was pronounced.' (17:17)

The outward meaning of this verse is that they are bidden to act viciously, while the *muhkam* on the same subject is the expression of the Exalted One:

> ...God bids (you) not to do abomination,' (7:27) rebutting the speech of misbelievers recorded (in the first half of the same verse):
> And when they commit an abomination they say, "We found our fathers at this, and god bade us do it" (7:27) And likewise is the phrase of the Exalted One:
> They (*i.e.* the hypocrites) forget God and He forgets them.' (9:68) The outward (meaning) of *nisyan* (forgetfulness) is that which is opposite of awareness, wile the outweighed (sense) of it is desertion. And the *muhkam* revelation of the Exalted One on the same subject is His phrase:
> '...The Lord is never forgetful,' (19:65)
> and the words of the Exalted One:
> '...My Lord does not go astray nor forgets.' (20:54)

Razi refers more than once to how various sects apply the term *muhkamat* to the verses agreeing with their own persuasion, and the term *mutashabihat* to the verses disagreeing with their persuasion:

> And know that this is a very important passage. And we say that all the people of different persuasions assert that the verses agreeing with their own persuasions are the *muhkamat* and that the verses agreeing with what their adversaries say are the *mutashabihat.* The Mu'tazalite say that the verse:
> ...so let him who will, believe; and let him who will, disbelieve...(18:28)
> is *muhkam,* while the verse:
> But ye will no will, except God the Lord of the worlds should will. (81:29)
> is *mutashabih.*

And the Sunnite reserves the position in the matter. A similar observation is made at a little distance from the above:

'And then we find the matter so that every one of (this or that)

persuasion is clinging to it (*i.e.* the Qur'an) according to his own persuasion. The Jabari (*i.e.* Compulsionist or the Predestinarian) clings to the verses signifying Compulsion (*i.e.* Predestination), such as His phrase:
'We have placed a veil upon their hearts lest they should understand it, and in their ears dullness of hearing.' (6:25:17:48:18:55)

And the Qadari (*i.e.* the Free-Willers says, 'Nay! This is the belief of misbelievers,' arguing that He, the Exalted One, has said this regarding the misbelievers by way of censure in His (other) phrase:

'And they say, 'Our hearts are veiled from what thou dost call us to, and in our ears is a veil,'(41: 4) and in another place (in the phrase):
'The say, "Our hearts are uncircumcised"...' (2: 82)

And he who affirms the doctrine of *ru'ya* (God's visibility) clings to His phrase:

'Faces on that day shall be bright, gazing on their Lord.' (75:22)

While he who negates it, clings to His phrase:

'Sights perceive Him not...' (6: 103)

And he who affirms to doctrine of Jihar (*i.e.* God's location in space) clings to His phrase:

'They fear their Lord from above them.' (16:52)
and His phrase:
'The Merciful settled on the throne,' (20:4)
while he who negates it clings to His phrase.
'...There is naught like Him...' (42: 9)
And so everyone gives the name *muhkamat* to the verses that agree with his own persuasion and the name *mutashabihat* to the verses that oppose his own persuasion.'[10]

What position does the Qur'an assign to man? When God had created Adam he told the angels that Adam would be His Khalifa, His representative or vice-regent on earth; He had breathed His spirit into Adam and commanded them to bow before him.[11] In another verse[12] men and jinns—that is, all creatures—are stated to have been created that they might serve (Him). The children of Adam are elsewhere declared to have been preferred to all creatures.[13] What appears to be the most realistic statement from the point of view of actual human experience is the following:

> 'We formed man in the best fashion and then thrust away all to be the basest of the base except those that believed and performed good works—for them there is unmeasured—reward.'[14]

The full implications of all the passages quoted above have not been explained in the Qur'an itself, and they seem to be no more than *obiter dicta* in a context where God's omnipotence and the certainty of punishment for the evil-doer are constantly repeated and emphasized. But almost equally constant are references to people who refused to believe and obey, and who rejected and inflicted sufferings upon the prophets sent to them. Even with a full and unqualified acceptance of God's omnipotence, the impression cannot be repressed that man is capable of deliberately chosing unbelief and disobedience by implication, possessing a power of choice that God's omnipotence does not eliminate.

This is what a study of the Qur'an uninhibited by traditional theology, would suggest. But even before theology and jurisprudence had been developed, its study was influenced by other factors. 'Fatalism, the supreme negation of human free will, was the most noticeable metaphysical concept embraced by pre-Islamic Arabs.'[15] An inclination to believe in predestination already existed when the Qur'an was revealed, and it is reasonable to suppose that more importance would be attached to passages in the Qur'an which implied predestination than those which made allowance for free will. Still, we find a group upholding man's power of choice, and the views of this group were elaborated by the Mu'tazila and the Shi'as. The first and the most outstanding among the Mu'tazila was Wasil ibn 'Ata (d. 748).

He held that to regard the Qur'an as uncreated was inconsistent with belief in one God, because it meant the association with God of someone other than God. He denied that God predestined human actions. Death and life and all the vicissitudes of life came out of God's *qadar* (power), but it was unthinkable that man should be punished for actions he had committed by the will of God and for which he was not responsible. We must assume that man has freedom of will and possesses power over his actions. Later adherents of this school established man's responsibility for his actions by showing that good and evil can be perceived and distinguished by the intellect. An-Nazzam (d. 845) taught that God could do nothing to a creature that was not for the creature's own good and in accordance with strict justice. Out of such ideas were evolved the Shi'a doctrines that God is apart from any evil actions and all His acts are in accord with wisdom and righteousness. God is all-powerful, but He does not necessarily do all the things he has the power to do. Man is a free agent, good and evil are matters of judgement by man's reason, and his actions must be judged by themselves without reference to any law which declares them good or bad.

The orthodox, or the majority, held and still hold the view that there can be no necessity upon God, even to do justice. He is absolutely free and man must accept what He does. Man does not have the capability to distinguish between good and evil, and can know them only through God's teachings and commands. Abu Hanifa (d. 767) and after him Maturidi (d. 944) do recognise that man possesses free will and is, therefore, rewarded or punished for his actions. No explanation is attempted of the nature of predestination and free will They are stated side by side as equal, if contradictory facts. Abu Hanifa admits that evil deeds are by the will (*irada*) of God—otherwise they could not happen—but he cannot bring himself to say that they are by the 'good pleasure' of God. It was not, however, the question of predestination and free will that was the main concern of the generality of Muslim, nor were they much concerned with the logical and philosophical consistency of their beliefs. The omnipotence of God had to be maintained even if it meant denial of free will to man even in a relative sense, and the Qur'an as the Word of God was as sacrosanct as God Himself. The Mu'tazila, who differed from the majority, were not free thinkers in the modern sense of the term, and they used their influence over al-Mamum (813-833) to have their views given an official semblance and their opponents persecuted. The test question was whether the Qur'an was created or uncreated; in other words, whether even the Word of God could be associated with God or not. The 'uncreated' Qur'an has strong affinity with the Christian Logos—the Word that was with God, the Word that was God—and the 'created' Qur'an is a concept in harmony with the physical facts of revelation in a particular social and historical context. But ultimately the belief in the 'uncreated' Qur'an prevailed, and with it the tendency to give the Qur'an the nature of an Absolute, and ignore its historical character.

When the orthodox were compelled to resort to dialectics, they used it as a means to defend the already occupied position. Al-Ash'ari, whose position represents a reaction from the Mu'tazila, attempts to raise a purely rationalistic theology to the level of the Qur'an, the Sunnah (or example of the Prophet) and the Companions. He adopted the middle course in the matter of predestination and free will. In the language of his day, the power to act was identical with the power to create; human actions were creations. Al-Ash'ari held that only God can create; man's power produces no effect at all on his actions. God creates in man power (*qudra*) and choice (*ikhtiyar*). Then he creates in him his actions, corresponding to the power and choice with which he has been endowed. So the action of man is created by God, relating to initiative and production, but it is acquired by man. By such acquisition is meant that man's action corresponds to the power and choice already created in him, without his having the slightest effect on the action. This accounts for the free will or the consciousness of it which tries to entail responsibility upon man.

Al-Ash'ari's reasoning is mere quibbling with words, and does not carry conviction. It received, however, the approval of the majority and was regarded as a decisive refutation of the Mu'tazila. But al-Ash'ari did not more than use the weapon of dialectics in defence of orthodoxy. It was left to Imam Ghazali to employ the argument of personal experience. His primary conception is, *volo ergo sum,* I will, therefore I am. It is not thought that impresses him but volition. God, the Creator wills; so does the soul of man. They are akin, therefore man can know and recognise God or, as a Tradition says, 'He who knows his own soul, knows his Lord.' It is also recorded in a Tradition that the Prophet said. 'God, the Most

High, created Adam in His own form (or likeness),' which is confirmed by the Qur'an (38:72). From this Imam Ghazali concludes that there is likeness between God and man in essence, quality and actions. The spirit of man rules the body as God rules the world. The human body is the microcosm as the universe is the macrocosm. But God is not simply the soul of the universe. He is the Creator of all by His will, and he sustains and destroys all by His will.

Once the orthodox had come to a conclusion in regard to predestination and free will, no further speculation on this question was permissible and, therefore, none was permitted. It was the sufis who then took the initiative. Muhiyuddin Ibn 'Arabi, or Shaikh-i-Akbar, the Great Shaikh (1165-1240), is regarded as the founder of sufi metaphysics, the basic doctrine of which was the Unity of Existence, *Wahdah-al-Wujud*. But Ibn 'Arabi has little to say about predestination and free will. His conception of unity must have made this question appear irrelevant. The sufis gradually accepted his doctrines, and they find poetic expression in the works of Jalaluddin Rumi. But one his followers, Shaikh Abdur Razzaq Kashani (d. 1329), who was also an independent thinker, has discussed predestination in some detail.

We are not concerned here with his metaphysics, except that he establishes a correspondence between the universe and man as between a macrocosm and microcosm. His exposition of predestination centres round the interpretation of three terms, *qada*, *qadar*, and *'inaya*. *Qadar*, which is usually taken to mean decree or command, Shaikh Abdur Razzaq explains as the existence of universal types of all things in the world of Universal Reason. *Qadar*, the usual meaning of which is measuring or apportioning, is for him the arrival in the world of the Universal Soul of the types of existing things. After being individualised in order to be adapted to matter, these are joined to their causes, produced by them and appear at fixed times. *'Inaya* is, broadly speaking, Providence, and covers both *qada* and *qadar*, just as these two comprehend everything that is actual. In other words, *'inaya* is the divine knowledge, embracing everything as it does, universally and absolutely. Further, while the essence of *qada* is part of the *'inaya* of God, its entelechy *(kamal)* is in the world of Universal Reason. Shaikh Abdur Razzaq identifies the Preserved Tablet, referred to in the Qur'an, with the Universal Soul, for on it are preserved, unalterably, all the general conceptions which are on their way to the individual heavenly souls.

It is the world of *qadar*, of the soul, which sets everything in motion.

The relationship between the macrocosmic scheme and predestination and free will is highly complicated, with a remote first cause and an infinity of intermingling secondary causes as we approach the physical plane. It is possible for man to look at these last only, and so to assign absolute creative and decisive power to his own will, or to look at the first cause and become a fatalist. He must, therefore, preserve a balance and hold by both. The complete cause of anything into which human will can enter must have an element, among others, of free will, which sets all other elements in motion. Shaikh Abdur Razzaq seems to imply, though he does not clearly state, that man has in him an element of the divine nature there must be freedom also in man—one of its emanations.[16]

The mystics cultivated the belief that the true *wali,* the man of God, could rise to a position where, through his *du'a,* his prayer to God, he could become a participant in the governance of human affairs. It was faith in the potency of the *wali's du'a* which made people flock to him, and the number of legends about the miraculous powers of the *walis* effaced the distinction between the natural and the supernatural, the possible and the impossible, in people's minds. Shaikh Nizamuddin Auliya is reported to have said that everything happened according to God's will; but this rather fanciful statement, is also attributed to him that while God's command descended from above, prayer (du'a), went up from below, and if they clashed, the one with greater power would have things its own way. What deserves serious attention, however, is the view implied in Shaikh Abdur Razzaq's speculations, that in considering the question of free will and predestination we must look at things from the microcosmic and the macrocosmic level. Putting things in our own terms (tough without the explicit support of any traditional authority), we could say that the macrocosmic span of existence extends from Creation to the Day of Judgement. With reference to this span, God's will is absolute, its fulfilment immediate. Human existence is here a purpose within the Purpose of God's will. The microcosmic span of human life extends from birth to death. God's will is operative here too, but, as Shaikh Abdur

Razzaq says, with an infinity of intermingling, secondary causes. We see it as law and justice, as moral command and obedience within the opposite poles of good and evil, which are necessary for meaningful existence at the microcosmic level. There is an essential harmony, an essential unity between the macrocosmic and the microcosmic, but the same thought-processes, the same type of reasoning, would not apply to both, as the laws of macrophysics do not apply to microphysics, and *vice versa.* This interpretation of Islamic belief, like Islam itself, would be true only for those who believe. It can be rejected by those who doubt or deny it. Such persons, or groups, or societies who offend against God and His will both at the macrocosmic and the microcosmic level, who, to use the language of Muslim theology, deny God's unity, His omniscience, His omnipotence, and who associate others with God or deliberately adopt evil ways, ignoring the final judgement, deserve to be punished. The duration of such punishment is indicated in macrocosmic terms as eternal, if the denial of God is deliberate and absolute or, in microcosmic terms, as depending on God's will and His mercy, if the offence against God and his commands is mitigated by awareness of sin and repentance.

A fresh study of Islam, uninhibited by previous thinking, began with Syed Ahmad Khan, the founder of the Muhammadan Anglo-Oriental College, which later became the Aligarh Muslim University. He held that any Muslim who possessed adequate knowledge could exercise the right of interpretation, and himself exercised this right in a manner that exasperated the *ulama.* But on the question of predestination and free will he argued on the same lines as Imam Abu Hanifa or Imam Ghazali, though not without a modern touch.

'I think, and anyone who sets aside the principle of adherence to authentic opinion will most certainly agree, that the *ulama* have misconceived the nature of the Qur'an. This has tow aspects; one: that it is the Qur'an, revealed by God. It is my belief that the Qur'an is, word for word, the revelation of God. The other aspect is the determination of its meaning, the eliciting of its purpose and intention. From this point of view the Qur'an is like something composed by a man with full power and beauty of expression, and just as we examine what such a man says and decides and what he intends and means to say, in the same way we would literally interpret the Qur'an, and for this purpose recognise no distinction between the language of the Qur'an and the language of man. For, after all, the Qur'an was revealed in a human language, the tongue of the people of Arabia, and so, though it may be entitled to reverence on the ground of its being a divine revelation, it is, for purposes of understanding and interpretation, no different from something uttered by man.'

Syed Amad Khan's views on predestination and free will, which should have made it possible for the Muslim to be guided by his conscience and not by tradition, appear to be dialectical and essential superficial.

> 'That First Cause which possesses true knowledge of all the conditions under which it acts is what we call *Taqdir.* That is to say, according to our thinking, *Taqdir* is God's knowledge. So if that First Cause, on the basis of true knowledge, says that such a one has been guided and such a one misguided, such a one has been created that he may go to heaven and such a one that he may go to hell, that is perfectly correct. Reference to this to itself is due to its being the First Cause, and statement of the results is based on its true knowledge. This does not mean that any agent (*i.e.* the person who was created for heaven or for hell) was necessarily acting under compulsion.''[17]

Dr. Iqbal's doctrine of Personality, of man fashioning himself into an assertive and creative power under God, held out great promise. He went so far as to say,

> 'Raise your Self to such heights that God, your Self beholding,
> Should ask of you, Tell Me, what is your Will.'

But this exaltation of man ends in what is no less than an intellectual collapse. For the Selflessness to which the Muslim should aspire, is nothing beyond the observance of injuctions in regard to prayer, fasting, *zakat* and pilgrimage, an observance that has been a habit for centuries.

In one sense a Muslim has no freedom at all: he has been created only that he might serve God,[18] and God has acquired him body and soul, with all else that he possesses.[19] In another sense he enjoys the greatest freedom, for belonging as he does to God, it releases him from every form of bondage. This is the interpretation that has been put on these verses by the sufis generally. In practice, every Muslim who believes that he must live according to the shari'a, which comprises the creed as well as the law, follows the shari'a as defined by his sect or by one of the four schools of jurisprudence (Hanafi, Shafi'i, Maliki and Hambali) which are recognised as orthodox. But the law has curious anomalies. The ruler is not bound by the *shari'a* in the sense that he is not answerable to the community, the *millat*, or the divines, but only to God, and he must be obeyed unless he forbids the religious practices enjoined by Islam and upholds *kufr*, or unbelief. The officers of the ruler who have to carry to his commands are answerable only to the ruler. A Muslim who holds, but does not propagate, heretical beliefs commits no cognisable offence. A Muslim who disregards traditional practices or taboos, is answerable only if he claims that he possesses theological status and maintains that his own views or practices are more correct than those prescribed by tradition. The Qur'an enjoins abstinence from intoxicating drinks, but the *shari'a* does not—in India, at least—forbid the smoking or eating of opium. A Shaikhul Islam of Turkey is alleged to have declared that a man who drank coffee was a *kafir*; nevertheless coffee became a favourite beverage. The flesh of the pig is among the things absolutely forbidden, and Muslims have abstained from it in all countries and all times, but no punishment has been prescribed for it, and drinking wine or liquor is a sin that can be atoned for by repentance, but not an offence punishable under the law. Adultery is a sin as well as a legal offence, but the evidence required to establish guilt would make it almost impossible to prove the parties guilty unless they themselves, or one of them, made a voluntary confession. But the niceties of the law are based very largely on tradition whose validity is as often as not open to question, and on interpretations which are valid only if recognised by the ruling authority as well as by the consensus of the majority. In India, the majority of Muslims followed and the state enforced the Hanafi system of law, except where rulers and their subjects were *Shi'a*; in Egypt, the Shafi'i system has been followed. According to the Qur'an, a Muslim should show gratitude to God by enjoying all that has been permitted: 'Eat and drink and do not waste; indeed, God is not a friend of those who waste'. This is modified by another passage: 'You will not attain the good (or righteousness) unless you spend out of that which you love.'[20] The intention of the Qur'an, if all such statements and modifications were taken together, would appear to be that men should lead a clean, healthy life, requiring each one to do what is known to be good and avoid what is regarded as evil,[21] on the understanding that God does not place on anyone a burden heavier than he can bear,[22] a principle which would apply to religious observances, conduct and needs of physical life.

NOTES

1. There are references in the Qur'an to a book or tablet, with meanings which differ according to the context.
2. These extracts have been taken from D.B. Macdonald, *Development of Muslim Theology, Jurisprudence and Constitutional Theory*, Lond., 1903, Appendix I.
3. From '*jabr*', meaning 'compulsion'.
4. Dr. Daud Rahbar, *The God of Justice*, E.J. Brill, Leiden, 1960.
5. That is, punishment in this world and the next.
6. Rahbar, *op. cit.*, pp. 63-64.
7. The references here is to the prophets sent and the successive revelations.
8. Rahbar, *op. cit.*, pp. 112-113
9. Azad, *Tarjuman al-Quran.* Edited and translated into English by S. Abdul Latif, Asia Publishing House, Bombay, 1966., Vol. I.
10. Rahbar, *op. cit.*, pp. 201-203.
11. Qur'an, 38:72 and 2:28.
12. Qur'an, 51:56.
13. Qur'an 17:72.
14. Qur'an 95:4-6.
15. F. Rosenthal, *The Muslim Concept of Freedom*, E.J. Brill, Leiden, 1960.
16. *Encyclopaedia of Islam*, Art. 'Abd al-Razzaq.
17. Tahzibul Akhlaq, Mujtabai Press, Lahore, 1894, pp. 235-36.
18. Qur'an, 51:56.
19. Qur'an, 9:112.
20. Qur'an, 3:86.
21. Qur'an, 3:106.
22. Qur'an, 2:286.

24

Islamic Influence on Indian Society

I believe there would be much less misunderstanding among the representatives of the different cultures of the world if we examined more closely the nature of what we call influence. Influence is not imposition, or a free gift of ideas and goods to those supposed to need them or a borrowing and lending or imitation of the ways of one people by another. It is something really indefinable and can take the most devious ways. We look for it in obvious and concrete froms, in architecture, music, painting, literature, where it is least genuine and seldom enduring, and we generally come to the wrong conclusions. For instance, would it be accounted an influence of Islam, which is rightly taken to be a democratic religion, that the caste system should become more deeply rooted than ever before among the Hindus? But that is what did happen. The Muslim sufis in Iran and Khurasan initiated in the 10th century a movement of taking Islam from the classes to the masses. Muslim sufis in India continued this movement. Goswami Tulsi Das, through his Ramayana, made the veneration of Rama the religion of the masses in north India, and as an indirect consequence strengthened the faith of the masses in the caste system as an unalterable, divine dispensation. Would this be considered an influence of Islam? We would says yes, if we regarded an influence of Islam? We would say yes, if we regarded the idea of taking religion to the masses as the essential element, and say no, very emphatically, we valued the democratic tendencies of Islam. Or again, take the case of the poet-saint Kabir. He attacked both Muslims and Hindus for making religion exclusive. We cannot be sure whether he himself was a Muslim or a Hindu; to what influence, then, can we trace his

---

From *Education and Traditional Values.*

determination to attack and ridicule exclusiveness? Islam, as a missionary faith, enjoins the eradication of false belief, and I would say that Kabir's attitude is an instance of Islamic influence. But, then, Kabir accused the Muslims of holding false beliefs, although they professed Islam. A third instance is even more illuminating. I have often heard it said that in north India Muslims have been the most outstanding masters of vocal and instrumental music. But music is, according to Muslim religious law, one of the frivolities, and for this reason, addiction to it has been condemned. The only explanation I have been able to think of is that the Muslim who took up music would have been one of the damned, both in this world and the next, unless he achieved the highest excellence. That would give him a status in this world, and he would have the confidence to expect forgiveness in he next. But would we call this the influence of Islam?

So let us not try to simplify matters where the reality is complex and, for that reason, all the more fascinating. Let us assume—what was most probably also true—that the Muslims wanted to keep Islam and the Musim way of life to themselves, and that the Hindus had no desire whatever to be influenced by the Muslims. Then let us see what changes took place.

One I have already mentioned. Religion became the religion of the people. Then, the spoken languages of the people became literary languages. We have the beginnings of Hindi, Bengali, Gujarati, Punjabi and Sindhi literature. Further, the city became the centre of culture, tailored clothing came into general use, simplicity was discarded in favour of a life enriched and complicated by a vast increase in the articies of daily use, manners became elaborate and were, so to say, codified in the form of a recognised etiquette. None of these changes, except perhaps the first, can be regarded as due to the influence of Islam, but the changes would not have taken place when they did if Islam had not become one of the religions of India.

Spoken languages benefited because Muslim rulers, while not exclusive in their patronage, had no reverence for Sanskrit and no reason to venerate the Brahmans, who were generally the only people who learnt and could speak it. On the other hand, the Muslim sufis wished to propagate their ideas, and they could do this only in the language of the people. They were not interested in the Hindus but in the Muslims of the lower classes. The Muslims thus made a wide breach in the ramparts behind which the linguistic prestige of Sanskrit—and also, let us remember, of Arabic and to some extent Persian—was entrenched. As early as the first decades of the 15th century, a Muslim sufi was asked why he was so favourable to Hindi. And about a hundred years earlier people had seen that when Persian verses failed to produce a mood of exaltation in Shaikh Nizamuddin of Delhi, the singers took up some Hindi folk song, and the Shaikh was soon in rapture.

Islam is averse to luxury of any kind, and the life of the good Muslim should perhaps be more simple and austere than that of the Hindu. But the cultural expression of Islam has been the exact opposite, and Islam has almost everywhere promoted urban life and luxury. This was, perhaps, inevitable when religion required the congregation of the faithful in the mosque preferably five times a day but at least once in a week. Muslims have to live together, a msque has to be the central feature of every Muslim settlement. In India, specially during the first two or three centuries, the Muslims could maintain themselves as a ommunity only in the cities. Their ruling classes had to strike the imagination of the people. And so we have both a multiplication and a rapid development of cities, and of the glamorous products of craft and industry. From this flow the other changes—the demand for many and excellent products of all kinds, even to the extent of having a pair of slippers costing Rs. 50,000/-, the cultivation of elaborate manners, and so on.

I have already indicated how the evolution of an elaborate and extravagant city life can be traced back to some features of Islam. Hindism is not congregational. There were large cities in the Mauryan and Gupta periods: there have, indeed, to be cities, if there is to be any civilisation. But the Hindu ideal—and my own, if it comes to that—is life away from the city, away from noise and dust and worldliness, where one can live in peace and think. I remember reading somewhere that the Vedas should not be studied and recited in cities. There is, therefore, according to Hindu standards, worldly advantage but no religious merit in city life.

And now I come to the intriguing question of the use of tailored clothing. There is a Sanskrit word for tailor, but I have not found evidence of tailors having been generally busy at any time previous to the settlement of the Muslims. Men and women draped cloth around themselves, or tied it where just draping could not be depended upon. The tailor may have existed, but he could be dispensed with. The Muslim, on the other hand, cannot say his five daily prayers without the help of the tailor and his craft, and the Muslim woman would lose all rights and status if the tailor did not enable her to clothe herself completely up to the wrists, the neck and the ankles. Rulers set the standard of respectability, and non-Muslim women had to pay the price of respectability by employing tailors and wearing a minimum of tailored clothing.

Finally, though it is not my business to discuss the influence of Hinduism on the Muslims, I must say that if I were an eighteenth or early nineteenth century Muslim, I could easily have become that public nuisance called a reformer. I could have said, 'Islam is buried deep beneath Hindu influences; let us dig it out, clean it and see what it really looks like!'

25

The Indian Muslims after Independence

At a party given during the U.N. General Assembly Session in 1949 I had the pleasure of being placed next to the Turkish representative. He looked at my name card, saw that I was a Muslim and at once asked, 'Are there still any Muslims in India?' The impression then created does not yet seem to have been removed and it is believed that the subcontinent had been divided between Muslims and Hindus, with all Muslims on the one side and all Hindus on the other. This belief is completely wrong. There are not only Muslims in India, but over 40 million of them and their number is increasing. They are found in all walks of life, in the Government, in the teaching profession, in other liberal professions, in trade and industry and in the rural areas. They are not only there but believe they ought to be there by right of being children of the soil and free citizens of a free country.

The reasons why India was partitioned is a painful subject not only for the Hindus, but for a vast number of Muslims, both in India and Pakistan. I do not propose to discuss here the reasons for the partition. But two facts, it is necessary to remember, because of their consequences. The party which demanded the creation of Pakistan, 'a separate homeland for the Indian Muslims', was the Muslim League. In the election held early in 1946, which proved decisive, it secured 425 out of 492 seats reserved for Muslims in the Central and the different Provincial Legislatures. It could be said, therefore, that Indian Muslims were overwhelmingly in favour of Pakistan. But the franchise was limited to the propertied classes, and those who voted for the League and its policies did not know for what they were voting, because the League

---

From *Islamic Influence on Indian Society.*

deliberately avoided defining what was meant by the creation of Pakistan. It insisted that the right to 'a separate homeland for the Muslims', to be called Pakistan, should be conceded first. The voting for Pakistan was thus a leap in the dark and can hardly be regarded as a considered move.

The other fact that needs to be remembered is that there was an uprooting of the populations in three Muslim majority and one Muslim minority province. Most of the Hindus in Sind, all the Hindus in the North West Frontier Province and West Punjab were forced to migrate to India and the Muslims in East Punjab to migrate to Pakistan. An incredible amount of rioting and bloodshed accompanied this partition and migration, and the situation created by this has to be borne in mind when considering the position of the Indian Muslims who remained in India after partition.

We still wonder what would have happened to these Indian Muslims but for Mahatma Gandhi. He was in Delhi when the riots took place, when the refugees from Pakistan streamed into the city carrying with them stories of the atrocities committed against them. Mahatma Gandhi insisted that the Muslims who wished to remain in India should be provided complete security and full citizenship rights. He went on a fast which he declared would end only with his life unless all his demands in regard to the safety of the Muslims were accepted and the necessary action taken. While his influence was enough to calm down feelings of most Hindus, and it was possible to help a large number of uprooted Muslims to settle down, there were some who regarded him as a traitor to the Hindus and it was at the hands of one such person that Mahatma Gandhi lost his life. It is significant in this connection that no outstanding persons or groups in Pakistan made any effective attempt to ensure the security of the Hindus or to enable those who did not wish to migrate to stay on. If they had done so, the lot of the Muslims, immediately after partition would have been much easier. The decision in regard to exchange of populations applied only to Eastern and Western Punjab. A large proportion of the Hindus in the North West Frontier Province and in Sind would have stayed on if they could. On the other hand, there would have been much less of immigration of the Hindus of East Pakistan into West Bengal and anti-Muslim sentiment in eastern and northern India would not have been constantly revived.

This is how the history of the Muslims in free India begins. What has happened since?

As a preface to everything else, it has to be stated that the meaning of the formation of two independent states was not realised by Muslims on either side of the frontier. They did not understand why there should be restrictions on travel, why a person should not be able to hold property in both countries, why non-Muslims in India should have any objection to Muslims maintaining relationships as before with the members of their families who had migrated, in fact, why the establishment of Pakistan should be resented in any way by non-Muslims in India. On the other side, while the vast majority of the non-Muslims, were willing and able to suppress their resentment, there were also elements among them that were actively hostile, and to them it seemed that the Congress Government, and above all, its leader, Jawaharlal Nehru, was objectionably pro-Muslim.

The security of Muslims in India has been endangered by these actively hostile elements, and by the attitude of the government of East Pakistan towards its Hindu citizens. The maintenance of law and order is the responsibility of the State Governments, which have shown on occasions that they were not sufficiently alert. It has appeared, also, that attacks on Muslim populations, wherever they occurred, were planned and might have been prevented if prompt action had been taken. But those who planned the attacks always prepared the ground by spreading rumours that created a strong sentiment against the Muslims, and made the neutral non-Muslims indifferent to the fate of the Muslims attacked. It must be remembered, however, that these attacks have always been more or less local, and while at first they created such panic that some Muslims of the affected areas migrated to Pakistan, this tendency has gradually weakened, and Muslims have stuck to their place in spite of riots and attacks. From the time immediately following the partition, the Muslims have not felt and have not been generally insecure. They have had full faith in the Central Government, and the Central Government has done all in its power to ensure their security. The war of September in 1965 has strengthened the position of the Muslims by showing that they are as patriotic Indians as the non-Muslims, and we may say that the problem of the security of the Indian Muslims has been solved. With the war has also come a full realisation of the fact that India and Pakistan are two different states, and not merely one country divided into two because of a quarrel that should be forgotten.

The problem of employment is closely linked with the problem of security, but is much more complicated.

The factor that has caused the greatest complication is the habit inculcated in Indian Muslims by the British government in its own interest of expecting special consideration from the government in the matter of service. After the establishment of the Congress in 1885 and the growth of its influence, British administrators began to patronise the Muslims of the upper classes and tried to wean them away from the national movement with offers of reservation of seats in municipal and legislative assemblies, separate electorates and employment under the government. The tendency to complain that the Muslims had got less than their due was encouraged and, what was much more dangerous, the Muslims were made to believe that if it came to competition, they would have no chances against the Hindus. All the concessions made for the Muslims as a minority and a supposedly backward community continued till 1947. Thereafter, special consideration was shown only to the really backward communities, listed as Scheduled Castes, and the Muslims were left to get what they could on merit. This made the Muslims of the upper classes feel that they had been thrown to the wolves of unemployment and starvation.

A second factor was the land reform policy of the Congress Government, of taking land away from the landlords and giving it to the peasants with full proprietary rights. The indication that these reforms would be carried out was given in 1937, when the Congress first came to power in a majority of the Indian provinces. The landlords were mainly Hindus, but there was a large number of Muslims also who depended, as landlords, on the rents they received from the tenants. The far-sighted among the landlords either disposed of their land or established large farms and gardens, and thus obtained exemption from the application of the law when it was enforced. But most of the Muslim landlords, specially the smaller ones, did nothing to save themselves. A large number of lawyers also, whose practice depended on litigation among the landlords, lost their main source of income.

The demand for Pakistan was made principally by the upper class Muslims. The vast majority of Muslim officers in the government who were given the choice of serving in India or

Pakistan chose to go to Pakistan. A large number of businessmen also transferred their business to Pakistan. Those of the upper classes who did not migrate immediately after partition found an easy way out by migrating to Pakistan later on in search of employment. In some services this caused a marked reduction in the number of Muslim applicants. For quite a number of years very few eligible Muslims appeared for competitions or selections for the administrative services, the army, navy and air force, and in the engineering services, because it was much simpler to migrate. This was a third factor complicating the problem of employment. But it is also true that in the first years after partition quite a number of Muslims, specially in the police service, were thrown out to restore the balance in favour of the majority community, which had not been given its due share by the British administrators in order to provide jobs for Muslims.

During the last ten years, the situation has gradually changed. The number of Muslims recruited to the higher grades of the administrative services is still negligible, because that class from which recruitmemt was made has mostly migrated to Pakistan. The number of Muslims in the armed forces and the police is slowly increasing. Overseers and engineers who formerly migrated are now looking for jobs and finding them in India. It is difficult to give any statistics, because recruitment is not on a communal basis, but even a person in my position, who is concerned in a minor way with selection for posts of different kinds or to whom people looking for employment come with requests for recommendation, does not meet or hear of many competent young men who are unemployed. International business houses and industrial concerns which formerly followed a policy of employing Muslims in Pakistan and non-Muslims in India are now throwing open their doors to Muslims in India. Old Muslim business houses in the main trading and industrial centres are now in much better position, and more and more enterprising Muslims are building up businesses of their own.

Employment is not an Indian Muslim problem only. It is an acute problem for all Indians because of the limited opportunities and the rapidly increasing population. It is inevitable that there should be great pressure on the sources of employment that exist and, therefore, suspicions of discrimination. What can be said with assurance, however, is that Indian Muslims are not its only victims.

Caste prejudices, linguistic and regional prejudices provide ample reasons for practising discrimination, and perhaps Muslims do not suffer more than others because of it. Discrimination is least in evidence in employment under the central government; in the states its pattern varies.

One important point to be remembered in this connection is that independence has brought about a social revolution, and sections of the population that were denied opportunities in the past are now coming up and demanding their rightful share. In Muslim society, only people belonging to the upper classes were regarded as deserving of interest and consideration. In the whole movement for education among Muslims during British rule there is hardly any reference to the needs of the poorer classes. It was considered improper, even ridiculous for them to demand equality of opportunity in education, and society looked askance at those who did get education. Now the oppressive weight of the upper classes has been removed, and our democratic government is really sincere in providing opportunities of education to the largest possible number of its citizens. At the present time, while the remnants of the old upper class may be complaining, the hitherto suppressed classes are coming up, in education and in economic life. Unless the Muslim interest is identified with the welfare and prosperity of the upper class Muslims, an investigation would perhaps reveal that the Muslims as a whole are better off than they were before.

How do the Indian Muslims stand in the matter of education?

It is the function of the state to provide opportunities and the state is performing this function to the best of its ability. The Indian Muslims on their side are taking advantage of the opportunities offered. There is a definite desire on the part of the state to encourage Islamic Studies, and while some of the Universities have departments of Islamic Studies, almost all have departments for Arabic, Persian and Urdu. On the other hand, institutions like the Theological Seminary at Deoband, are flourishing. They are not supported by the state, but they have more funds and more students than they had before. A movement for organisation of religious education at the elementary level was started about ten years ago and is now showing encouraging results. Generally speaking, the Indian Muslims have not only taken what was given to them. They have actively participated in the framing of educational policy, for themselves and for the people as a whole.

The third major problem of the Indian Muslims is that of political and cultural survival.

The ideology of the Muslim League and the demand of a separate homeland for the Muslims was based on the assumption that the whole Muslim community possesses a common political and economic interest. But even a superficial consideration of the distribution of the Muslim community in the country and the many economic classes of which it is constituted would at once disprove this theory. The Muslim landlord and the Muslim agriculturist could not possibly have the same economic interest, nor the Muslims in the free professions the same interest as the craftsmen. But the possibility of uniting the Muslims on the basis of a common allegiance required the rejection of all, and specially of political relationships with non-Muslims has been exploited to the full by the Muslim League because the Muslims were a separate electoral body, and the franchise, as I have already stated, was limited. But now there are no separate constituencies for the Muslims or any other community, and the question arises as to what the Indian Muslims should do to ensure their political survival.

There is still a Muslim League party in a southern state, but anywhere else in India a purely Muslim political party would not be able to achieve anything and would only antagonise the other communities. But is there any risk, and fear of loss in the Indian Muslims not being organised as a separate political party? I do not see any. In a democracy, where government has to be the government of the majority, a small party working for its own interests can serve no useful purpose, when these interests themselves are likely to be inconsistent with each other, because the party has a religious and not an economic or political basis. On the other hand, if we are agreed that democracy is an Islamic principle, that the organisation and promotion of social welfare is an Islamic duty, the Indian Muslims can serve Islam and themselves best by associating themselves with persons and parties who aim at making democracy as real as possible and at achieving the maximum of social justice and social welfare through the legislative and administrative action of the state. There has been this kind of association. Rafi Ahmad Kidwai, who died in 1956, is still remembered as one of the ablest administrators the Indian Government had, a man of swift decisions whose trust in his subordinates made it a stimulating experience to serve under him. His generosity was limitless, and his regard for fair dealing so great that his bitterest political opponents came to him for justice. He came from a family of landlords, but it was he who took the lead in the abolition of landlordism. Maulana Azad, free India's first education minister, was another outstanding figure, a man of great learning and courage, who often stood for justice against immediate political interest, and has left a deep impression on the Indian people. It is impossible to believe that Muslims would sacrifice their own interests if they cooperated with and gave the lead to parties working genuinely for the highest human interests.

Muslim culture would also derive enormous benefit if the Indian Muslims worked for common ideals in cooperation with the other communities. There has, no doubt, been an element of cultural self-assertion in Hindu nationalism. There was a tendency to look at the remote past and incorporate its qualities in the image of new India, and this revivalism was directed more against the Muslims than against the British, because the Muslims had been culturally dominant for a far longer period. The form of revivalism that annoyed the Muslims most was the rejection of the Urdu language and the propagation of Hindi. Urdu had been built up as a literary and conversational language by the joint efforts of both Hindus and Muslims; its rejection in favour of Hindi made it seem that the whole contribution of Muslims to Indian culture was being rejected, and the culture of free India would be exclusively Hindu. There is no point in discussing and passing judgement here upon a whole historical process. The present-day reality is that the movement of revivalism among the Hindus has failed to lead anywhere. Hindi as defined in the Constitution would have been acceptable as a national language almost without question, but the revivalist character given to it by certain dogmatic and reactionary advocates has produced a sharp reaction. On the other hand, there is no doubt that in certain vital areas, such as the state of Uttar Pradesh, where Muslims form a substantial minority and in Delhi, administrative action has gone against professed policy and the teaching of Urdu in schools has been almost entirely stopped. But in some other states of India, Urdu is getting the official recognition and support to which it is entitled and there is ample evidence now of a reaction in favour of Urdu, which will gather force because of the attractive qualities of the language itself. Urdu is, in fact, the most widely spoken language in northern India and is recognised as the language of polite conversation. Even those who cannot themselves speak it well enjoy hearing it spoken and Urdu poetry has a fascination that none can resist. In Mushairas, or assemblies where poets recite their verses the crowd is always larger than can be accommodated, and there are many in the crowd who have only a vague understanding of what the poets say. But their enjoyment is real, for Urdu poetry has become symbolic of the free personality, of intensity of feeling and of a moving beauty of expression. It has given a language to love, which is the most human and most creative of emotions; it has given form and meaning to those situations in which the passion for life discovers itself. Since Urdu poetry is a projection of Muslim culture, those who appreciate its values cannot but pay homage to Muslim culture, and realise its significance for the refinement of their own life. More and more people are beginning to understand that unless Indians as a whole are to adopt a cheap imitation of European and American culture, there is no alternative to a revival of the culture created by themselves during the medieval and early modern period, a culture that is distinctively their own. The cultural survival of the Indian Muslims is thus being promoted by the movement of events.

26

Gandhi and the Muslim Masses

One of the saddest topics of conversation now among those who knew Mahatma Gandhi personally or participated actively in any of the movements led by him is the manner in which Indian sentiment and government policy have drifted away from what were considered Mahatma Gandhi's principles. There is no positive rejection of these principles in favour of others; there is no desire to understand them. They seem to be things written with smoke on the sky which people observe and read and pass on. Is this because the Indian people have the habit of forgetting their benefactors, or is it because this particular benefactor upheld principles that are no more in tune with the times?

The Hindu mind is generally impressed by a life of simplicity and self-denial. Not to desire and not to possess, to live unharassed by fulfilled and unfulfilled pleasures is for the Hindu in theory always and in itself the best of condition; but in fact the Hindu is quite like other human beings, with an uncontrolled multitude of desires and hopes. Theory and fact have both had their place in Hindu life throughout the ages and have never been reconciled, though the Hindu has a logical mind which tries to link up everything with everything else—human life with the movements of the stars, or with the events of previous lives to explain the whole as well as the details of all that happens to him and to his world. In Mahatma Gandhi's life practice was identical with principle, but the principle, the moral and intellectual predisposition was traditional and Hindu. The admiration Hindus felt for him because of his abstinence, his achievement of mastery over the flesh followed a traditional pattern; except in a few cases

---

From *Islamic Influence on Indian Society.*

there was no urge to identify the practice with principle, to be like Mahatma because of admiration for him and his way of life. Now that the Mahatma is no longer there, the Hindu lives like other normal human beings, and admiration for the Mahatma has to be pulled out of the depths of the subconscious.

On the Muslim simplicity makes no impression, and abstinence or self-denial he regards as a form of ingratitude to God unless there are obvious and compelling reasons for it. The Muslims did not like Mahatma Gandhi's way of life, and his dress and diet seemed to them idiosyncrasies inappropriate in a leader of men. Mahatma Gandhi's tolerance of other ways than his own did not affect the Muslim's attitude, because he had no doubt that his own way was the better way. The Hindu masses felt that they must do what was expected of them by paying homage to the traditional qualities of the saint in Mahatma Gandhi, and this homage was paid so constantly by such large numbers that the Muslim could easily convince himself that he would always have to remain at a distance, because he could not pay the same kind of homage.

I went to the Sabarmati Ashram at Ahmedabad in June 1926, as one of a party of four headed by Dr. Zakir Husain. I was deeply impressed by Mahatma Gandhi himself, but felt completely out of place in the Ashram. There was an atmosphere of deliberately cultivated poverty, an almost oppressive consensus on doing without everything that was not essential for life and health—no smoking, no tea, no tasty food, no colourful dress. Mahatma Gandhi and the children laughed, but no one else. The only person who was officially permitted to drink tea was Imam Sahib who had come with Mahatma Gandhi from South Africa. We were sent to his hut in the afternoon and took tea there. But when I asked his permission to smoke, he made a wry face and said, 'Smoke if you cannot do without it'. I put away my cigarette, feeling ashamed at my weakness. But I could not forget that I shared this weakness with a large part of the civilised world, with people who enjoyed themselves and yet had accomplished great things and whose normal life gave ample evidence of creative and useful activity. Was that a sign of weakness, a moral fault? Was the Sabarmati Ashram a pointer to the path which the rest of the world must follow if it was to save itself from destruction or moral collapse? These questions arose in my mind and I could not find answers favourable to the Sabarmati Ashram.

Mahatma Gandhi had two standards, one for himself and for those who pledged themselves to the 'ashram' way of life and to participation in all that was done to realise 'truth and non-violence', and another standard for those who acknowledged his leadership in the struggle for Indian freedom, who were willing to spin, to wear hand-spun, hand-woven cloth, to profess and practise non-violence but wished otherwise to live as they were used to. He was relentless with himself and with the followers of the first kind, the 'disciples'. One can only guess at the inner history of the first Ashram at Sabarmati and the second at Sevagram, near Wardha, but Mahatma Gandhi was not given to living on illusions and he could not have been satisfied with his experiments in monastic living. Why, then, his persistence in regarding it as the higher way of life?

One could explain away Mahatma Gandhi's dressing as he did by saying that a genuine leader of the Indian people would have to dress like the mass of the people, who were too poor to wear anything more than a loincloth. His diet could not be explained in the same way, because the poor man's diet is dry bread or cooked or uncooked cereals, not fruit and milk. Mahatma Gandhi's belief in the efficacy of spinning could be justified on economic grounds, but these were not the only grounds for his belief. He was beyond doubt sincere. He deduced all the details from first principles, and he was as firm in his belief in the correctness of his deductions as he was in the fundamental principles themselves. We cannot take his belief and practice into parts, and decide for ourselves which were meant for his own time and circumstances, and which for all time. As a Muslim and a student of Indian history I have come to regard every aspect of Mahatma Gandhi's belief and practice as inevitable, as historically predetermined. For the same reasons I have to regard some of the externals he emphasised as tragic impediments to the full expression of the universal in his beliefs and his personality. The traditional Hindu concept of the good life was too deeply rooted in his nature for him to grow out of it.

To understand the working of Mahatma Gandhi's mind, let us begin with the enunciation of the universal principle, now regarded as a platitude, that human life must be a reflection of the moral law. Those who accept this principle must assert and seek to realise in personal and social life values which would make the moral law effective and operative, in other words, establish truth, justice, beauty. From his boyhood Mahatma Gandhi had an awareness of right and wrong which developed into an unusual moral sensitivity. His intellect was subordinate to his moral instinct. He had been made to take a vow when leaving for England that he would not touch meat. He found it very difficult to keep his vow, but when he discovered a vegetarian restaurant and met vegetarians in London, the vow receded into the background and he became intellectually converted to vegetarianism. He read about it, wrote about it. It seemed to activate his mind. Nothing else seems to have done so. He took no interest in politics or in social problems during his stay of about three years in London. Scholarship, literature, art did not influence him at all, now or later. He was affected only by what explained, justified, confirmed what he believed and wanted to continue believing. It is remarkable how very limited his reading was. The Bible, the Qur'an, the Bhagvadgita, two works of Tolstoy, Ruskin's *Unto this Last*, about make up the total of what he read, and he read nothing presenting a different view from his own in life or religion. Morally he was capable of admitting his own mistakes, of judging himself from his opponent's point of view with an incredible frankness and openness of mind, but he seemed to have no inclination whatsoever towards the exercise of his critical faculty in the consideration of intellectual problems. Once the moral issue was clear, the only function his intellect performed was to communicate to others what his moral sense dictated. It was a horse harnessed to a cart that had to use all its strength in pulling the cart in a particular direction it could not browse or wander on its own, seeking lush pastures. It had to keep to the road, to see nothing but the road.

The energy released by this harnessing of the intellect to a moral purpose was tremendous. The young barrister who broke down while pleading a simple case in a small cause court in Bombay was within a few years organising resistance to racial laws in South Africa in a spectacular fashion, and facing men and situations with astonishing courage and resourcefulness. On his return to India, as he gradually came to the forefront, he adopted the methods of 'satyagraha' (firmness in truth) which he had evolved in South Africa. His advocacy of the peasants' cause in Champaran and Kheda, of the workmen's cause at Ahmedabad were successful exercises in satyagraha, and a preparation for the struggle known as the Khilafat and Non-cooperation movement. From 1919 onwards the Indian National Congress looked to him for guidance and inspiration, his personality became the symbol of India's moral and social awakening and the promise of national freedom. But in course of time a subtle change took place. The 'Salt Satyagraha' of 1930 was the result of a search for an issue on which to fight the British government and, as compared with the Non-cooperation movement, was very much the cause of a political party, even though the masses as a whole would have benefited from its success. So was the 'Quit India' movement of 1942 which, in addition, was inconsistent with the principle followed by Mahatma Gandhi in the Boer War and the First World War, that the British government's embarrassment and preoccupation with what seemed to it a life and death struggle should not be taken advantage of.

It is clear from these instances, historic in themselves, that Mahatma Gandhi's methods evoked sincere and widespread response where the injustice he sought to remove was obvious, and the more limited his objectives, the greater was his success. His endeavour to give a moral character to the Indian people's struggle for freedom made his opponents—both Hindu and Muslim—suspicious where the issues were mainly or entirely political, such as the question of separate electorates or reservation of seats in legislative assemblies for Muslims or the demand for Pakistan. It was a hindrance to him personally also, because he could not think and act on the same level as his opponents; he sought to apply moral principles where only such tactical moves as would put the opponent in the wrong or reduce the damage that could be done were called for. On the other hand, there is no doubt that Mahatma Gandhi's championship of the untouchables removed a cancer in the Hindu social system and gave the status of full citizenship to millions who had been regarded as sub-human for thousands of years. His 'constructive programme' was a very efficient means of integrating the urban and rural elements of the Indian population and of harnessing the enthusiasm of thousands of men and women. It also provided a direction—not followed after independence— for the planning of Indian economy. But here again, the identification of moral principle with economic policy proved a hindrance, The idea of full employment and of every individual being a productive unit are economic ideas, not to be mixed up with spiritual ideals.

Spinning yarn and wearing hand-spun hand-woven cloth, if proposed as temporary measures, the encouragement of village industries, if not confused with opposition to industrialisation, might have stimulated inventiveness, promoted small scale industries and given a healthy direction to Indian economic development. Elevation of spinning to a form of worship, idealisation of a life where medicine and surgery could be dispensed with implied a commitment to particular views which could be shared by only a few, and these few would be under a psychological pressure to cultivate a pride that would provoke resistance if not ridicule.

And yet criticism such as this is no more than the ant of expediency biting the elephant of absolute sincerity. In particular, the Indian critic with an essentially European intellectual background is more anxious to show the sharpness of his teeth than the breadth and comprehensiveness of his vision. Consider Mahatma Gandhi's insistence on simplicity in the context of a society where the lords and masters have practised senseless extravagance at the cost of the masses, or of a democratic society with a planned economy where the import of nylon yarn is more important than the import of books, and all cavilling at the ideal of simplicity looks short-sighted and foolish. Consider the traditional diet of the vegetarian Hindu, the frying, the over-cooking, the mad hunger for sweets, and it will be apparent that Mahatma Gandhi's advocacy of a simple diet of preferably raw vegetables has taught dietetic good sense to a far larger number of people than all the doctors put together.

The drive for development of village industries failed, the idea of education through work could not be realised not because the schemes were basically defective but because inventiveness and discernment in the one case and sincerity in the other were lacking. The 'ashram' way of life did not justify itself beyond producing a band of workers who were more devoted than wise, but Mahatma Gandhi succeeded in transforming himself and his capacities into the most perfect instruments for the achievement of the ends to which he had dedicated himself. Satyagraha, as he understood and practised it, was always an effective means, but one person, however intense his belief, however great his power, cannot change ways of thought and action that have been customary for ages and have become second nature. He is entitled to our reverence and admiration not so much because of the measure of his success but because of the passion with which he tries.

One of the cherished aims of Mahatma Gandhi was the attainment of Hindu-Muslim unity. The political aspect of this unity would have been an adjustment of rights and opportunities to the satisfaction of both parties. This was obviously of crucial importance. But no adjustment could be made unless both parties felt the compulsion, the absolute necessity of making it, and while the British ruled it was open to extremists and persons who could not repress the bargaining spirit to prevent an agreement being arrived at. The Congress leadership gradually came to the conclusion that the third party, the British government, would have to be removed before Hindus and Muslinis could be made to agree. The Muslims, however, felt quite reasonably, that questions left over for settlement till after the British had left would be decided by a majority vote and the spirit in which negotiations about rights and opportunities had so far been conducted did not justify any optimism about the majority opinion. The nationalist Muslims were willing to take the risk, and it was mainly because of their support that Mahatma Gandhi adopted the Congress point of view. Judging from what ultimately happened, he would have thrown his whole weight in the balance, which means he would have fasted to death, to ensure that the Muslims got not only a fair but a favourable deal. But what if he died before India became free? What if the Hindus refused to listen to his advice and resisted the moral pressure he exercised? The final result of the confrontation of Hindus and Muslims was the partition of India, to which the Mahatma was forced ultimately to agree by those closest to him, Maulana Azad alone excepted. Here, if anywhere, Mahatma Gandhi failed. Here, if anywhere, lies his claim to a more than human greatness.

The whole political history of mankind can be resolved into a struggle between justice and self-interest. The Melian dialogue of Thucydides has been repeated constantly by tongues and hearts, Socrates has died many times. Mahatma Gandhi stood for justice against the self-interest of both Hindus and Muslims. In an atmosphere of suspicion it is impossible for anyone to say and do nothing that will cause misunderstanding. The Muslims were willing to do anything at his behest when he was leading the Khilafat movement. From 1923 onwards, when both the communities were busy staking their claims, Mahatma Gandhi was continuously accused of seeking to give a moral status to what were really the demands of the majority community. It was only when the killings started in 1946 that he stood forth as the only vocal and effective champion of human love and sympathy. His endeavour to bring Hindus and Muslims together as one people united in goodwill and trust is one of the epic struggles in history, where the tragedy or inevitable failure is more meaningful and inspiring than the satisfaction of accidental success, and where the martyr's death is the victory of his cause,

Historically, Mahatma Gandhi represents the utmost limits of Hinduism's expansion from within. His political and social activity was inspired by his interpretation of the moral and spiritual duties of a Hindu. His predecessors in spiritual leadership, Aurobindo Ghosh and Swami Vivekanand, spoke and wrote with far greater fervour and a more obvious dedication to the spiritual values of Hinduism. But their sphere of activity was intellectual, their spiritual fervour did not lead them into the social world, with its injustices and aberrations from the right path. They accepted the fundamental unity of religions, but the form of Hinduism which they represented was not free from what the pure theist would call animism and idol-worship.

Mahatma Gandhi treasured some myths because of the moral lessons to be derived from them, in essence he was a pure theist. He believed as a Hindu that all religions are true, but he went further and asked all believers to be true to their own religions. His acceptance of the Muslim was not based on expediency or humanism or any concept of natural justice. He believed that, as a Hindu, he was under a moral and spiritual obligation to give equal status to the Hindu and the Muslim, and the Jamia Millia Islamia of Delhi is one of the results of his endeavour to induce Muslims to make their lives and activities an embodiment of the ethical values of Islam. One wishes that Mahatma Gandhi had investigated more closely and from an objective intellectual standpoint the origin of his concept of Satyagraha; he may have found that the Bhagvadgita and the Qur'an were saying the same thing. His view may not have been accepted by the Muslims or the Hindus, but he would have stimulated the urge for a general revaluation of values and promoted the unity for which he was willing and, ill fact, surrendered his life.

27

Guru Nanak Through Muslim Eyes

Every religion has an essence and attributes, a core of ineffable spiritual experience and attributes that begin to be acquired as soon as the attempt is made to communicate it through language and give it visible form in modes of worship and social institutions. The attributes make the spiritual experience a part of the historical process, and the whole existing system of habits, traditions and economic relationships begins to act as an assimilating, modifying, equalising influence. The history of Sikhism should be considered in this light. We are, however, not concerned with Sikh history here, not even with the confirmation of the original experience by the nine succeeding Gurus, but only with Guru Nanak, and with the question whether he was, or was not affected by Islam and the spiritually most potent form Islam had taken in India, sufism.

The features which appear common to Islam and Guru Nanak's teaching are belief in one God, at once transcendent and immanent, the God of all mankind, not to be represented by any physical symbol; the equality of all men as men; the organic fusion of the spiritual and worldly life, of worship with the fulfilment of social obligations; a community life based on work, worship and generous sharing of what is earned, a sadh sangat, or organised community living as an expression of the religious ideal, and dhikr, the repetition of God's name as a form of prayer. The easiest explanation of these common features would be to describe Guru Nanak's environment, the monotheism of the Muslims, the prevalence of a socially unjust and morally indefensible caste system, the propagation of their ideas by the

---

From *Islamic Influence on Indian Society.*

sufis, the preparation of the ground for a synthesis of beliefs by the Bhakti movement and then to show how, the Muslims and the Hindus being what they were, it was impossible for Guru Nanak to identify himself with the religion of either. This is what is normally done as regards the essence of Guru Nanak's teaching. An examination of the attributes of the historical process which gave Sikhism its known form could be made to prove either that Sikhism is a more than half Islamic belief lost in its Hindu environment or a reformed Hinduism in which certain Islamic doctrines, particularly the ideas of a casteless society, were adopted as a measure or reform.

Such explanations may appear adequate so far as the facts, the external factors, are concerned. There is plentiful evidence in history of the assimil ation by one people of the ideas and beliefs of another, also of conversion for the sake of advantage or because of a genuine change of heart. But there is also evidence in history of a spiritual experience, a revelation which becomes a creative force and gives birth to a new religion and a society with its own *elan vital*. It is the nature of the new religion and the strength of the *elan vital* by which we estimate the quality of the original spiritual experience.

According to Islamic belief, there is an essential faith revealed directly to all the peoples of the world through a prophet or messenger. Logically, every such messenger has to be the last; he cannot declare his revelation to be incomplete or ask his people to wait for another messenger. Belief in the one God is the essence of this universal, basic faith. According to the knowledge we possess at the moment, monotheism was first preached by Pharaoh Amenophis IV (1380-1362 BC). In one of his hymns to the supreme God, Aton, he says:

> How much is there that thou has made, and that is hidden from me, thou sole God, to whom none is to be likened ! Thou hast fashioned the earth according to thy desire, thou alone, with men, cattle, and all wild beasts, all that is upon the earth and goeth upon feet, and all that soareth above and flieth with its wings.
>
> The lands of Syria and Nubia and the land of Egypt—thou puttest every man in his place and thou suppliest their needs. Each one hath his provision and his life-time is reckoned.[1]

The Egyptian people were not as spiritually sensitive as their Pharaoh, and belief in the one supreme God, Aton, did not survive Amenophis IV. But belief in the 'sole God, to whom none is to be likened' appears again and again. However, if we examine the religious history of the Jews, the Christians and the Muslims, this belief in the one God is either accepted as a theological dogma and becomes a habit, without stimulating the believer's mind or it is what the sufis called an 'occurrence of the heart', a kind of revelation by its own nature direct, independent and original. If this could be true of a professedly monotheistic community like the Muslims, it would be patently wrong to assume that belief in the one, true God, as ardent and overpowering as Guru Nanak's could have been communicated in any sense or manner. An imaginative reconstruction also of social life in the Punjab of the fifteenth and sixteenth centuries, with Muslims exercising political authority in their own interest and committing excesses every now and then that hurt the religious sentiments of the Hindus, would not make it appear plausible that their monotheism would attract the sensitive Hindu. During the three hundred years or more during which Muslims had lived in the Punjab before Guru Nanak was born, Muslim monotheism would have ceased to be a striking novelty and become a commonplace. And we have no evidence of Guru Nanak having come into contact with any Muslim during his impressionable years who could have transformed the commonplace into a striking novelty. The revelation that came to Guru Nanak must have been as direct and immediate and as independent of history and social circumstances as the religious records of the Sikhs show it to be.

Shortly after his enlightenment Guru Nanak is reported to have uttered the cryptic phrase, 'There is no Hindu, and no Mussalman.' This can be taken to mean that he thought both Hindus and Mussalmans had strayed away from their true paths. But with the effects of his own experience fresh in his own mind, he would have been more inclined to a positive assertion than to a critical appraisal in his later hymns. 'There is no Hindu and no Mussalman' was perhaps another way of saying that 'There is no Hinduism, no Islam; what is valid is my own vision, my own dispensation, which I have just received.' And if Guru Nanak did mean this, we should not take it as a rejection of Hinduism and Islam but as a revelation of the inevitable conflict between direct and transmitted experience.

Hinduism is not under consideration here. The Muslim sufis who claimed to know God for themselves had to beware of expressing too clearly and openly what their experience necessarily led them to believe. Mansur Hallaj paid the penalty for declaring that he was 'the Truth', and his example served as a warning to others. They generally confined themselves to rejecting the 'books', the faith as learnt by a process of transmission, and to putting in its place the 'condition', the spiritual state, in which man is in direct contact with his Creator. 'The sufi is he on whom conditions pass that are known to God only, and who is with God in a way that is known to God only', another sufi, Abu Sulaiman al-Darani, has said, and where relationship with God is so ineffable and so direct, the recognition of an intermediary seems out of place.

This is the conclusion we must draw from all that Guru Nanak has said about God. So far as Islam is concerned, he made this clear in his reply to Mian Mitha:

> The first name is that of God; many prophets are at His gate!

This is not a denial of any prophet; in fact, it is a confirmation of the Islamic doctrine that prophets have been sent to all the peoples of the world. It also indicates, however, that the acceptance of any particular prophet implies acceptance of a transmitted spiritual experience, and if one is to do that, one will be confronted with the situation of many prophets to open one gate, and whom among the prophets could one choose? It could be said, in parenthesis, that acceptance of the Muslim prophet would have meant not only acceptance of the whole religious tradition of the Muslims but a repudiation of his own spiritual experience and an abdication of his freedom to say all that he felt to be necessary and true.

Only someone who has experience of revelation, or an 'occurrence of the heart' is, presumably, aware of its nature, but even he cannot communicate it except through language. Once language is used, associations irrelevant to the experience are introduced. One cannot refer to God without using a name, but when any name is used, beliefs of others who have used it earlier inevitably become a part of the spiritual context and indicate a strong similarity if not an identity of belief, which can be very misleading. On the other hand, any name of God that has become a part of common speech cannot be disowned without a rejection of the validity of all the spiritual experience associated with the name, which may not be intended. Neither Kabir Saheb nor Guru Nanak had the choice of not using any of the names of God already current, and because they used both the Hindu and the Muslim names the impression is created that their spiritual function was to present a synthesis of beliefs which could claim to be a higher form of truth because it was not exclusively Hindu or Muslim and could be acceptable to both. But this is a form of rationalisation which, however it may support the ideal of Hindu-Muslim spiritual unity, does not reflect the truth. Theology always divides, genuine spiritual experience always unites; Guru Nanak's spiritual experience was a unifying force because it was genuine, it does not claim to be genuine because it was a unifying force. We must not get involved in Arabic and Sanskrit, in history and philosophy, because Guru Nanak used Hari, Murari and Rahim and Sat Kartar as names of God. They are only aspects of a spiritual experience which took him from Attributes to the Essence. We cannot escape the confusion created by language; but we must do all we can to avoid a too straightforward identification of words and names with an experience which is, by its very nature, incommunicable.

Guru Nanak's insistence that none should be associated with God and that He should not be represented by any physical symbol is obviously logical and inevitable if we regard his revelation as original. He was the founder of a new faith, not a religious reformer. He was not a believer in an existing religion who quoted the scriptures to justify emphasis on some values as against others; he was his own authority for saying what he did. There was no reason why lie should accommodate or placate those who believed in the religion within whose fold he was born, or those of other religions who heard him preach. There was no reason why he should appeal to history and show that there were others who believed as he did. He was not supporting Muslim beliefs in attacking idolatry. It must have been obvious to him that the harsh practice of breaking idols and temples had made some Muslim rulers very unpopular, and Muslim rulers still had the opportunity of continuing this practice, which his own tolerant nature would not have allowed him to endorse.

The equality of all men before God appears at first sight to be a clearer case of borrowing from Islam than even the idea of one

God, or to be a continuation of the attack on the caste system which was one of the facets of the bhakti movement. As regards the first possibility, Islam no doubt ordains an egalitarian society. But there was nothing egalitarian about Muslim society in India. Divisions on the basis of race and descent were recognised, in particular the difference between the Central Asian Turks and Tajiks, the Pathans and Indian Muslims. The Saiyyads were honoured above all others, whether they deserved it or not. Differences of rank could be ignored only at great risk. The democratic Muslim salutation 'As Salaam-o-Alaikum' was for equals in status only. It was not used in the court; and elsewhere, if there was a too pronounced difference of rank or status, it would have to be combined with a bowing and placing of the hand on the head which would neutralise its egalitarian quality. The Mehdavis, who insisted on practising equality because it was enjoined in the Qur'an offended kings and courtiers and were bitterly persecuted for this among other reasons. The equality advocated by the bhaktas was more spiritual than social; it depended for its acceptance on the good sense of man, not on a clear and absolute command of God, the God of all mankind. The form in which Guru Nanak preached the equality of men could only be an 'occurrence of the heart', intimately connected with his belief in the one God.

Another point of resemblance between Islam and Guru Nanak's teaching is the concept of 'sahaj', of a desire for right living which is fostered within man with the help of tendencies inherent in his nature, as against asceticism and self-mortification practised because man's nature, with its multitudes of pestering desires, is held to be the greatest obstacle to his self-realisation. In Islam the spiritual life is based on nature, and 'God does not demand of any (human) being more than he is able to bear.' Asceticism and self-mortification are forbidden. But here, as in the belief in one God, Islam affirms what is a universal tendency. The Buddha condemned both self-mortification and self-indulgence, and advised only such a tightening of the string of human nature as would enable it to produce the note proper to it, which would not happen if the string were stretched too tight or left too loose. The oracle of Delphi, whose guidance formed the basis of Greek religious life, advised the observance of balance. The teachings of Zoroaster and Confucius also commend normal living; their ideal is the householder who works, maintains a family and worships with a sincerity which suffuses his whole life. This simple ideal, however, does not impress, because there is nothing spectacular about it, and it has had, therefore, continually to contend against an exhibitionism which has been persistently but falsely considered the hallmark of spirituality.

The ideal of the householder who worships God with sincerity and serves his fellow-men was obscured among Muslims by the Umayyad rulers and the Arab tribes who looked upon Islam as their patrimony and established their claim by the acquisition of political power. The sufis did their best to restore it to its just position. Shaikh Abu Bakr Shibli defined the sufi as one who regarded all mankind as relatives whom he had to serve and maintain, and even the preacher could not ignore the saying of the Prophet that the man who earns his livelihood is a friend of God. Islam raised the status of the craftsman wherever it spread, but there is no doubt that lust for power and the inability of the pious and the truly religious to impose restraints on it upset the social standards and ideals of Islam. One could say that the injunction of Guru Nanak, 'Kirt karo, Nam japo, vand chako' was as relevant for the Muslims of his days as for the members of any other community. If we look for an exact parallel we find it not in the practice of the Muslims but in the sanctification of man's worldly vocation by Martin Luther (1483-1546), a contemporary of Guru Nanak's in far-away Germany.

Another point of resemblance is between the sufi concept of the shaikh and Guru Nanak's concept of the Guru. Here we are confronted with a complex pattern of parallel spiritual movements and questions arise that need elaborate discussion. And perhaps the first question would be to determine what Guru Nanak meant by the term 'Guru', when he himself had no spiritual instructor or guide. Did he mean God, as the eternal source of guidance and light, or an idealised human guide, whoever he might be? This is a question for Sikh theologians and philosophers to settle, or decide not to settle.

Guru Nanak's organisation of community living was not basically different from the khanqahs of some sufi orders. But here again we have an idea that is logical in itself and almost universal. Men who share a belief and a way of life inevitably devise ways and means of community living, and the vihara, the ashram, the monastery and the khanqah represent the similarities as well as the characteristic differences of the ideal of community living.

It may appear strange that a Muslim should argue against the view that Guru Nanak was influenced by Islam. But the belief that 'Din', the true religion has been revealed to all men is one of the basic doctrines of Islam, and this belief is confirmed, not weakened by the assertion that Guru Nanak's teachings present an independent, original spiritual experience. The Sikh is not obliged to the Muslim or the Muslim to the Sikh, and their faith in their own religions should be all the stronger because of any confirmation of the one by the other. If they walk steadfastly on what is their true path they will discover that their paths and the goal are the same. That discovery will itself be a spiritual experience, an 'occurrence of the heart', a fulfilment of what God, in a story related by Maulana Jalaluddin Rumi, said to Moses: 'You have been sent to unite, not to divide'.

NOTE

1. A. Erman, *The Literature of the Ancient Egyptians*, Methuen, London, 1927, p. 290.

28

The Discovery of India

Discovery is a fact; it is also a feeling. There is a rich opportunity for any Indian who travels round the country to see what he has not seen before and to immerse himself in the feeling, approaching ecstasy, of becoming a new and a large person. Our culture has prescribed travel. The Buddhist visited holy places; the Hindu performs the pilgrimage to Amarnath, Rameshwaram, Dwarka and Puri, to Badrinath and, of course, to Banaras; the Muslims pay homage to piety at the tombs of saints, far and near. Now it is almost an obligation imposed by loyalty to the state for the Indian citizen to travel around the country and strengthen the sentiment that binds him to it. It is not enough for him to live in the country, for living can all too easily become a vegetative process. He must discover it, and make his discoveries a vital aspect of his life.

The plains constitute such a large part of the country that those who pass through them and even more those who live in them are disposed to regard the Indian landscape generally as flat and monotonous, and to think of the hills as providing the only variety. Those who are frequent visitors to the hills think more of the cool climate and the comfortable living. But anyone who wishes to discover India must remember that he has, at the same time, to discover himself, to seek for harmony between nature and his own moods, to understand the language of dawn and sunset, of trees and the breezes that live in them, of flowers and butterflies and birds. 'The morning of Banaras, the evening of Oudh, the night of Malwa' have for centuries been regarded as symbols of beauty, as moments when man feels at one with nature. These symbols can be multiplied by anyone filled with the urge for discovery till they

---

From *Education and Traditional Values.*

become a part of his being. The Emperor Jahangir was among those continuously desirous of communion with nature. Many of the spots he noted as remarkable were developed into gardens during his own time or later. We also, if we are sensitive and observant, can find such spots along our many roads, and transform them into landmarks of aesthetic adventure.

The character of civilisation and culture in various parts of our country is as diverse as the natural landscape. We incline too easily to talk of an inner unity, which means unfortunately, that we avoid the intellectual and spiritual effort necessary to understand, appreciate and enjoy the diversity. No two styles of building could be more different than the temple and the mosque, and there is no easily accessible inner unity that can relieve us of the cultural responsibility of delving deep into the mystery of how both can be houses of worship. To associate the temple with Hinduism and the mosque with Islam may be factually correct, but it does not make the understanding of temple and mosque architecture automatic for the Hindu and the Muslim. House architecture has lost its character because of the growth of large cities and the change of habits in the urban population, but many towns still have an individuality of their own which will not escape the observant eye.

If any programme of the discovery of India is to be made, one should begin with the nearest groves of trees. There may be nothing to see there, but they would be ideal places for the first lessons in aesthetic appreciation, in getting the feel of the Indian atmosphere. The nearest stream, with the inevitable dry ravines, reminders of the process of corrosion that is continuously taking place, could come next, with circuitous rambles along the water-channels and boundaries of corn fields. Sight-seeing, when it begins, can be much more meaningful after the preliminary local excursions in the discovery of oneself, of nature, and the creations of culture.

Let us begin with these last, because they are visual representations of long processes of the search for knowledge and harmony, for the realisation of the eternal in what is itself physical and transient. The cave, the free standing *stupa,* the temple and the mosque symbolise attitudes and modes of worship, the mausoleum is man's response to the challenge of death and time, the garden is a call for communion with nature. These are parts of our heritage where the self of India is reflected. To see the typical examples of these we must traverse the whole country and visit its modern towns as well.

The geological structure of the Deccan plateau, with its immense rocks, provided the best opportunities for cave architecture. There are caves at Nasik, Bhaja, Bedsa, Karle, Ajanta, Ellora and other places, and all have their individual qualities as works of art. The common features are the degree of faith necessary to undertake such a task and the exactitude of what must have been calculations in a void. The larger caves must have taken decades to hew out of the solid rock; the Kailash temple at Ellora was chiselled out of a rock by four generations of craftsmen. There is no evidence of any after-thoughts, any change of design. And though they were meant for monks, who were supposed to have given up the world, the caves do not convey the impression of isolation from the life around. On the contrary, representations of the world are generally there, in some very striking form. In the Chaitya cave at Karle there are parallel columns of pillars surmounted by human figures symbolising the glory and the sensuousness of the physical world. In Ajanta, of course, the canvas is larger, comprehending all the variety and the rich colours of life. The gateways of Sanchi *stupa* present almost every type of activity and are about the fullest record of the various aspects of social and economic life of India in the second century AD.

Cave sculpture was gradually replaced by architecture in the north and the south, but certain traditions were continued. Sculpture remained dominant, determining the character and outline of even the largest structures. The Konark temple in Orissa, the Hoysalesvara temple in Halebid and the Dilwara temple in Mount Abu represent the finest and most elaborate combination of sculpture and architecture. The multiplicity of forms and ornamental motifs is staggering. The calculations were astonishingly exact. Sculptors and stone-masons worked on the ground, and every sculptured piece was fitted into the place where it belonged. The *silpa shastras* were never wrong in the proportions they prescribed, and the sculptors and stone-masons, repeating their formulas as they worked, never made a mistake. The planning was as marvellous as the beauty of the finished detail.

We shall never, perhaps, be able to reproduce fully the spiritual experience that went to the making of the temple. We admire the architectural conception, the art, the inwardness. The temple possessed all these aesthetic and spiritual qualities, but it was also something more. It was a fusion of physical, the sensuous, the transient and the eternal, a spiritual unity that was greater than the sum of its constituent elements. The Temple of the Sun at Konark, so ambitious in design that it could not be completed, is perhaps the greatest challenge to our understanding. It represents the twelve-wheeled chariot of the sun, drawn by seven horses, and is a mysterious blending of the sacred and the profane, of allegory with gross physical fact, of the profusion of creation on the exterior and absolute silence and formlessness within. The great temples of Madura and Tanjore, apart from the religious significance which they possess, also present a new concept of the vastness of the country, teeming with life and cultural activity. Their lofty *gopurams* overshadow the shrine, their tanks and courtyards were planned for multitudes of worshippers. Without any change in the ritual or the social system, religion seemed to have become the religion of the people, and to comprehend their limitless preoccupations, hopes and aspirations. Their significance is supplemented, in a way, by the Qutab Minar and the Buland Darwaza of Fatehpur Sikri, which are political in character and embody the determination to achieve power and glory by fusing all the diverse elements of the country into one body politic.

The Muslims insisted on maintaining their identity as a community. There is much to be said for and against this attitude. But what is important is to remember that the problem still exists for all of us as individuals and also as members of communities. Do we contribute more by being like the rest, by merging our personalities in the large or small social or religious group, or by asserting our individuality and beginning a series of reactions by giving expression to what is unique in us? The Muslims did not isolate themselves. They created new forms in music, in literature, in the minor arts, in architecture, in social life, and much of their contribution was due to their self-assertion in matters of belief as well as taste.

Muslims can pray on any piece of land that is clean and level, and where they do not commit trespass by praying. Mosque architecture is, therefore, entirely incidental and has nothing to do with the requirements of the faith. The construction of mosques became necessary because of the varying climatic conditions and because social and political symbols are indispensable, and the practice, once begun, was continued. But idolatry was forbidden, and the prohibition was enforced with a rigid fananticism by pubic opinion. The mosque could have naturalistic ornament, but no human, animal or allegorical figures. The architect was, therefore, thrown back on forms of beauty that arose out of symmetry and proportion, and the combination of arches, domes and minarets. But the variety achieved even under these restrictions is quite astonishing. The Jame Masjid of Gulbarga is all a covered area, with a multitude of domes; The Jame Masjid of Delhi has a covered area of 200 by 90 feet and an open courtyard of over 250 feet side. In the Jame Masjid of Fatehpur Sikri an attempt has been made to combine pillars, reminiscent of temples, with arches and vaulted roofs, and the Jame Masjid of Ahmadabad indicates the intention to endow the mosque with the inwardness of the temple.

The Muslims bury their dead, but the grave should, according to the rule, be a small mound of earth that will disappear within two or three years. However, the religious injunctions in this respect were disregarded by all except the poor, and kings and powerful noblemen erected mausoleums for themselves in order to keep their name and prestige alive. But the mausoleum had to possess some meaning, to indicate in some way the attitude towards life and death, and to give this attitude an individual quality. The Mausoleum of Iltutmish, near the Qutub mosque, is a small structure, and its interior surface is covered with inscriptions in many styles, as if cultural and spiritual values had been the monarch's chief concern. Tughlaq's tomb is by contrast the quintessence of self-assertion, the mailed fist of a warrior who had not known weariness or fear. Sher Shah built a mausoleum for himself at Sassaram in an artificial lake, expressive of all the power of his personality, his imagination and his vast ambitions. The Taj Mahal, though it has an Indian ancestry and could have been conceived and built only in India, has attained the height at which the spiritual and the physical meet, at which all the arts, all aesthetic standards, all tastes, all longings for beauty and immortality merge and take a precise form. Here architecture has achieved the highest. Beyond it there is only the 'garden of mystery'.

This 'garden' is a spiritual hypothesis, but it has also been associated with the physical world. It has been the forest where the scriptures were studied, where self-discipline was practised, where illumination was attained. It has been the meadows and groves and streams where people went to purge their minds of the dross of town life. Later it was formalised. It became a pattern of water-channels, terraces, flower-beds and fruit-trees. It was enclosed, but it also gave a perspective on the surrounding landscape. Because of the prerequisites, of which the most important was the availability of water, it could not be just something around the corner. The location of the formal garden was the result of patient search, the reward of courage, imagination, planning and successful execution. The sun sets everywhere, on mountains, plains, lakes and seas. Everywhere during some season or in particular climatic conditions the play of colour assumes magnificent and mysterious qualities, but the sunset as seen from the Chashma-i-Shahi in Srinagar is a profoundly moving experience. However, it was not the Chashma-i-Shahi Jahangir thought of as he lay dying. He thought of Verinag where, as the night approaches, the spirit can lean back for all eternity on a cool and friendly hillside.

There is no end to what we can discover of India once we have prepared ourselves for the adventure. We shall not all discover the same things or respond in the same way to the challenge to our understanding. But India will be all the richer for every sincere attempt made to discover her secrets and to become intellectually and spiritually aware of what she represents.

29

Approach to the Study of Medieval Indian History

It has been said that he who raises a fence fences out more than he fences in. Every historian with imagination and the desire to inform must be embarrassed by the feeling that no matter how comprehensive his account is, it is still only an infinitesimal part of what could be told. And he cannot write unless he prescribes limits for himself. The metaphorical fence is always and inevitably there. His only alternative is to impress in every way he can that the territory he has fenced in is part of a landscape, and is only a part of a larger whole. In other words, he must make it clear that only the history of the human world and all aspects of human life is history, and although we have to select, to write the history of particular countries or of particular periods of the history of different countries of the world or to investigate particular aspects or problems of history, we must place our subject of study as much as possible in its world context. Otherwise history may become a mere shadow-play, a tangle of silhouettes in space, unrelated to any context.

In studying and teaching Indian history, we must bear in mind the events and movements of contemporary world history. The revolt against ritual and practices that were divorced from spiritual purpose and ethical principle, which is reflected in the philosophical ideas of the Upanishads and the teachings of the Buddha, forms part of a world movement which may be callled a spiritual revolution. The Maurya empire belongs to a series of empires which seem to have a close relationship with, or one may

---

From *Education and Traditional Values.*

even say were either the cause or the result of, the spiritual revolution. These empires, if we analyse them, consist, in one respect of an administrative and military structure plus centres of trade and industry plus trade routes plus naturally irrigated agricultural land. In another respect, they consist of a union of tribal religions and cultures under the aegis of an imperial religion and culture. These empires and imperial religions, in a later phase which begins with the expansion of Islam, take the form of the religious world-state, which we could analyse as world religion plus world government. The northern races in Europe and the Turks in Asia, after a process of large-scale racial migrations, took over and maintained the idea of a world religion, but broke up world government—the Khilafat among Muslims and the Holy Roman Empire among Christians—into actually independent kingdoms. By the time this happened in the Muslim world, religious belief and practice had acquired what some would call definiteness and others rigidity, and it was one of the recognised functions of the ruler to maintain orthodoxy and to suppress heresy and, anything that could be called polytheism and unbelief. But the ruler himself had no religious status and could give no opinion in matters of religious law.

In order to understand the form assumed by the Turkish state in the Indian environment, we must view the position of India in the world context from another angle. India lay between two international trade-routes, one which connected the lands around the eastern Mediterranean with China, and passed across northern Iran and Turkestan, and the other which connected the eastern Mediterranean countries with Java and Sumatra, and passed along the southern coasts of India. The Taxila-Khyber-Kabul route in the north and the western and eastern seaports of South India in the south were the links connecting India, with the two international trade-routes. Only a power that was expanding along the sea-routes would attempt control and occupation of the South. Indian seaports. In the north, any power that was expanding along the trade-routes would find it advantageous or necessary to occupy at least the Sind valley. From 518 BC, when it became a province of the Achaemenian empire, the Sind valley went to the winners of every contest for power in Central Asia and Iran, the Greeks, the Parthians, the Sakas, the Kushans, the Huns, the Arabs, the Turks. In some cases the momentum of expansion was exhausted after the occupation of the Sind valley, in others it carried the expanding power into the Punjab and beyond. In every case it was a trade-route that gave the direction to movements of expansion by its offer of inducement and opportunity.

It has become so commonplace to talk about the relationship of history and geography that we hardly give any serious thought to it. But even if we do, we think of mountains, rivers and plains, not of the trade-routes. We forget that these routes formed the link between the areas of raw material, production and exchange, between the field, the manufacturing centre and the market. Mountains, forests, rivers could create obstructions, but goods found ways of flowing in and out. The map of India as made by the trade-routes is not necessarily the same as that made by the mountains, rivers and plains, and certainly not the same as nationalist ideology would like us to draw. South India was, from long before medieval times, more closely connected with West Asia and the Mediterranean than with north India; the Deccan was a self-sufficient unit and foreign travellers of the early middle ages have observed that the merchants of the Gujarat seaports concerned themselves more with the trading centres of the Persian Gulf than with north India. If we made a close study of the major and minor trade-routes of India we might come to the conclusion that the desire or the need for control of particular trade-routes was the real instigator of expansion policies and wars, and not religion or any abstract of power.

We must also examine, more closely than we do, the people with whom we are concerned, their character as a society, their occupations, their scale of values. If we do this, we might feel strongly inclined to rejection the classification of Hindu and Muslim as having no inherent significance. The Muslims were not one mass, solidly united by a common religion and an identity of social and material interests, but a community weakened by internal tensions and conflicts of interests, and liable, at any time, to a disastrous disintegration. We might find that the Hindus could not even be called a community, because of the deep rifts produced by the working of the caste system, that the rulers and warriors, the traders, the artisans lived in almost separate worlds, without any effective means of communication. The multitude of local dialects and the size of the country strengthened the social compartment-alisation. Megasthenes noted that the Indian farmer quietly went on with his work, while armies fought around him. Would the farmer be anxious to take the side of a Hindu army against an invading force? And what would be the interest of the merchant, the moneylender and the artisan looking for employment?

An examination of the dominant ideas among those we classify as Muslims and Hindus will further clarify the position. The Muslim ruler, during the period with which we are concerned, was the guardian of the *shariah,* but his private life—his extravagance, his wives, his slave-girls, concubines, his drinking and other kinds of indulgence—was not subject to the laws and conventions which applied to the generality of the Musilms. He could be admonished by reckless preachers because of sinful living, but could not be deprived of his position and authority. In his public capacity the ruler was looked upon as a safeguard against dissension and anarchy, and could therefore exercise an unrestricted right to reward and to punish, and to use his discretion in ensuring the security and welfare of his subjects. It is unthinkable that the despotism of such rulers should not have produced reactions. One kind of reaction is known; it is notorious: subservience. Those who had not the moral stature to resist cringed before the ruler. Among these were courtiers, government officers of all ranks, the official ulama, and all seekers after personal benefit. They were the vocal element, and they interpreted motives and events for the greater glory and power of the ruler. The ulama, apart from the theological support they gave to the ruler, clipped the wings of religion, reducing its dimensions to fit the framework of the law. This produced another kind of reaction which is identifiable, the rejection, on moral and spiritual grounds, of the ruler, his minions, his system of government through violence and terrorisation. This reaction is found among the learned and the pious, the righteous ulama and the sufis. It could not, naturally, assume a political or a recognisable social form. But there was, in all probability, a third kind of reaction which did, and which has been confused with heresy and sectarian violence. It would take me far afield if I discussed this matter at any length, but to give just one illustration: it would have been impossible for Hasan-bin-Sabbah and his organisation to find as many dedicated fanatics as he did who would assassinate persons of eminence against whom they had no personal grudge, if there had not been a widespread feeling that the political and social system of the Hanafi Sunnis was so monstrously oppressive and unjust that it deserved to be destroyed at any cost. This is, of course, a conjecture, and it may be wrong. But it would still be quite reasonable to assume that the despotism of Muslim rulers produced, as a reaction, tensions and feelings of deep unrest within the Muslim community.

Among the Hindus, caste was something final and fatal. The isolation of the various castes was so complete that all tensions seem to have been eliminated. It was possible even to postulate a supra-social unity which would comprehend the rigid divisions of the caste system. In any case, the question how it was possible for a handful of Turks to overrun north India from the Sutlej to the estuary of the Ganges within a decade has to be answered in an objective and convincing fashion and if the operation of the caste system is not the answer, the correct answer must be found if we are to understand medieval Indian history.

We may assume that the intrusion of a powerful foreign element would have upset the balance which the divisions of the caste system helped to maintain. But how powerful and how foreign were the Turks who established the Delhi Sultanate? Even a cursory examination of the resources of Shahabuddin Ghori in men and material would show that his empire and his hopes of survival were built on sand. The degree of foreignness of the Turks is something that has still to be investigated. If the Qutub monuments are regarded as evidence—and I would personally regard them as more valid than the statements of any contemporary historian—the understanding and cooperation between the Muslims who desired to build the mosque and the minar and the Hindu stone-masons who set up these buildings was unique and marvellously creative. As the buildings were planned and completed within four years of the occupation of Delhi, we should assume that both parties knew each other well, both by contact and hearsay, rather than the contrary. The existence of a Muslim settlement at Badaun is known. There was probably another at Ajmer. And there may have been others of which we do not have any direct evidence. The Delhi sultanate was not established by strangers, even though its establishment was accompanied by violence and bloodshed.

Once the sultanate was there, it had to create an environment conducive to its maintenance and survival. Could it depend entirely on the Muslims? There were a very small minority, not united by any common purpose, and not dependable, according to the accounts of the Muslim historians themselves. In the army, the cavalry was mainly, if not entirely, Muslim, and it was the most effective arm. But what about the supply services? And even if the rulers, the army officers and the soldiers were all of one mind, can a government maintain itself entirely and continuously on the strength of an army? We attempt to make assessments of what may be called the national character of the sultanate and Mughal governments by counting the number of Hindus in his office, because only the high officers are mentioned in the chronicles. But many other factors have to be considered in order to make a fair assessment. Outsiders have never been looked upon with favour by the village communities of India, and we have little reason to presume that the rural chiefs would have been submissive and cooperative even when the overlords were Hindus. They would have been even more suspicious and hostile when the governors and revenue officers were Muslims. But what about the population of the towns, the artisans, the merchants, the capitalist moneylenders? Muslim civilisation has been urban, and Muslims settled mainly in the towns. It was their relations with the urban population of the Hindus that mattered most to them, and it is these that require attention and study. If I may hazard a conjecture here, such study will most probably reveal that the Hindus derived what advantage they could from the new situation, the Muslims being dependent on the artisans, the merchants and, most of all, the capitalist moneylenders, while the normal life of the Hindu continued entrenched within the social system and established practices, with only an occasional, even if violent, disturbance.

It would be an obvious mistake to assume that Muslim sentiments were uniformly or continuously influenced by political considerations. The rulers—Turks, Pathans, Mughals—were a minority almost always guided by their particular interest. They never felt obliged by religion or by altruistic motives to share their power with the generality of the Muslims, and the generality of Muslims were not bound to the rulers by any ideals of loyalty. They wanted employment and other benefits, of course, but they also hoped and prayed that the ruler would not inflict suffering upon them. The political division that mattered normally was the division of ruler and subjects, and this should not be confused with the division of Hindus and Muslims on grounds of belief or prejudice.

But the intrusion of a new element in Indian life did have its effects. These, were, however, mainly indirect, and they form a more interesting and more important subject of study than political developments.

We know that Islam is a missionary religion, and assume that there has been missionary activity on a large-scale wherever Muslims are found. As the number of Muslims in India leads us to conclude that most of them must be converts, it is natural to suppose that there were organised efforts to convert Hindus. There are some indications that such efforts were made. Fanatical rulers also used force. But that meant an infinitesimal reduction in the number of Hindus, and would have had no other effect on their society. What we see, from the eighth century onwards, is a vast and growing ferment. This must have had many causes, but perhaps the most potent among them was a movement that arose among Muslims when conformity to one of the four schools of jurisprudence began to be insisted upon. The leaders of this movement were sufis. They propagated what they held to be the essential doctrines of Islam among the Muslim masses. The official ulama were concerned with the maintenance of orthodoxy and the observance of religious injunctions. They were not interested in bringing to the Muslim masses or to individuals in distress the hopes and consolations of religion. This the sufis accomplished through personal contact and new liturgical forms. By the time the sultanate was established, sufism had become a fairly strong and general movement. The sufis propagated sufism, which was their version of Islam, among the people in the language of the people.

There is a great deal of literature in the local and regional dialects of north India that bears witness to the extensiveness of the effort to bring religion to the people. The concept of the Unity of Existence or of Immanence, which became more and more the central feature of sufism and therefore of Islam as the vast majority of sufis preached it, helped to remove a great ideological barrier between the Muslims and the non-Muslims.

The movement of taking religion to the people had two opposite results, so far as the non-Muslims are concerned. One is symbolized in the philosophy of Kabir Saheb, who questioned the right of the Hindus and Muslims to practise exclusiveness in any form; the other result is symbolised in the *Ramayana* of Tulsi Das, which was an attempt to take Hinduism to the Hindu masses, and which strengthened immensely not only the beliefs but also the social system of the Hindus. The only period comparable to the fifteenth and sixteenth centuries in spiritual ferment is the age of the Buddha, an age of great heart-searching and moral awakening, of insistence on the elimination of non-essential differences and distinctions, of a reaching out towards unity at a purely human level. The medieval period was not a period of spiritual and social hibernation of the Hindus.

Having come to this point, the historian has to answer a very fundamental question. Whose history is the history of medieval India? Is it the history of the Indian people whom we now see united in one state, under one Constitution, or is it the history of a large number of good and bad Muslim rulers, or of Muslims plus Hindus as unintegrated units or of Muslims only, struggling to maintain themselves in power in a land which resisted their attempts to make it their own? The answer to this question must be given clearly and without mental reservations, because it will determine our whole attitude towards Indian history. If medieval Indian history is not the history of the Indian people, it can only have an academic antiquarian value, and we must habituate ourselves to regarding Indian history as beginning with the establishment of British rule. Otherwise we shall be following the ridiculous example of the author of *Five Thousand Years of Pakistan.* If we believe, however, that medieval Indian history is the history of the Indian people, we must frankly admit the implications, and they are many.

It will probably not be possible to avoid using the terms 'Hindu' and 'Muslim', but we must see to it that they do not imply any value judgements. Our value judgements must apply to persons, to ideas, to actions, and our criterion must be a conception of the common interest of the Indian people. This is, of course, not easy to define as yet, when we are used to thinking in terms of communities. But constant endeavour to impress upon our minds the image of the Indian people as a whole will gradually clarify our vision. The use of the terms 'Hindu' and 'Muslim' is in fact a simplification that enables us to evade the exercise of our imagination and the strain of objective thinking. If we classify the Delhi Sultans and the Mughal emperors as Muslims and judge them as such, our task is easy, and we do not need to challenge the attitude of our historians. If, on the other hand, we judge them as Indian rulers, we shall first have to cultivate in ourselves the attitude that would give us the right and the competence to judge. We shall have also to read the minds of medieval ancestors, to examine their actions not only in the light of our documents but also in the light of what these ancestors could not state and our historians could not imagine because of their compartmentalised thinking. We shall have, to restate ambitions and policies in terms of ideas, and evaluate them as ideas, even though that might lead us to express unorthodox or unpopular opinions.

I think an example or two will make my meaning clear. The causes of the downfall of the Mughal empire is a question that has been asked and answered hundreds of times. But we do not ask what this downfall meant for the country as a whole. Was it a matter of indifference to India and her people, or did it bring relief from oppression or was it a fulfilment of the desire of Providence that the British should come and rule, so that the Hindus might by and by oust them and come into their own after centuries of deprivation? Or was it a calamity from which all suffered, for which all were responsible because of what they did or failed to do, and because of which India had to suffer the consequences of alien rule? It is not my purpose here to answer this question, but this question must be posed and must be answered with all regard for historical truth, for logic and consistency. And we must also remember that the answer would matter very much in determining our future as a people.

Let us look at the period of Mughal downfall from another angle. Aurangzeb's fanaticism is listed as one of the causes of Mughal downfall. But was he a fanatic or a statesman who was caught in a relentless grip of circumstances? A religious fanatic is one who pursues some religious purpose, fiercely and recklessly. A political fanatic is one who strives to achieve a political aim, whatever the cost to himself and to others. Was Aurangzeb a religious fanatic. If he was, is not something more than the dislike of music, the destruction of temples and the levy of *jiziya* required as evidence. The dislike of music may have been the reaction of a puritanical mind, which is not undesirable in a ruler who wishes to concentrate on administrative work. The destruction of temples was an ugly but almost routine punishment for overt rebellion or suspicion of subversive activities. As regards *jizya,* I am sure in my own mind that it could not have been levied under a strict interpretation of Muslim religious law. In any case, the question must be considered also from this point of view. But let us set aside, for a moment, the issue of its religious validity and examine the levy of *jiziya* from a purely administrative and economic point of view. No government can dispense with taxation, and if abnormal expenditure has to be covered by taxes, much thought has to be given to the form of the additional taxes. Muslim law has determined what taxes can be levied. A new tax could have been opposed by Muslims on religious and by Hindus on economic grounds, and it may have fallen on many who did not possess the ability to pay. The *jiziya* had some traditional justification, and it could be argued that it would fall on those whose taxable capacity was highest. The levy of the *jiziya* was a serious mistake, but cannot the decision to levy it be considered as a choice between evils and not as an act of outright fanaticism. It was one of the many unjust taxes levied, but while we condemn it, let us not forget that the *chauth* levied by the Marhatta chiefs cannot be justified merely because it was secular tax and was levied indiscriminately. An administration that assumes the minimum responsibilities of government is entitled to levy taxes; where no responsibilities are assumed, taxation in any form is unjustified.

Was Aurangzeb a political fanatic? He did pursue his expansionist aims with a fanatical persistence. But what were these aims? We have, in recent years, felt indignant at the idea of foreign powers having possessions in India, the D.M.K.'s cry for secession made us furious and we have been angered by the demand for a Punjabi Suba. Today we do our thinking with the help of newspapers and the mouths of politicians; three hundred years ago all such thinking was the function of a few persons, or of just the ruler himself. After attempt had been made to establish outposts at Kandahar and Balkh, and there had been continuous expansion southwards., the decision to incorporate the territories of the Deccan sultans in the Mughal empire cannot be construed as extravagant ambition. The suppression of elements subversive of the empire was necessary if a unifying administration was to be maintained. Before we pass judgements, we must pause to make sure of our criteria, and also be confident that we have the courage and the objectivity to apply the same criteria to all those whom we judge. For instance, if we condemn the Mughal empire or its last effective ruler, we must be willing to consider whether those who were instrumental in crippling its administration offered something better to the country, whether the Marhattas, the Jats and the Sikhs were inspired by higher ideals, possessed the ability to realise them and therefore evoked widespread and deep sympathy among the Indian people as a whole. It is very easy to condemn failure and applaud success if we base our judgement on facts which we have ourselves selected. But do we serve the truth and our own higher interests by doing so? Have we not fortified ignorance and prejudice, blurred our perspective and weakened the moral foundations of our national life already by not looking at all facts, all aspects of situations and problems?

I am myself aware, that while claiming to be an Indian citizen, I think and feel most of the time as a north Indian. A professor of a south Indian university accused Bengali historians of having exalted the Gupta dynasty far beyond its merits and kept the achievements of south Indian dynasties out of the picture. I felt that his way of thinking was a classic example of academic regionalism. But so is mine, even though I identify myself with a larger region, and I must confess I would resent a south Indian telling me that Akbar and his ideals meant nothing to him. In fact his statement would be justified, even if it were made in retaliation. We mention the south in connection with the first appearance of Muslim Arabs, with the origin of the *Bhakti* movement, with the military achievements of Alauddin Khilji—as if the south was unexplored enemy territory which it was a glorious thing to overrun and plunder—with the wars between the Bahmani Kingdom and the Vijayanagar empire. Does this prove that we regard the south as an integral part of India during the medieval period? I am not satisfied that it does, and therefore there must be something basically wrong with our perspective. I fear there is something wrong with my own perspective. It was only after taking classes in medieval Indian architecture for over a year that I realised I had completely omitted south Indian architecture. I have studied it, I have as high a regard for it as for Indian Muslim architecture and am deeply moved by its aesthetic values, but I have quite unconsciously allowed myself to be blinded by the tradition of ignoring the south, or still worse, of regarding it as fundamentally alien to the north. I hope my conscience will not let me rest till I have made amends.

There are, of course, many other questions that require thought. Why was there no movement in India comparable to the European renaissance: why were no attempts made to organise production on more profitable lines, when there was no shortage of capital or skilled labour and the desire to acquire and accumulate wealth was as strong as anywhere else; why was there no development of political ideas, no cultivation of public spirit, no experimentation in political organisation, when there was no lack of moral sense or of intelligence or of a desire for ordered living? Any of these problems would be a study in itself—and of great significance for us today. But we seem reluctant to undertake such studies, and I fear the main reason is that we think of India and the Indian people in parts and have no comprehensive image of the Indian people as a whole. It is for the historians to project this image before politicians have made it difficult or impossible.

To conclude, Indian history must be studied and taught in the context of world history. We must have far more detailed knowledge than we possess of the geography of our country, and specially of the major and subsidiary trade-routes. We must not regard 'Hindu' and 'Muslim' as self-explanatory terms, but investigate the structure and character of what are called the Hindu and the Muslim communities. This investigation must comprehend not only beliefs and practices but also the dominant attitudes and ideas. The establishment of the Delhi Sultanate was the culmination of various types of relationships and contacts extending over 500 years, and we cannot have a correct perspective on the early phase of Indian Muslim history unless we have adequate knowledge of the situation in the twelfth century. The influence of Hindus and Muslims on each other was both direct and indirect, and the indirect forms require to be analysed very carefully. Finally, unless we have decided in our own minds that medieval Indian history is not the history of the Indian people, we must courageously examine our present criteria of judgement and develop a perspective on persons, policies and events of the past that will enable us to understand and forgive and to obtain a clear vision of the past and the future.

30

The Meaning of Indian History

Can we discuss the meaning or meanings of Indian history before we have considered whether history itself has any meaning? Is history just information about the past or is it true knowledge? Are the events and actions which we call history facts like the observed facts of the natural sciences from which we can deduce laws? If they are, have laws been deduced from them? If they are not such facts, what is their value? I must confess that I have evolved no philosophy of history of my own and would not regard any philosophy of history as more than an opinion, possibly deserving of deep consideration. I am only a student of Indian history, and I have, in my endeavour to understand Indian history, come to ask myself the question: In the light of our history, what is it to be an Indian?

I know I could be confounded by the rejoinder: In the light of the history of human life on this earth, what is it to be human? Until we have answered this fundamental question, how can we ask what it means to be an Indian? I appreciate the pertinence of this question, but like everybody else I have tried to be human without first arriving at a precise definition of homo sapiens or, as the Arabs called him, 'the talking animal'. I feel that, without enlarging our field of observation to such an extent that we are confused by its vastness, we may well consider the record of homo sapiens within the part of the world we call Indian and arrive at conclusions which will help to ensure his survival with the freedom, the dignity and the materials of comfort which he obviously desires. To put it in another way, I am an Indian citizen who if deeply concerned about the present and future welfare of

---

From *The Meaning of Indian History, Basu Memorial Lecture.*

his country and who is looking to history for guidance in his approach to problems that appear to be important.

'What is it to be an Indian'? If you look back you will find that there have been few occasions in our history when that question seems to have been asked even symbolically and few persons who have asked it. We are naturally inclined, in our study of history, to concentrate on achievement, and we try to form an idea of what we are by a process of logical deduction from the nature of our achievements. We forget, however, that our history is not all achievement. It is also a record of failure. We have, for instance, periods in which the idea of India as one country seems to have faded out of people's minds, when thoughts and activities were confined within localities and regions and our country was a conglomeration of isolated unites or a welter of forces in blind and meaningless conflict. For achievement we depend upon the fortunate accident of persons with vision and creative power being born among us, and we may not be able to give such persons the support and the trust they deserve if we have not prepared the ground for them by reflecting on the reasons why our political unity has been often so short-lived and why we have not been able to give enduring form to any concept of a common interest. Akbar was a statesman who felt the need for such a concept. He asked himself the question whether the religious and worldly tendencies of men had any common ground. After a search an inquiry which, for its uninhibited quality and comprehensiveness, has few parallels in history, he placed before those who were closest to him his idea of a basic, national faith-—belief in one God and goodwill towards all men. We relate now in derision or pity that he wanted to establish a new religion and failed, as he deserved to. But was it Akbar who failed or those around him who, in spite of an otherwise unconditional loyalty, would not agree to recognise that political obligations must have a spiritual basis and service of the state the quality of a moral command? We are no better than Akbar's associates, and do not appreciate the relevance of his ideas for our own times.

We have agreed, in our Constitution, to allow our citizens the full right to believe in and to practise their particular religion. The only limitation is that they do not encroach upon one another's right. This attitude is a reflection of our conduct as a people in matters of religion throughout our history, and it has been strengthened by a fairly general conviction that all religions have the same aims and lead to the same goal. We have given a modern form to this conviction by assuming a fundamental unity of all religions and by giving our state a secular character. But while the contemporary solution to the problem of religious diversity may be regarded as having grown naturally out of a tradition of coexistence and tolerance, the acceptance of this diversity has consequence which should not be ignored. People who believe in and practise a particular religion inevitably cultivate the feeling of belonging together in a special sense. There may be those among them who are religious only when they are engaged in contemplation or prayer or the performance of some religious duty, and are not otherwise influenced by religious group feeling. There may be conflicts of belief or interest within a religious community which produce the impression that its religion is not a unifying force. But by and large the presence of a felling of 'we' and 'they' within each religious community cannot be eradicated by the practice of tolerance, however, consistent and sincere it may be. And to this extent, therefore, the diversity of religious beliefs injects an uncertainty in the concept of India and Indian.

But, you will ask, need this uncertainty be given any serious consideration? There are Protestants and Catholics in Great Britain. The religious-minded among them do not hesitate to assert their differences, and a close examination of sentiments may reveal the existence of fairly deep-rooted prejudices. But this does not conflict with the feeling of belonging together, or what Ibn Khaldun called 'asabiyah', among the British people. That may be quite true. But Great Britain and other countries whose history has been completely different from our own, cannot be cited as parallel cases. What is more important, religion is among us only one of the diversifying factors. We have languages which are, except Urdu, languages of states, and provide claims to a cultural identity to many major units of the Union of India. The feeling of belonging together in the religious community which constitutes the overwhelming majority of the Indian people is thus modified and may under circumstances be neutralised by regional cultural loyalties. Our states, were largely accidental divisions created for purposes of administrative convenience. They have now, by our own will, become political and cultural entities. We have to ask ourselves whether they will or will not in course of time reproduce the picture of India which we see during long periods of our history.

One result of the sanctified diversities of religion, language and culture has been not only to obscure the meaning of Indian history but to create doubts about there being such a thing. In spite of our common citizenship it seems obvious that if we do not continuously ask ourselves the question. What is it to be an Indian, Indian history will become a vague background of regional histories and concepts of India will be evolved which will be inconsistent with each other and inconsistent with any reasonable concept of the whole. We shall have no common standard for the evaluation of persons and ideas, for the interpretation of events or for objective assessments of any kind. Another result of the recognition of diversities has been that a definition of the term 'Indian' cannot be imposed, except in the legal sense and as laid down in the relevant clauses of our Constitution.

Whenever I have raised the question. What is it to be an Indian? I have been asked for my own definition. I have avoided giving it because I do not regard myself as possessing the right to give finality to the concept of an Indian. History tells me that we are still in a process of becoming, and any anticipation of the ultimate result of this process would be a hindrance in its working itself out. A study of the sociological history of the Indian Muslim has convinced me that they cannot be defined in terms of religion and culture. If they are denied an identity their reaction is strong and hostile; if they are declared to possess an identity, they become allergic to almost every form, except certain religious practices, in which their identity is recognised. This would, I believe, be true, *mutatis mutandis,* of most constituent elements of the Indian people. We may satisfy ourselves by talking of an overriding spiritual unity which compensates for the existing diversities of religion and culture, and hope we shall not be cross-examined on this point. But if our history is to have meaning and formative influence, every possible emphasis must be placed on the process of our becoming as distinguished from being Indians.

I have already referred to the risks involved in sanctifying the diversity of religions. On the other hand, I am convinced that it would be disastrous if we adopted a policy of enforcing unity and uniformity. What part, then, should religion play in the process to our becoming Indians? You as educators are aware of the consequences of the elimination of religion from education. We have, characteristically, attempted to solve the problems created by secularism by setting up committees to report on how moral values could be inculcated without reference to religion. I participated some years ago in a seminar organised by this institute, to consider how the moral values of the different religions could be so isolated as to become useful for prophylaxis and proper motivation in education. As chairman of a panel of thirty teachers, all Hindus, I thought of beginning the proceedings by asking the members how many of them had made a study of Hinduism. Only three held up their hands, and of these three only one appeared to me to be homo sapiens of the normal kind. I do not remember what the report of the panel was, but what we felt was that there was nothing to do till Hindus had become proper Hindus, able to state with some precision what they held to be the moral values represented by Hinduism and able to withstand elementary cross-examination. I am quite sure that if the panel I had to deal with had consisted of members professing any other religion the fate of the panel would have been the same.

If in the face of this appalling ignorance of religion we still talk of diversity of religions, it is obvious that we are not thinking of genuine religion. If we go still further and talk of an overriding spiritual unity we are only professing allegiance to a myth. It is open to us to say that religiousness is not an essential quality of an Indian, and strive for a frank admission of this fact. But the initiative in this must be taken by the members of every religious community within their own communities in the first instance, and they must be prepared for a possible revival of religiousness as a reaction to this move. What history indicates is that there has always been, within each community, an upper stratum of intellectual and freethinkers, and the sophisticated among us are the heirs and successors of the upper strata of the different religious communities who now share a common language, English, and enjoy the protection of the law. But so far as I have been able to observe, these sophisticated persons play safe. The freedom they claim to have achieved is at a lofty intellectual level; they seldom reject custom and established practice, and so almost always remain ineffective. Another refuge of the sophisticated is the advocacy of the fundamental unity of all religions. It has even been thought that a syllabus of religious instruction could be drawn up by taking the common elements of all religions and fusing them together to form an adequately edifying whole. But a unity or religions can only result from a unity among believer. We cannot tell the believers in any religion to which part of their beliefs they should assign priority, nor can we ask them not consider any belief fundamental out of regard for believers in other religions. So either we should have no religion at all, but only committees in perpetual session for devising a syllabus and creating an atmosphere for effective moral instruction, or we should invite believers in the different religions to ask themselves the question, 'What is it to be an Indian? And find an answer that will be valid under any given circumstances.'

What I mean will perhaps become clearer if I give an example. In the Jamia Millia we have emphasised that identity and unique character of every religion, and have done what we could to provide instruction to every student in his own religion. I have not been satisfied with what we have been doing, and least of all with the teaching of Islam. I have protested in several ways, discreetly and indiscreetly. But attitudes, specially in matters of belief, which have become established and are taken for granted can be changed only by some revolutionary method, and I could not exceed the limits of peaceful provocation. Some two years ago it occurred to me that the point to emphasise in the teaching of Islam is not the benefits that Islam ensures to the Muslim in this world and the next but the benefits that non-Muslim cannot only expect but demand from the Muslim because of his faith in Islam. In other words, it is not what the Muslim hopes to get which matters but what he is commanded to give to Muslims and non-Muslims alike. I discussed this idea with some of my colleagues, and suggested that it might be propagated in theory and through practice. But most of us are not normally religious-minded, and I do not possess the patience or the self-confidence of the preacher. So the idea is still germinating. The same idea could be planted and allowed to germinate in other institutions also, and it might ultimately bear fruit is stimulating and unifying answers to the question. How does my belief in my religion help me to understand and express in my thoughts and actions what it is to be an Indian? If this happens, the diversity of our beliefs will lead to a diversity of spontaneous contributions to the strengthening of our national life, and our beliefs will be not only diverse but also genuine.

Of course, the first reaction of the members of every religious community will be to calculate the possible losses. They naturally regard the claims of their own community as deserving prior consideration, and these claims can themselves never be fully satisfied. How can they, then, legitimately ignore the needs of their own community to fulfil those of others, and even if they do, what return will they get? The only answer is that we have been thinking on these lines for over a century, and we must now either admit that nationhood has been forced upon us by a handful of persons who thought differently, or we must accept the social and religious obligations imposed on us by freedom and the need to remain a fully integrated people.

Underlying all aspects of the problem of integration is the question to whom we owe our primary loyalty. Here our history has hardly anything to show in terms of achievement, and religion has been perhaps the most important force in drawing our attention away from a serious consideration of this question. The Hindu dharma assigned government to a caste, and isolated this caste by defining the duties of the other castes. The dharma was not the only operative force and examples can be quoted to show that all rulers did not belong to a particular caste, and that there were communities and guilds which engaged in occupations so alien to each other from the point of view of the dharma as warfare and trade. But whether we regard the dharma as representing only theory and not practice or both theory and practice, the primary loyalty was to the particular dharma of the individual or the caste group and to society or the political community as a whole. Among Muslims obedience to the commands of God has been without question the overriding duty, but it could never be determined in any actual situation what the commands of God were. The Quran has laid down that affairs of government should be settled by consultation: in practice, the ruler was an autocrat and the law gave him indirect support by making opposition almost impossible under law and religion. The exponents of the law had only the status of officially recognised theologians and could not assume an independent position in political affairs. There was also a long and hallowed tradition of righteous men, scholars and mystics, who condemned the government of their times as based on injustice and advised Muslims who cared for the good of their souls avoid all contact with kings and courtiers and government officers, If we consider only facts and not law and doctrine, we find the both Hindus and Muslims were very confused in their ideas of loyalty: The dominant notion during the period just preceding the British occupation of our country and for quite some time after it was that one must be loyal to him whose salt one had eaten, that is, to him who had conferred some material benefit. Whatever we may think of this as a sentiment governing personal relationships, there is no doubt that it is subversive of every general concept of moral obligation and common political and social interest. I know that among Muslims it was the greatest obstacle to political awakening. So what we learn from our history is that the consequences of not evolving a concept of loyalty that creates social and political solidarity can be disastrous, and we must have a concept of loyalty that is both clear and effective if we wish to avoid disaster.

We must, in fact, go further. We must recognise and affirm that our state is a moral entity, that its interest is not a material but a moral interest, and that any opposition to the government must be inspired by a deep sense of loyalty to the state. The clearest statement in history of opposition to a government in the interest of the state and to a society in the interest of a higher ideal of life is the defence of Socrates. That is a statement made for all time. We could adapt it to our own circumstances and draw upon our own faiths for the strength necessary to uphold the ultimate values. Faiths then will take on the character of faith, of moral commands, of categorical imperatives, and slough off dead tissues of myth, tradition and custom. We will not insist that religion needs to be embodied in the particular ideals and practices of this or that community. In India religion will become the faith of the Indian, of the human being who looks beyond himself, who has the courage to face the consequences of sacrificing the immediate benefit to the ultimate and who believes that his state demands of him an absolute loyalty to moral values.

To sum up this extremely rambling discourse: Our history tells us that the different types of communities into which our country has been divided have constantly been building fences around themselves. These fences have sometimes been broken by religious leaders and by statesmen, but the tendency to build fences has again and again reasserted itself. We can eradicate this tendency only if, in matters of faith, we think constantly of what we must give to others because of our faith and not of what we have and may keep to ourselves, and if, in matters of material concern, we give priority to the interest of the country and the people as a whole. The right approach will gradually become a habit if, as I have suggested, the consideration of all matter is under the auspices of the question. What is it to be an Indian?

In this context, the educator appears to be the arbiter of our country's destiny. Politicians, because of the very nature of their function, deal with masses, and in our country they have found an easy road to success by identifying themselves with religious communities or economic, linguistic, regional or local groups. Unfortunately, historians have followed the same line. The case of the individual has gone by default. In history we find that he has been considered liable to fall into error to such a degree that the right to discover the truth for himself has been denied to him. He was not considered entitled to a conscience of his own. In our own times, he is habitually reduced to an anonymous unit of a community, sharing its attributes. He is assumed to desire no character of his own distinct from that of his community. This is a situation in which educators must come to the rescue. It is their function to deal with individuals and not communities, with concrete human beings and not abstractions. They must reinstate the individual. They can, of course, do this only by first reinstating themselves as individuals. This is a task to be performed *not* by discussion and collective thinking but by each teacher drawing upon his inner resources under the guidance of his own conscience. I suggest that the first step in the formulation of this task is for the teacher to pose the question. What is it to be an Indian? And work his way to an answer.

31

The Middle Ages (AD 900-1450)

I

Histories which deal primarily with Europe divide historical time into ancient, medieval and modern ages. In this division, the medieval age, though possessing a political and cultural identity and definite characteristics of its own, is regarded mainly as a time of transition. If we look at the world as a whole, this division does not apply. In west Asia, India and China mature civilisations were taken over by new races. They changed their form and might have acquired a fresh impetus. But though large and powerful empires were established, beliefs, organisation and skill remained largely stagnant. The centuries with which we are dealing in this chapter form a kind of watershed, with the European peoples following a fresh line of development, and the Asian peoples retaining the old course and gradually losing political vision and economic initiative, The centre of gravity of human civilisation begins to shift westwards from the twelfth century.

By the middle of the ninth century, the Abbasid Khilafat was on the decline, the power of the Khalifa having passed into the hands of' Turkish generals who intrigued and fought to govern in his name. Early in the eleventh century, Iran, Iraq and the larger part of Asia Minor came under the rule of the Seljuk Turks. With the disintegration of their empire, the whole of west Asia was divided up into small principalities, This fragmentation was the main reason for the early successes of the Crusades, which began in 1096-97, and continued with long and short intervals for nearly two hundred years. About the middle of the twelfth century, the

From *World History*.

Turkish empire of Khwarizm. sprang up in the central Asian steppes and expanded southwards toward Khurasan and Iran. This empire went down before the onslaught of the Mongols under Chenghiz Khan (1155-1227), who had mustered all the power of the Mongol tribes under his authority. He conquered Peking in 1215, and then turned westwards. In 1219 he overran Turkestan, Khurasan and Southern Russia up to Dnieper. It is impossible to imagine the ruin caused by his hordes. Every city in Turkestan and northern Iran was destroved, and the more flourishing the city the more thorough the devastation. Of the population, only the artisans were spared, and these only to be deported to the conqueror's capital. The rest of the people were massacred without mercy. In 1258, Chenghiz Khan's grandson seized and utterly destroyed Baghdad, leaving hardly any trace of civilized life and activity. A little more than a century later, Timur the Lame (1370-1405) built an empire with its capital at Samarkand on whatever was left among the ruins, repeating all the horrible massacres perpetrated by his ancestor Chenghiz. His empire included Turkestan, Iran, Asia Minor, Syria, Russia till Moscow, and northwest India. Such an empire could not be kept together and it broke up as soon as Timur was dead.

One of the successor states of the Seljuk Empire was established in Asia Minor, with its capital at Brusa, by the Osmanli Turks. The Osmanlis took upon themselves the function which the Seljuks had attempted to perform, of defending and expanding the Muslim world. Once they had established themselves in Asia Minor they advanced westwards. Adrianople was conquered in 1366 and became their capital. Mohammed II (1451-1481) conquered Constantinople in 1453.

While this may be considered a military advance on one frontier of the Muslim world, there was continuous retreat on another. During the latter half of the tenth and the first half of the eleventh centuries, the Arabs in Spain proved themselves most successful as rulers and creators of civilisation. Then the Christian kings of Castille began to recover their lost territory. Toledo was taken in 1085, Cordova in 1236, Seville in 1248. About this time the small kingdom of Granada was flourishing, but it was a small and isolated political unit. It survived till 1492, when the last of the Muslims, or Moors as they were called, were driven out of Spain.

Egypt escaped from the attacks of both the Crusaders and the Mongols. Here the Fatimids established themselves in 969, and their rule lasted till 1172. They were replaced by the Ayyubis (1169-1250), the dynasty founded by the famous Sultan Salahuddin. The Ayyubis were followed by the Mamelukes (1252-1517), and it was the first Mameluke Sultan, Baibers who beat back the Mongol advance in northern Syria.

The history of north India from the end of the fifth century onwards was very largely influenced by tribal migrations. We hve seen that the Gupta Empire was overthrown by the Huns. Harsha succeeded in resisting the immigrant tribes, but his dominion did not extend far into the Punjab. After him the stream of immigrants flowed steadily into the country. Most of the Rajput tribes are really foreign elements absorbed in the Indian population according to the requirements of the caste system. The history of north India till the Turkish invasion is mostly a record of the attempts of the Rajput chiefs to establish themselves. Some of them, like Raja Bhoj, have become legendary figures. But real advance was made only in the south. Here, in spite of suicidal wars with the Pallavas, the Chola dynasty, founded about 846, was able to expand its power. Under Raja Raja I (985-1016) and Rajendra I (1016-1044) the Cholas extended their influence up to the Ganges in India and across the seas to Ceylon, Malaya and Indonesia.

The first Muslims to come to India were Arab traders. In 711-12, the Arabs took possession of the Sind valley, but did not advance further. Even in the valley their power soon declined and disintegrated. In the ninth century, the immigration of Turkish tribes into Turkestan and Iran had already begun, and while Turkish nobles were becoming all-powerful in the Abbasid court, the Samanid Sultanate was established in north-western Iran and Ghazni became the nucleus of another kingdom. The Turkish invasions of India were a continuation of the migration of tribes which began in the fifth century. The difference was that the Turks were smaller in number, that they considered themselves representatives of a religion and a culture and could not be assimilated within the social system of India.

Mahmud of Ghazni (998-1030) raided India seventeen times and carried off as booty all the accumulated treasures in the temples of north India from Banaras to Somnath. He must have had full knowledge of the country, and though it seems his armies contained

Indian elements, his destruction of Mathura proves that he had the barbarian's jealousy of the achievements of civilisation. He was not anxious to acquire territory and his occupation of the country up to the Ravi was mainly to protect his line of communications. By the second half of the twelfth century the situation had changed, and Mohammad Ghori invaded India with the object of establishing his power here permanently. He took possession of Dellii in 1196, and 10 years later his deputy, Qutubuddin Aibak, became independent ruler of his Indian territories.

The Sultanate thus founded expanded rapidly along the trade routes eastwards and southwards. In spite of the Mongol raids, which became persistent from about 1235 onwards, the Sultans of Delhi extended their dominion to the Deccan plateau and beyond, and the Sultanate attained its maximum limits about 1334. Then it began to break up, and by the end of the century every one of its provincial governors had become independent. The provincial kingdoms were mostly engaged in wars with each other, but some also became rich and prosperous. Among the most flourishing states of the fifteenth century was Vijaynagar, founded late in the fourteenth century. We have evidence of its wealth and splendour from many sources.

Like India, the political destiny of China was also moulded by the pressure of Mongol tribes in the north-west. After the downfall of the T'ang, there were five dynasties ruling in the Yellow River basin, and the first state that was of any considerable extent and power was established by the half-Mongol Liao dynasty (937-1123). To the south of the Liao territory, the Sung established themselves in 960. They were attacked in 1126 by Mongol tribes, but a prince of the dynasty who fled south-eastward founded another state with Hangchow as its capital. In 1205, Chenghiz Khan was proclaimed "Emperor within the Seas." The empire established by him, which reached the zenith of power and prosperity under Kublai Khan (1259-1294), included China, Burma, Annam, Tibet, Central Asia and Europe up to the rivers Theiss and Weichsel. Kublai Khan's subjects do not seem to have been as happy as the glowing accounts of the European visitors to his court would lead us to believe. There were famines and revolts, and in 1368 a Buddhist monk, Chu Yuan Shang, headed a rebellion against the dynasty and drove it out of Peking. The Ming dynasty (1368-1644), founded by him, introduced agrarian and financial reforms and also extended the frontiers of the empire. In 1382, Yunnan was conquered and six years later the Mongols were driven out of Karakorum. In the reign of the emperor Cheng–tsu (1405-1424), Chinese prestige was restored in the southern seas by means of naval expeditions, Sumatra and Ceylon were made to acknowledge Chinese overlordship and missions were sent as far as Aden and Hormuz.

In Europe, the disorder following upon the break-up of the empire of Charlemagne was remedied in part by the kings of the House of Saxony. Otto I (936-973) consolidated his power and was crowned Roman emperor in 962. Charlemagne had conquered part of what is now known as Westphalia and Bohemia, Austria, Hungary and Slovenia. These territories were inhabited by tribes with their own organisation. One of the problems of an emperor was to enforce recognition of his authority by the tribal chiefs, another to protect these territories, which formed the frontier of Christian Europe, against the attacks of the Scandinavians in the north, the Wends in the east and the Magyars in the south-east. To attain the full prestige of a civilised and Christian ruler he had to have a status in Rome corresponding more or less to his political position. The frontiers of Christian Europe were slowly extended to the north, the east and the south-east, but the tribal chiefs and their territories maintained their identity. In Italy and in Rome the emperors failed to acquire lasting influence. The papacy was under the influence of the emperors from 963 for about a hundred years. Then it slowly recovered prestige through measures of reform and assertions of a supreme religious status independent of the emperor. Frederick I (1152-1190) and Frederick II (1211-1250) were men of vision and imagination. They were, therefore, anxious to centralise authority and to assert their rights as the supreme secular rulers against the Pope. Both Empire and Papacy suffered because of the conflict. The power of the emperors was divided up between the princes. On the other side, papal claims provoked strong resistance, the result of which was that some Popes had to live at Avignon in France as exiles from 1305 to 1378. The exile was followed by a period (1378-1417) when there were two Popes at the same time, one at Avignon and the other at Rome.

One reason for the defeat of the Popes was the rise of monarchies in France and Engand. France was an ill-defined area at the beginning of the tenth century. Hugh Capet became king in

987, and his dynasty gradually expanded its possessions and built up its power by supporting the rising middle class and the cities. In the thirteenth century, France acquired importance in European affairs because of participation in the Crusades and in the controversy over the extent of Pope's authority. It was, in fact, a French king who forced the Pope to live at Avignon. But France suffered considerably in the Hundred Years' War with England, which lasted from 1338 to 1453.

England was occupied by the Romans in the second half of the first century BC and became a Roman province. Early in the fifth century AD, the Romans withdrew from the country, which was then conquered and colonised by German and Scandinavian tribes. It was again conquered in 1066 by William of Normandy. His successors ruled both England and the French possessions inherited from him. Security against foreign invasions and the small size of the country enabled the kings, some of whom had an extraordinary regard for the forms and conventions of government, to create a system of constitutional rule. The history of England is unique as an experiment in political organisation.

The Crusades form a turning point in the history of Europe. They were nominally holy wars waged for the reconquest of Jerusalem from the Muslims, in fact they were the result of a strange combination of motives. The Normans, a Scandinavian people, who first settled in Normandy (France), conquered England and began their attacks first upon Arab possessions in the Mediterranean and then on Epirus (north-western Greece). They joined the Crusades from the very beginning, and used every opportunity to realise their ambition to conquer the whole of the Byzantine Empire. The Italian cities, Venice, Genoa, Pisa also joined in the Crusades. Each of these cities was interested in establishing its own maritime empire and making as much profit as possible out of the religious fervour of the kings and nobles who did the fighting. The Venetians even succeeded in converting the fourth Crusade (1204) into an attack on Byzantium. This city was looted and destroyed and a large number of the inhabitants massacred to enable the Venetians to establish a Latin empire that would give them greater liberty and privileges than the Byzantine emperors were willing to agree to. The Popes were engaged in conflict with the emperors of Germany, and hoped, by proclaiming Crusades, to get the support of the whole Christian world and add to their prestige and authority. Last among the participants and the largest in number were the knights and noblemen. They were led by kings and emperors who desired fame and honour, but were moved even more by the need to divert the attention of their nobility, so that they might establish or extend their power in their own countries. Their efforts led to the formation of nation-states.

II

The main line of development in all the religions we have described was towards the determination of the correct beliefs and the creation of institutions through which the way of life required by the beliefs could be established. These beliefs and institutions together make up what is called the orthodox form of the religion. We have seen that among Buddhists the Sangh was constituted, but a large number of sects came into being because it was difficult to decide in many matters what the Buddha had taught. Buddhist orthodoxy was the orthodoxy of separate sects. Christianity was spread by the Church, and its orthodox forms were represented by the Byzantine and Roman Churches. As soon as Christianity was recognised by the Emperor Constantine, orthodoxy began to be enforced with the help of the state. The Muslims had the advantage of possessing in the Quran and the remembered acts and sayings of the Prophet most of what was needed to make the faith clear to the believer, but among them also, public opinion and sometimes the power of the state was called upon to support orthodoxy.

The vast majority of people need to have the feeling that they believe in the right things and act according to the correct laws. They become the support of orthodoxy and the political and social order which safeguards orthodoxy. But there are also people who feel that they are not being true to themselves or to their religion if they merely repeat what they are told and perform prescribed acts in the prescribed way. They think that those who follow the orthodox religion do so out of habit; they do not believe with their heart. So they endeavour to understand everything for themselves, to get the truths of their religion directly and personally from the source, and they speak almost as if they were the first exponents of their religion. They do not always reject the orthodox creed, but they do claim to know what is important and what is not, and to have the authority to define and declare the true spirit of their religion. Such people are called mystics. They may or may not preach what they believe, they may or may not try to reform others. They may or may not give a systematic form to their ideas. They may become recluses, ascetics, or devotees or they may live like ordinary people, serving God and man in the way that appears most suitable to them. Mysticism has many forms and also many degrees, but the distinctive quality common to all of them is the intense personal realisation of truth.

This period, which we have called the Middle Ages, is also the age of mysticism. We see it in almost every religious community and it seems, like the spiritual revolution, to be a worldwide movement. Why it became an outstanding feature of this period is difficult to answer. It represents obviously the desire for a purer and more intense spiritual life. The distance in time between the believer and the founder of the faith was so great, the established religious ideas and institutions so much an accepted form that the earnest and sensitive believer was forced to look within himself for the sources of truth. The idea of the religious world-state among Muslims and Christians expanded the religious community to such dimensions that it became spiritually necessary to organise small units of like-minded people who could live the ideal life for themselves. The monastery, and its Muslim form, the *Khanqah,* appear inevitably as the social and in many cases the economic expression of the mystic tendency.

Among the Christians there was from the very beginning a strong ascetic tendency, a feeling that everything physical and material was impure. This was the first form of mysticism, and also the most enduring and characteristic form. Contact with other beliefs and ways of life led to the assimilation and adoption of doctrines and ideas and the creation of sects. The mysticism of those who remained orthodox became more intellectual. This tendency implied the understanding of the Christian religion from a point of view that did not contradict but was still different from the teaching and the attitude of the Church. It became more pronounced because of the study of Aristotle, stimulated by contact with the Muslims. St. Anthony (250-356), whose achievements in self-mortification became a by-word, represents the first type of mystic; St. Augustine (354-430) was the type which sought and attained both spiritual and intellectual satisfaction. St. Bernard of

Clairvaux (1091-1153) was the typical ascetic, preacher and admonisher. In St. Thomas Aquinas (1225-1274), who taught that revelation was a means of apprehending theological truth and was not opposed to other means of attaining knowledge, we see the influence of Aristotle and Muslim scholasticism.

Christian mysticism took three other distinct forms. One was of dedication to the spiritual life through love and service of fellow-Christians. This is represented by the monastic movement, which may be described as an attempt to regulate the life of mysticism and asceticism. The origins of monasticism go back to the sixth century, when St. Benedict founded the first monasteries in Europe and called them schools for the service of the Lord. Every monastery had an abbot at its head, and a community of monks who led a self-denying and hard life, but not one of great austerity. St. Bernard of Clairvaux founded a new order on the lines of St. Benedict, but with much stricter regulations. In the thirteenth century, monasticism took a new turn through the establishment of mendicant orders, the Franciscan (1210), the Dominican (1215), the Carmelite (1245), and the Augustinian (1256). Those who belonged to these orders were called friars instead of monks, they did not attach themselves to the monastery or live a secluded life. They served those in need outside the monastery and endeavoured to influence people, directly by their personal example.

The second form of mysticism became prominent in the thirteenth century, though its traditions are much older. Hugh St. Victor (1096-1141) made the Augustinian monastery of St. Victor near Paris the centre of mysticism in the twelfth century, and its influence was widespread. In Germany, mysticism seems to have found very fertile soil. Mechthild of Magdeburg (1207-1282), a woman who was the first to use German as a literary language, and Meister Eckart (*c.* 1260-1327), who for the first time attempted to philosophical ideas in German, were outstanding figures. Such mystics gave a personal touch to the teachings of Christianity. There were also mystics like Johann Tauler (1300-1361) who formed a society known as "The Friends of God." This led to the formation of other societies and communities with their own rules of life. Thomas von Kempen (1380-1471) wrote a book, *On the Imitation of Christ,* which has become a religious classic. Jan van Ruysbroeck (1294-1381), who was closely associated with Tauler, is regarded as the father of mysticism in the Netherlands.

The third form of mysticism has more the character of a reform movement. It seemed to some deeply religious persons that the Roman Church had fallen prey to worldliness and the desire for pomp and power. It was not what a Christian church should be. St. Francis of Assisi (1182-1226), the founder of the Franciscan Order, was a mystic who was perfectly orthodox. His burning faith, his life of self-discipline, poverty and dedicated service was an open condemnation of the wealth and power of the Church. In England Wyclif (1328-1384), and in Bohemia Jan Hus (1369-1415) were reformers of a different type. They studied the Bible, got their inspiration, their idea of Christian life, from the source, and set it against both the teaching and the practice of the Church. Wyclif and Hus were the forerunners of the Reformation and the Protestant sects, with which we shall deal in the next chapter.

The study of Greek and Roman literature produced the movement of humanism, represented during this period by the poetry of Petrarch (1304-1374). In humanism we see a new conception of man, of man's destiny, of religion and of culture which had also a subtle mystical quality.

Mysticism appeared among the Muslims as an ascetic movement during the seventh century. The mystics were called 'Sufis', a term about the origin of which there is no general agreement. Their way of life came to be known as *Tariqah,* which means "Path." The first Sufis sought to bring every word, act and thought into harmony with the Divine Will. As Sufism spread, and the process of teaching and learning began, it became necessary to formulate ideas and experiment in methods of self-discipline for attaining the ultimate spiritual goal. Scholars have looked for the non-Islamic ideas that have found their way into Sufi beliefs, and have found the influences of Christianity, Neo-Platonism, Buddhism and, in India, the Vedanta. But the essential thing to realise is that while orthodox religions—Buddhism, Christianity, Islam, Hinduism—tend to reject one another, mysticism looks for support and confirmation, because it does not have any established authority behind it. Sufism in Islam and mysticism in all other religions developed complete systems of thought, but the essential feature of mysticism is personal spiritual experience. This cannot be borrowed; and even if we discover similarities in the expression given to the knowledge, derived from this experience, the experience itself, if it is genuine, still remains personal and original.

If the qualities or the teachings of mysticism have a universal character, the reason is that the mystic tendency is inborn in man, that truth is universal, and its realisation inevitable.

The earlier Sufis, and most of the later ones, insisted that the *Shari'ah,* the orthodox creed, should be scrupulously followed. Orthodoxy among Muslims was never organised in the form of a church, and open opposition to it might have undermined religion altogether. But we see in Muslim religious history a development that is not seen in any other religions an acceptance of the fact that both religion and mysticism are according to nature, an intellectual and spiritual reconciliation of orthodoxy with mysticism. This was due very largely to Imam Ghazali (1058-1111), who studied theology, dialectics, logic, science and philosophy, and finally came to the conclusion that direct realisation was the only means of attaining the highest truth. He did not reject other means of knowledge; he ranked them according to their potentialities and limitations. He thus achieved a synthesis which was not only logical and satisfying but also stimulated moral and spiritual effort. Islam became in a large measure a mystical faith.

The Sufis believed that the Sheikh, the master or teacher, was indispensable for spiritual guidance. This brought up the question of personality. Here also Imam Ghazali seems to have given the lead. The Prophet Mohammad, on whom had been bestowed the highest revelation, was the Perfect Man, but between him and the ordinary man there were other types of personality, to be classed according to their ability to realise truth through direct personal experience. Sheikh Muhiyuddin Ibn al-Arabi (1165-1240) elaborated the theory of personality to include among the Perfect Men all those who had fully realised their essential oneness with God, the prophets, the elect among the Sufis, and all who had received the divine light.

The importance of the Sufis increased with time. They set the standard of moral conduct, of the spiritual and social qualities that should distinguish the Muslim, of the manner in which the ideal of service should be realised. The symbolism they adopted gave literature an unique opportunity of fusing the spiritual and the beautiful, of identifying God with the Beloved, and the highest virtue with the greatest love. Sufism is perhaps the most valuable contribution of Muslims to human culture.

The relation between the master and the disciple, and the idealisation of the master as the source of spiritual knowledge led to the growth of what are known as "Orders," each of which had its particular discipline. The Qadri, the Chishti, the Suhrawardy, the Naqshbandi and the Moulvi Orders are the most well known.

Side by side with these orders, most of which were founded in the eleventh century, we find other movements for the reform of personal and social life. There was the movement for the practice of *Futuwah,* a term which has been translated as "Chivalry." *Futuwah,* as used by the Sufis, meant "placing others above oneself," and found expression in liberality, self-effacement, rising above disappointment, showing indulgence to the faults of others. Qushairi, in his *Risalah,* has given accounts which show that in several cities groups of people who had resolved to live according to the ideals of *Futuwah* were formed. Ibn Batuta also mentions small communities or brotherhoods which he came across in Asia Minor of people who practised the same profession, lived together in *Khanqahs* and supported each other in the cultivation of particular virtues. The guilds, in their ceremony of initiation, included an oath to follow the code of conduct, the *Futuwah,* prescribed by the guild.

Mysticism took another form in India which was a very significant development in belief as well as in culture. The devotional attitude, *bhakti,* appears for the first time, perhaps, in Mahayana Buddhism, and it is recognised in the *Bhagvadgita* as a means of union with the Divine. But if mysticism is considered as dedication to the higher life, we could go even as far back as the *Upanishads.* There are, however, certain features in the *bhakti* movement of the seventh, eighth and ninth centuries which distinguish it from earlier movements of a similar nature and link it up with the mysticism of later times. This new feature is intense, personal devotion to a particular deity, a love so passionate as to embrace every moment and every aspect of life. The songs of the Adyars, who were Siva worshippers, and of the Alvars, who worshipped Vishnu, have a deep and moving religious quality. Ramanujacharya, who lived in the twelfth century, gave a philosophical background to devotional religion in his theory of modified dualism. He challenged the monism of Shankaracharya, and advocated a view of life and the universe which was not so intellectual, and which provided ample opportunity for the vitalisation of religious life by bringing into play all the higher emotions. Ramanujacharya's followers further developed his philosophy, gradually taking up a position which was opposed to the formal ritualistic religion. This brought *bhakti* more in line with Sufism.

There is reason to believe that the *bhakti* movement in south India was part of a reaction against Buddhism and Jainism. The intellectual attack on Buddhism was led by Shankaracharya. He achieved remarkable success, but that would not have been possible, perhaps, without assimilating some elements of Buddhist thought and religious practice. The extent to which this assimilation can be traced in Shankaracharya's own teachings is, however, a matter of personal judgement. It has also been suggested that the *bhakti* movement was influenced by Christianity and Islam. This, again, is a matter of personal opinion. Students of comparative religion are rather hasty in drawing conclusions about "borrowing." Ideas can be borrowed, but they have to be assimilated into a system, and this system can neither be coherent nor deep-rooted if the ideas adopted are not organically related to it. The "borrowed" idea must be original enough for borrowing to be possible.

The existence of a Christian community in south India large enough to exercise any influence has been doubted. But the settlement of Muslim Arabs in the coastal cities and in some trading centres in the interior did create a new situation. Certain elements pre-existing in the religious thought of the Indian people surged into prominence, certain moral values, regard for which is inherent in human nature but which Brahmanism had kept suppressed, could now be asserted. When Turkish rule was established in the north and the Deccan, it was inevitable that the *bhakti* movement should be drawn towards the centre of gravity, and Ramanand (1400-1470), who himself belonged to Banaras, spread it in the north. Here the Sufis, had already established themselves, sometimes in advance of armies and rulers, and prepared the ground for a rich and creative spiritual life.

The Turks who invaded India desired to have the support of Muslim public opinion, and to prove that they were adding to the glory of Islam. But they were concerned with conquest and dominion, not with proving the moral quality of the Muslim religion and way of life. The Sufis were not concerned with political rule. They endeavoured to represent Islam and the Muslim way of life. They were not missionaries. Their duty was "the stringing together of hearts" alienated by political policies or injured by injustice and cruelty. They were the first to adopt ideas and practices that appeared to them of use in the spiritual striving, and the first to transform the belief that God was immanent in all His creation into a doctrine of the unity of mankind.

In the Far East, during this period, we see the emergence of Amida. Buddhism, and its propagation by Eshin (942-1017) in Japan. Later, another form of Buddhism, known as Cha'n, which taught an active, assertive way of life, was introduced in Japan and became very popular. In Tibet, Tsong-kha-pa reformed religious life by eradicating worldliness and moral laxity among the priests. He placed the Tibetan priest-state under the dual rule of the Dalai Lama who had political authority and the Tashi Lama, who was given religious authority.

One of the forms in which the mystical element in human nature found expression in China under the Sung and Ming dynasties was landscape painting. There were schools of painting supported by academies or the government, there were artists who kept themselves entirely free. Every style represented a way of life, a spiritual mood. Ni Tsan (1301-1374) was both painter and poet, and each one of his landscapes was accompanied by a poem which expressed in words the mood that inspired the landscape. Side by side with mysticism in art we see an effort to humanise ideologies and beliefs, and Chu Hsi (1130-1200) founded what is known as Neo-Confucianism, by combining the teachings of Confucius with Buddhism and Taoism.

At the same time as mysticism, a development was taking place in Europe which was to have tremendous results and to give an entirely new character to political organisation. This was belief in law, legal rights and, the moral obligation to act according to correct legal procedure. The first laws, recognised as man-made, were laid down in Greece and Rome. From the second century AD, as we have seen, the Romans began to devote special attention to the study of law, and Roman law was codified in 527. Its study was taken up by the Roman Catholic Church, whose own canon law closely followed the Roman model. The Germans, the English and the French had their own customary law, which was coordinated with the feudal organisation of society. It was this feudal organisation, with its system of relationships whose existence depended on a strict regard for rights and duties, which gradually made people not only follow but believe in the law. This belief was the basis for assertion of authority as well as resistance to it, and political thought and practice arose out of and depended upon this belief.

III

The problems of administration which confronted all the earlier empires have already been pointed out. There are no changes anywhere during this period which imply any great alteration in the system of government. But there are three different situations, one represented by the Muslim world, the second by China, and the third by Europe.

The pattern of government of the Abbasid Khilafat was not improved upon anywhere in the Muslim world. Everything continued to depend upon the ruler, and the ruler depended on his advisers, military commanders and supporters among the nobility and the learned men. Nobility was not hereditary, but all those in government service, whether civil or military, were given land in place of a cash salary, which reduced both the revenue and the control of the state. The collection of revenue was entrusted to district and provincial governors or to special officers, and revenue accounts were checked. The judicial system continued as before, under the Abbasid Khilafat, but the actual practice of the government as well as the application of the laws lagged very far behind not only the spirit but the letter of the law. The whole organisation of the government, the expenditure on king and court, the taxes, the methods of collection, the punishments, all were more or less contrary to Islamic law and government was reduced to an exercise of judicious policy and force. It is only among some of the sects that we find new political ideas, but they have a predominantly religious colour, and these sects also cultivated a fanaticism which made them into a destructive element and aroused bitter opposition. The *Siyasat Namah* of Nizam al-Mulk Tusi (c. 1000-1091) is a manual of guidance for statesmen which avoids all discussion of principles.

The administration of the Delhi Sultanate followed the general pattern of the Abbasid Khilafat and the other Muslim states. Its besetting difficulty was lack of resources, in particular of cash resources. The splendour of the court could not disguise the fact that large armies, or the officers necessary to enable the government to extend its functions, could not be paid, and the practice of assigning the income from land instead of giving a cash salary tended to reduce the total income of the state. What was worse, it put the cultivator at the mercy of the landlord, who was not concerned with improvement because he could be transferred at any time. The fault did not lie with particular kings or statesmen. The requirements of a large administration were greater than the economy could bear, and politically the large state was always in danger of going to pieces because the sentiments of loyalty and solidarity were not strong enough and communications were difficult to maintain. On the other hand, a reduction in the size of the state implied a reduction in its resources, and in the volume of trade, for trade is always hampered if goods have to cross many frontiers. Sultan Alauddin (1296-1316) cordoned off a large area, the agricultural and other produce of which could not be hoarded or exported, in order to lower prices. He succeeded in his immediate aim, but it is not known what effect this measure had on economic life, and for how long.

Another weakness of the political organisation was that it was the rule of a small minority, consisting of the sultan and a group of nobles loyal to him. There were sometimes rival groups waiting for the opportunity to seize power, and if there were not, the possibility of such groups being formed was always there. Conflicts were, therefore, very bitter, and opposition could only take the form of rebellion. If a rebellion did not succeed, it was suppressed with the utmost harshness in order to prevent further rebellions, and this made political life a desperate gamble.

The state was in principle subject to the *shari'ah,* according to the standards of which all political measures were judged. Because the Sultan dispensed honours and privileges and appointed the Sadr ul-Sudur, or Chief Qazi and judge, and approved the appointments of Qazis, he had a hold over just those people who had the prestige and the knowledge of the law which would enable them to pass judgement on his actions. But we have instances of Chief Qazis and learned men speaking out their mind when asked to do so. Far more influential, however, than those learned in the law were the Sufis. They did not accept honours and appointments, and almost all Sufis of the Chishti order carefully avoided relationship of any kind with the sultan and his court, and involvement in political issues. They would live in the *dargah,* where thousands of people of all sorts and conditions came to pay their respect to them and ask for their blessings and guidance. It was the Sufi in the *dargah* who was the real symbol of peace and security, virtue and justice and of the sympathy and goodwill which is essential for social and cultural cooperation.

What is known as Indo-Muslim culture had its origin in the *dargah* of the Sufi. The first person to use Hindi as a literary medium was a Sufi, Sheikh Abdur Rahman. Sheikh Farid Ganj Shakar (1173-1265) is known to have spoken Hindi and Amir who is reported to be the first to attempt an assimilation of Persian and Hindi, was a disciple of Sheikh Nizamuddin Auliya. Sheikh Nizamuddin himself was the noblest example of piety, learning, culture and tolerance, and the influence he exercised over the citizens of Delhi was the envy of the tyrant and the greatest consolation of the common man. Sheikh Nizamuddin assigned different cities and regions of India to selected disciples who went and settled there and carried on the work of "stringing together of hearts". These Sufis and their successors took the lead in using the spoken language as the medium of writing and cultured conversation, and gave a shape to the ideal of spiritual unity and a common culture.

The governments of China had to face many baffling political and economic problems. There was, first, the question how far the state would be centralised. The answer to this question depended largely on the division of power between the civil officers, who desired centralisation, and the army, whose commanders desired the utmost power in the area under their command. Then there were the problems of the relationships between landlord and peasant, and between large and small merchants, where the peasant and small farmer as well as the retail trader had to be protected. The interest of the state lay in supporting the farmer and the retail trader, because the landlords and big merchants, while exploiting the poor and creating unrest, did their best to cheat the state out of the taxes due to it. Under the Sung dynasty, the expenditure on government and army continuously increased, while the revenues fell, metal was coined and paper money printed to meet the demand, and there was considerable inflation. To remove the distress created, schemes of reforms were put forward. Ssuma

Kuang (1009-1086), agrarian reformer and historian., proposed that crown lands should be rented out and that the landlords should be deprived of all property rights over their estates. Wang An-Shih (1021-1086), a statesman and poet, was entrusted by the Emperor Shen Tsung (1068-1085) with the reform of the administration when it became clear that the policy being followed by the government was injurious. Wang An-Shih cut down expenditure, raised the salaries of the smaller officials, provided for loans to farmers in order to save them from moneylenders, and opened state banking and barter offices. In spite of all opposition, these reforms remained in force for over fifteen years, during the lifetime of the emperor, and much that was good in them survived for another thirty-five years.

The rule of the Mongol dynasty was marked by the oppression of the peasantry, but at the same time the roads and the postal administration was considerably improved and foreign trade was encouraged. The Ming dynasty reorganised the administration and raised the political power of China, but it made no contribution to the theory of political organisation or any experiments worthy of note.

The third situation is seen in Europe. We have already referred to the conflicts between emperors and popes. One aspect of these was intellectual, the question as to who, in the Christian world-state, possessed the highest authority. Another aspect was political, and it concerned the appointment of the officers of the Church. The archbishops, bishops and abbots owned large landed properties, lived like princes and lords, and exercised the same powers. If they were appointed by the emperor, they would be subject to him; if they were appointed by the pope, the emperor would lose both authority and revenue. The popes were, in fact, more powerful than the emperors, because the whole Church recognised their absolute authority, and the question of investiture remained for centuries a matter of dispute.

The most important problem in organisation was created by feudalism. This system was established to prevent complete anarchy, but, as has already been pointed out, it led to a division of authority and power between kings, princes and nobles which interfered with political and economic development. In theory, the king (or emperor) was himself elected, and he had to abide by the conditions under which the great princes and lords held their lands from him. He was bound to consult them, and he could not go to war or get money or support of any kind from them unless they agreed. In practice because the king or emperor was himself the biggest owner of land and responsible for government, he had power enough to compel his vassals to obey him. But if some vassal, by inheritance or marriage, acquired a position where he could challenge the king's or the emperor's authority, he would do so. Attached to the big landlord were smaller landlords who held lands from him and were obliged in return to serve him in different ways. The lowest in this system of obligations were the serfs or peasants, who were mostly regarded as the property of the landlord whose lands they cultivated and around whose house they lived.

The unit of the feudal organisation was the manor, or the landlord's house. As the manor aimed at being a self-sufficient unit, needs of different kinds had to be provided for, and there was often a nucleus of trades within it. The feudal system may have been basically unjust and a hindrance to political growth, but if we bear in mind later economic developments, it will appear to have been an advantage that industry was decentralised and spread over the whole country. When opportunities for expansion came, industry and trade did not remain confined to the cities and prosperity was shared by the countryside as well.

The growth of trade with Byzantium and the Muslim world and the contact with the civilised life of the Near East because of the Crusades created a growing demand for luxuries. For this cash was needed, which the self-sufficient economy of the manor could not provide. One of the reasons for the decay of feudalism was the desire of the landlords to commute the services due to them from the peasants into payments of money. The peasants, under the feudal system, were obliged to work for their lord, and could attend to their own farms only when they had finished the work to be done on his land. For them the change also meant benefits, because they could devote themselves entirely to their own farms, and sell their surplus produce. There were bitter conflicts when, in the fourteenth century, the "Black Death" killed off one-third to a half of the population, and the landlords in some cases desired to revert to the original system of service. Other factors also worked against the interest of the peasant. In some cases, the landlords took possession of all the land in order to farm it out for fixed payments.

In other cases, they converted agricultural land into pasture for breeding sheep, which was much more profitable than agriculture.

Feudalism as a system did not possess uniformity, and for this reason political development followed a different line in the different countries and regions of Europe. There was everywhere an attempt by the king or the emperor to assert his authority. The dynasty of Hugh Capet, whose possessions lay in the Isle de France, around Paris, had to struggle against rival powers, and it was only in the fifteenth century that the whole of France was brought under its rule. In the course of this expansion, the French kings set up a machinery for the administration of justice and created a body of civil servants for the management of the royal domains. To build up their resources they sought the help of the towns, which in their turn were enabled to grow because of the royal protection. An assembly, known as the Estates-General, which represented the nobles, the clergy and the townsmen, met now and then and began to exercise influence on the government. But further progress was held up by the Hundred Years' War with England.

In England, William the Conqueror undermined the feudal system of relationships by asking all who held land to take an oath of allegiance to himself. He also called together meetings of the Great Council (*Magnum Concilium*), which included the great nobles, the archbishops and the bishops. When he wanted to levy new taxes, he would summon representatives of the gentry, the independent landowners. In 1215, King John was forced to sign a charter, which was supposed for some time, sincerely if incorrectly, to be the foundation of civil liberty in England. In the beginning the *Magnum Concilium*, which later came to be known as Parliament, met in three groups or estates, one of the nobility, one of the clergy and one of the commoners. In 1265, a Parliament was summoned to which two representatives from each of the towns were also invited. In course of time it became a rule to present petitions to the king, which had to be granted before Parliament agreed to the levy of new taxes. It was thus that a session of Parliament led to the making of new laws. By the middle of the fifteenth century, the procedure of levying taxes and making laws through Parliament had become habitual. From the time of Henry I (1100-1135) the king had begun to take over as much as was possible of the administration of justice. Henry II (1154-1169) attempted to gain full control of administration and revenue by reforming the judicial system. After him additions and changes were made, sometimes with the king, sometimes the Parliament, taking the initiative; and opposition between the interests of the king, the clergy, the nobles and the commoners tended to strengthen the practice of acting according to the law and custom of the land.

In the development of city life, as we know it now, Muslim civilisation marks an important stage. In Muslim Spain, great care, labour and resources were devoted to beautifying cities. Cordova, Seville and, later, Granada were outstanding examples of large, beautiful cities provided with civic amenities like running water, fountains and parks. In the Near and Middle East there were cities like Damascus, Baghdad, Samarkand and Bokhara that matched them in grandeur. The wealth of these cities was derived from both industry and trade, and they continued to flourish till the Muslims lost control of the Mediterranean in the eleventh century.

Trade with Byzantium and the Muslim world led to the growth of cities first in Italy and then along the trade routes of central and western, Europe. In the tenth and eleventh centuries, China and the Muslim World were the centres of industry, while south India and south-east Asia provided some natural products not available elsewhere. The goods brought into Europe by the merchants of Venice and Genoa consisted of cotton fabrics, silks, precious metals, precious stones, pearls, frankincense and myrrh, ivory, cloves, pepper, ginger and aromatic spices. Cane sugar was brought for the first time from Alexandria to Venice in 996. The Crusaders brought back with them a desire for luxuries, and in the twelfth and thirteenth centuries the growth of cities was very rapid. Venice, as we have seen, was founded in the sixth century. Genoa and Pisa came next, and were followed by Florence and Milan. From the eleventh century, cities in Germany began to acquire autonomy, with their own judicial system and market rights. Emperors and kings found it to their interest to help and protect the cities and promote their trade, just as the cities, which in most cases came into existence after a struggle with their feudal lords and were afraid of their interference, found it necessary to band together and ally themselves with the kings. Generally, cities obtained charters defining their rights and privileges; the Free Imperial Cities of Central Europe had the rights of self-defence, coinage and tolls. Some of the cities, like Magdeburg in Germany, drew up constitutions which served as models for others, and are of great historical importance. The cities in Italy, because of the absence of a central authority, grew into states.

At first all trade in Europe was confinea to fairs, mainly local. By the end of the twelfth century, along with national and international fairs, there were flourishing cities with permanent markets. From centres of commerce they gradually became centres of industry and began to influence political policies through their wealth. They attained the height of 'their prosperity towards the end of this period. The League of Lombard Cities in north Italy, formed in 1159, defeated the Emperor Frederick I in 1176. Lubeck and Hamburg combined, in 1244, to organise protection of the Baltic trade routes. About the beginning of the thirteenth century, the commercial cities of Italy established a system of consulates in the Mediterranean area; towards the middle of the century over 50 cities of the Rhineland formed a confederation for the maintenance of peace and prevention of hindrances to commercial development. The end of the century saw Cologne and the other Free Imperial Cities on the North Sea Coast, which controlled European trade with the Baltic and had offices in many foreign countries, organising themselves as the Hansa League. They were powerful enough to fight and win a war against Denmark in 1370. The Imperial Cities of south Germany were not so fortunate. They combined to fight against the neighbouring princes (1377-1389), but were defeated.

The growth of the towns and formation of merchant guilds went together. These guilds were associations of merchants and sometimes included master craftsmen. They controlled all the buying and selling within the town, kept an eye on all transactions to prevent price-cutting, hoarding and other malpractices, and helped members if they were ill or suffered serious losses. The guilds had also the character of fraternities. They protected their interests in law-courts, and looked after the widows and orphans of the members. The guild was thus the guardian of the town, of which its more important members were often the chief officers.

Side by side with the merchant guilds there grew up the trade or craft guilds. For a time it was difficult to distinguish between them. Gradually their functions were divided, and the trade guilds made themselves responsible for the interests of the workers, and for the maintenance of recognised standards of work in a particular trade. The trade guilds consisted of masters, journey-men and apprentices. The masters were those whose knowledge and skill had been formally tested and recognised, who had produced the "master-piece" and were considered competent to set up their own workshop and employ journey-men and apprentices. The journey-men were skilled workers who had not the means to set up their own workshops and worked for wages, while apprentices were boys who wished to learn the trade, and lived with the master, more or less as servants.

Before the end of this period, we find a conflict of interests between the merchant guilds and the trade guilds and within the trade guilds themselves. The causes and results of this conflict are too complicated to be described here in detail. Merchants invested money in particular trades by giving raw material and loans to those who carried on the trade as a cottage industry and gradually sought to gain control over them. There were masters of trades who were very successful and used their position to dominate the trade. There was exploitation as well as unemployment. The journey-men formed unions to protect their interests, while those who wished to dominate them sought the help of rulers. Ultimately, the guilds either disappeared or survived with their functions considerably reduced. The cities themselves lost their unique position as feudalism declined, though economically they continued to prosper.

European trade could not develop or the cities expand commercial activities without a proper medium of exchange. Feudal economy was based on local self-sufficiency and trading was by barter. The situation was changed, as we have seen, by the slow infiltration of luxury goods from the Muslim world, by the Crusades, which enabled thousands of people belonging to the upper classes to see what really civilised life was like and by the commercial relations, established on an increasingly larger scale, by the cities. The earliest gold currency in feudal Europe was Byzantine or Muslim, but its quantity was limited, and only gradually increased by trade. The supply of silver was larger, but great confusion was caused by the right of every feudal lord to mint money. The assessment of the real value of money was the special function of money-changers, who were to be seen at all fairs and markets.

The opposition of the Church to lending money on interest proved a great hindrance in the beginning to the growth of commerce, and till about the end of the twelfth century the Jews were the only people who lent money. But the pressure of economic circumstances forced merchants to devise means of lending and borrowing money on interest for investment in small and large undertakings. One of the means adopted was to form unions for this purpose. At the same time, banking was developed, and just as some merchants combined to purchase and distribute goods on a large scale, others pooled their cash to provide funds for such ventures. In the thirteenth century, ledgers began to be kept and bills of exchange, drafts and acceptances to be issued. Currency also began to be standardised. In the eleventh century, the mark became the unified currency in the Rhine area; in 1240, the cities around the Bodensee made a currency agreement among themselves, and about the middle of this century the gold florins, gulden, and ducats of Florence and Venice became current in Europe. But lack of sufficient gold and silver coinage remained a handicap till the discovery of the American continent.

In the different fields of knowledge, most of the work done in the earlier half of the period was in the Muslim world. Primarily, it was work of organisation and transmission, but there was also original contribution, specially in the matter of approach to knowledge, and in physics, optics, mathematics, medicine and, above all, historiography. Secondly, the dissemination of knowledge was far wider than it had been before. While there were centres of higher learning, such as Baghdad, Cairo and Cordova, where the most eminent scholars were engaged in studies as well as teaching, even the smallest town would have a school for basic instruction in religion.

One of the basic concepts of the Muslims was the unity of all knowledge. While individuals might specialise, science was a unity cemented by philosophy. This was an essentially religious attitude, but "on reading Islamic scientific works one is struck by a rationality of treatment that we associate with modern science… . Though the two great mystifications of early science, astrology and alchemy, were also pursued by the Arabs, the greatest figures of Islamic science, such as al-Kindi, Rhazes and Avicenna explicitly repudiated the extravagant claims of these pseudo-sciences." Islamic science had also a secular and commercial background, which "marked it off sharply from that of medieval Christendom, which was almost exclusively clerical"[1] and also from that of the Greeks.

The work in different fields of science and philosophy begun in the reign of al-Mamun was carried on in the many centres of learning. Farabi (870-950) wrote a celebrated commentary on Aristotle, and also commentaries on Greek works on ethics, psychology and science. He was also a mystic with Neo-Platonist leanings, a mathematician and a physician of repute. But perhaps what would distinguish him most from our point of view was his accomplishment as a musician and his treatise on the theory of oriental music. Ibn Sina (Avicenna, 980-1037) was renowned in medieval Europe for his commentary on Aristotle, but he was also a noted mathematician and astronomer, and has been revered for centuries in the Muslim world as the author of the *Qanoon,* and the supreme authority in medical science. Al Beruni (973-1048), philosopher, mathematician and astronomer was a scholar who translated numerous works from the Sanskrit and has left an invaluable account of India as he saw it in the early eleventh century. "He also did some accurate and delicate work on specific gravities which was not equalled before the time of Galileo in Europe."[2]

Another scholar distinguished for his versatile genius was Omar Khayyam (1007-1123). Among philosophers, the specialists are represented by Ibn Rushd (Averroes, 1126-1198), whose commentary on Aristotle was translated into Latin, and exercised such a deep influence, specially in the University of Paris, that his teachings came to be known as Averroism. Ibn Yunus (950-1009) established trigonometry as a separate science. The physicist, Ibn al-Hasan (Al-Hazen, 965-1039), did much original work on optics, including the reflection and refraction of rays, and we owe to him the theory that the eye is able to perceive because light rays enter the eye. Al Shirazi (thirteenth century) explained the formation of the rainbow. In chemistry, the Muslims discovered how to isolate many important chemicals, including sal ammoniac, saltpetre and a number of oxides, and learned how to prepare sulphuric and nitric acids. There can be no doubt that Muslim alchemy laid the basis for modem chemistry by performing this pioneering work.[3]

"Arabic astronomy was more practical than the Greek. A great many stars were named and catalogued. They (the Arabs) were better instrument makers than the Greeks and more accurate observers, but they made no advance in principles over Ptolemy... . Arabic physics was a considerable advance on that of the Greeks. The excellence of their craftsmanship and their mathematical aptitude stood them in good stead... . Arab medicine and biology show acute observation and report many phenomena that the Greeks did not observe. Medicine, however, was hampered by their religious objection to dissection, without which no great progress could be made. The Arab surgeons were skilled operators and invented a number of instruments."[4]

The Muslim geographers, al-Masudi (tenth century), al-Muqaddasi (tenth century), al-Idrisi (1100-1166) and Abul Feda (1273-1313) travelled more widely than the Greeks, and have left records which are valuable sources of information on a large part of the civilised world. Historiography was a science to which Muslims devoted special attention and Ibn Khaldun (1332-1406). was the first to evolve a philosophy of history based on an interpretation of events. He sought to discover the reasons for the rise, progress and decline of civilisations, and arrived at conclusions some of which anticipate philosophies and sociological theories of later times.

Among books written to please and instruct, the *Gulistan* of Saadi (1184-1258) has perhaps no parallel in the literature of the world. Nor does any other book present a more vivid and correct picture of what may be called the educated and liberal, but also worldly-wise, Muslim's philosophy of life. The *Masnavi* of Maulana Jalaluddin Rumi (1207-1273) is a treasure-house of religious thought and spiritual experience. Here, again, one would have difficulty in naming another book in world literature so catholic in its outlook, so intense in feeling and beautiful in expression, so distinctive as the product of a culture, and so universal in its spirit.

There were many centres of cultural contact between Muslims and Christians, and the contacts took many forms, but it is only now that the thick veil thrown over them by prejudice is being slowly lifted. The Roman Church, as we have seen, was the first to take up education, but this must have been very limited in scope. Expansion could take place only through the introduction of new material for study and the stimulus of new ideas. But the Church was anxious to safeguard its doctrines and to prevent the growth of opposition, and it was largely to strengthen its own position that it marshalled the Christians to fight against the Muslims for the Holy Land. But friendly contacts, specially for the purposes of commerce, could not be prevented, and in the eleventh and twelfth centuries large numbers of Arabic books were translated into Latin and could be used for study. It was in these centuries that universities began to be established and it would not be an exaggeration to say that the Muslims provided the foundation for higher learning in Europe. Translation of Arabic commentaries on Aristotle and Muslim scholasticism activated metaphysical and theological speculation. Constantius Africanus (died 1087) brought over all the Arabic works on medicine to Salerno and translated them. He founded a school of medicine here which attained great fame in the twelfth century. The numerals used by the Arabs were introduced to the western world by Leonardo of Pisa in the thirteenth century.

The medieval universities of Europe grew out of the cathedral schools established by the Church. The idea of an institution of learning where all subjects could be studied together was not a new one. But the new universities were more general and more systematic in their teaching. The universities of Paris and Bologna date from about the middle of the twelfth century, Oxford from 1167, Cambridge from 1209. Then came Padua (1222), Naples (1224), Salamanca (1227), Prague (1347), Cracow (1364), Vienna (1367) and St. Andrews (1410).

In China this period is distinguished mainly by the formation of academies of art and the excellence of landscape painting. But an encyclopaedia was prepared during the years 927-983, the study of history was pursued and Ssuma Kuang (1009-1086) wrote his "Mirror of World History" in many volumes. This is considered the highest achievement of Chinese historiography. Books on mathematics were printed in 1083, and Chin-Kiu-Sliao wrote over the nine parts of mathematics in 1247. An observatory was built in Peking in 1279. Realistic and social romances were written and the dramatic art was cultivated in the thirteenth and fourteenth centuries.

IV

In the history of skill, this period is one of transmission in a literal sense of the technical knowledge of the Chinese through the Muslims to the European peoples. We have already mentioned the discovery in China of magnetic action on the needle (and the possible invention of the compass), the introduction of silk and porcelain and the manufacture of paper. Gunpowder was made and used as an explosive in China in the twelfth century. The Muslims, who in the earlier period as well as this performed the function of acquiring, improving upon and transmitting the knowledge and techniques of earlier and contemporary civilisations, learnt the methods of paper manufacture, silk-weaving and other skills from the Chinese. Their own specific contribution consisted of improved chemical processes in the manufacture of steel, distillation, industrial production of sugar from sugar cane and of soda, alum, copperas, nitre and other salts for use in the textile industry, the invention, probably, of the compass and of the astrolabe, and the construction of windmills. These contributions, it must be remembered, were additional to what was already known and practised, and formed the basis of industrial activity and progress so long as it lasted, in the Muslim world.

The Muslims formed the main agency for the transmission of skills to Europe, though Byzantium also played an important part. The marriage of a Byzantine princess with the heir of an Emperor in 972 led to the introduction in Germany of the skills of goldsmithy, ivory carving, gold-filigree, and enamelling. Because of the Crusades, Europeans learnt the cultivation of varieties of wheat, maize, rice, lemon and apricot, and the techniques of the manufacture of cloths, clothing, leather and leather goods, silks, glass and sugar out of sugar cane. The first windmills were set up towards the end of the fourteenth century.

These techniques formed the starting-point of industry in Europe. They were soon improved upon and new inventions added. The horse-collar led to the replacement in the eleventh century of the ox by the horse for ploughing and transport of agricultural and industrial produce. Ease and speed of distribution enabled the exclusive cultivation of crops in climates and soils suited to them, and thus indirectly increased productivity. For instance, whole districts round Bordeaux in France were given up to wine-growing, and wine became the first bulk cargo. European industry was first concentrated in the monasteries. From the beginning of the eleventh century, trades and industries began to be built up in the cities. The reconquest of Spain from the Muslims, the havoc wrought in Byzantium by the fourth Crusade and the onslaught of the Mongols on the Muslim world considerably reduced competition, and after the middle of the thirteenth century Europe could export manufactured goods. But we must not forget the capacity of the internal market to absorb manufactured goods, which was due in part to the manorial system.

The use of power is essential for the development of industry. Water power was being used from very early times, and during this period in Europe it was developed much further. The use of mineral coal as fuel began about the middle of the thirteenth century in foundries in the Netherlands and north Germany, and blast furnaces began to be made in these countries and in England and Sweden in the fifteenth century.

The progress of industry also depends very much on devices that save labour and increase production. The cloth industry in Europe was among the first to benefit from the application of the mind to labour-saving devices. By the late thirteenth and earlier fourteenth centuries, a spinning-wheel with foot-drive was in use, and in England a fulling mill had been invented which trebled cloth production. An invention that does not appear impressive in itself made all the difference to the housewife and the tailor was the making of needles with eyelets instead of hooks.

The masterpieces of this age, which bear witness to the understanding and regulation of requisite mechanical movement are the "astro-nomical" clock sent as a gift in 1232 by the Sultan of Egypt to the Emperor Frederick II, the clock of the Nuremberg cathedral where, as the hour strikes, the Seven Electors appear and bow before the Emperor, and the clock of Charles V's palace in Paris, run by weights.

The most revolutionary and the most ominous invention of the period was gunpowder. It was used first in China as an explosive by being pressed into hollow tubes, first of bamboo and later of metal. It began to be used in Europe by the middle of the thirteenth century for fireworks. Early in the next century, the arquebus, the oldest form of the gun, was manufactured, and cannon with bronze and iron barrels which could throw balls weighing up to 750 lbs. began to be cast. Medieval armour and weapons could not be made unless the necessary resources in metal were available. War became costly, and only those could fight who were able to bear the cost. Industry and trade destroyed the economy and gunpowder the fighting strength of feudalism in Europe. The introduction of the compass, along with the stern-post rudder, gave that stimulus to navigation which led to the discovery of new lands, while the invention of printing by Gutenberg (c. 1397-1468) in 1445 provided the foundation for a far quicker dissemination of knowledge than had ever been possible before.

NOTES

1. Bernard, *op. cit.*, p. 196ff.
2. F.S. Taylor, *Science Past and Present*, p. 57 (William Heonemann, London).
3. S.C. Easton, *The Heritage of the Past*, p. 491 (Rinehart & Co., New York).
4. Taylor, *op. cit.*, pp. 56-58.

32

The Religious World-State (AD 200-900)

The period which we have called the age of spiritual revolution began in a large part of the civilised world after the settlement of the so-called Aryan tribes in Greece, Iran and northern India. In different ways and in different degrees these newcomers took over the ideas, the systems of organisation and the skills of civilisation and gave them a new form. The period of the spiritual revolution ends in the west with the destruction of the Roman Empire by barbarians, in the upsurge of new elements of the old peoples in Iran and India, and in the assimilation of new racial elements in north and south China.

In the west the barbarians had acquired the rudiments of the civilised life in their struggles against the Roman Empire. In west Asia the Arabs, who now appear as the bearers of the message of Islam, had had contacts with the civilised peoples of Egypt, Syria and Mesopotamia for a very long time. In India, civilisation had been spreading along the trade routes and the Guptas represent most probably a new stock of vigorous people able to carry civilisation forward.[1]

We now come to the age of the religious world-state. Like the spiritual revolution, the idea of the religious world-state as seen in the Muslim Khilafat and the Holy Roman Empire in Europe is the distinctive feature of this period and is the result of significant developments in belief and organisation. It has had far-reaching results and created problems which have not been solved till today. It let to bitter conflicts between religious groups and communities and between these and the state. It has also led to such ideas as one world of many peoples sharing certain fundamental beliefs.

From *World History*.

We shall first briefly review the main events of this period. In China, the Han dynasty was overthrown by peasant insurrections in AD 220, and there was anarchy in the country till AD 280, when the country was again unified for about 150 years by the Chin dynasty. But a really stable government was established only in AD 618, by the T'ang dynasty (AD 618-906), whose achievement in political and economic expansion, in art and culture is comparable to that of the Han. The reign of the Emperor T'ai Tsung (AD 627-649) marks the height of its power and glory.

In India, decaying Kushan power was wiped out by the Guptas, whose dynasty was founded in 320 by Chandra Gupta I. He was succeeded by Samudra Gupta (*c*. 320-380), a warrior, statesman and a man of culture, who united a large part of India under his rule. His successor, Chandra Gupta Vikramaditya (*c*. 380-413), conquered Gujarat and West India, so that all the important trade routes came under the control of the Gupta government. After the middle of the fifth century the Huns began their invasions and shattered the Gupta Empire, bringing ruin and devastation upon all the centres of civilisation. Under Harsha (606-646) there was a splendid recovery. After him, centralised administration in the north broke down, and the Deccan and South India, under the Chalukyas and the Pallavas, became the centres of cultural and political activity. But the kingdoms of this area wasted their strength in purposeless warfare.

In Persia, the Sassanians succeeded the Parthians in 224, and their empire lasted till 641. Their state expanded towards Mesopotamia, Arabia and Asia Minor, and attained such power and prestige as to become a byword for splendour. Khusrau Anushirvan (531-579) was recognised for centuries in the Muslim world as the model of the wise and just ruler.

The Sassanians were in perpetual conflict with the Byzantine Empire, the eastern part of the Roman Empire which survived the western by about 1,000 years. The Roman emperor, Constantine the Great, made Byzantium the capital of the empire in place of Rome in 330. The change was made because of the pressure of barbarian invasions. These invasions continued, and in 476 the western Roman Empire came to an end. The Byzantine Empire had to struggle for survival from 565 to 716. Then it developed its economic resources and its political and military systems and enjoyed wealth and prosperity for over three centuries. After this there was again a decline.

The successors to the western Roman Empire in Europe were small and large racial groups who fought continuously to establish themselves. Towards the end of the eighth century, the kings of the Franks succeeded in obtaining dominion over the whole of western Europe except the British Isles and Spain, and Charlemagne (Charles the Great) was crowned Roman emperor at Rome in 800.

The latest religious as well as political development of this period is the propagation of Islam and the rapid expansion of the Muslims. The Prophet Mohammad (570-632) left Mecca in 622 because of continuous persecution and established himself at Medina. Within 10 years Mecca had been reduced and a very large part of Arabia converted. Under the Caliph Omar (634-644), Palestine, Syria, Iran and Egypt were conquered, and the expansion continued under the Omayyads (660-750), till the Muslim state extended from the valley of the Indus to the shores of the Atlantic. Spain was conquered and the Muslims advanced into France. With the conquest of Crete (826), Sicily (827), Corsica (850) and Malta (870) their hold over the western Mediterranean was complete. The Omayyads were overthrown by the Abbasids in 750, and with them began an era of prosperity and intellectual achievement. But by the close of this period political disintegration had also begun.

I

With the spiritual revolution we see the emergence of a more advanced type of religious community. It can be divided into three units, (1) the body of doctrine and belief, (2) the members of the community who study and teach the doctrine and the particular way of life enjoined by the doctrine, and (3) the social and organisational form given to the community through religious law. The Buddhist, the Christian and the Muslim communities are representative in this respect and each of them has a history which has been deeply influenced by the development and by the interaction of the three units into which it was divided.

The Buddha did not recognise caste, or the ritual and rites which formed such an important part of religion in his time. But he did not teach how society should be organised and what observances should be introduced. This means that he did not attempt to create a new social order, a new religious society with its own laws, customs, ceremonies. On the other hand, compromises in matters of doctrine were made through allowing converts to continue believing things they believed in before, and no change was made in their way of life. This led to a wide propagation of Buddhism, but it also brought in an element of weakness.

But if Buddhism did not aim directly at creating a new social order, the belief that not only all mankind but all creation was one, that all men were equal and distinction could be achieved only through good works, gave a tremendous stimulus to cultural and commercial activity. The idea of the unity of mankind removed all those barriers which make men strangers to one another. It created the desire to see the wide world and to be of service, wherever and to whomsoever possible. The inculcation of generosity led to the donation of lands and properties and the dedication of works of art to the community. In China, where Buddhist missionaries went both overland and by sea during the first century BC, the religion found no approval among the educated and wealthy classes. When the missionaries turned to the middle and lower classes, their teachings gained widespread acceptance. The Buddhist doctrine of the after-life, according to which all oppressors and exploiters would suffer for their misdeeds in the next birth, and those who suffered in this life would be rewarded in the next, made a strong appeal to the harassed peasantry and the other classes which suffered from the wrongdoings of the powerful. The Buddhist missionaries did not interfere with the worship of the indigenous deities, and did not look with disfavour on the ordinary economic activities. They did not ask for too much dedication to moral ideals, because Nirvana did not need to be attained at once. It could be the result of lives of virtue in successive rebirths. The merchants made use of Buddhist monasteries as banks and warehouses, as places where moneys could be exchanged. They were, therefore, well-inclined towards Buddhism and gave money and lands for temples. The temples were able to settle peasants on these lands. It was because of this type of popularity that Buddhism became the state religion of China in the fourth century. We do not know what effect the spread of Buddhism had in south and south-east Asia but, judging from the architectural and artistic remains, the influence must have been considerable.

Like the doctrines of Buddhism, the doctrines of Christianity also took definite form only gradually. Christ does not seem to have prescribed any daily routine or any distinctive dress for his disciples. They had just to preach the word of God. This preaching revolved round two basic beliefs, the Christ through his sufferings had redeemed humanity and that the Kingdom of Heaven was at hand. If we could picture to ourselves the misery and the suffering of the lower classes and the slaves who had been crushed and exploited to the limit by the wealthier classes under the Roman Empire, we would easily understand what consolation and relief this teaching would have brought to them. Christianity was at first the religion of the poor and the downtrodden. As its influence rose to higher levels of society, it began to encounter criticism and opposition of different kinds. The Romans disliked it because of what seemed to them its unpolitical, and therefore unsocial spirit. The philosophically-minded failed to be moved by it because of its simplicity. The Neoplatonists disliked it because it was the religion of the masses. But Stoicism in a way prepared the ground for the acceptance of Christianity just among those people whose continued disapproval was likely to injure its cause. We do not know how far the stories about the horrible persecutions of the Christians are true, but there can be no doubt that they were persecuted. This strengthened their faith on the one hand and, on the other, put their oppressors in the wrong. Ultimately, because their numbers grew till it could be said that they were a unifying factor among the subjects of the emperor, Constantine the Great, in 327, recognised Christianity as one of the religions of the empire. Christianity was then able to exercise influence on the political and social organisation of society, and to undertake the task of preserving civilisation.

With the decline of the Empire the Christian faith seemed to be the only institution that was likely to survive, and the only force working to save both the moral quality and the material creations of civilisation. Two events serve as typical illustrations. In 390, St. Ambrosius forced the emperor Theodosius to perform public penance for having massacred 7,000 rebels, and in 452, Pope Leo I persuaded Attila and Hun to spare the city of Rome.

It would not be easy to understand how Christianity could appeal to the new peoples in Europe if we did not realise that, by the time the conversions began, Christianity was not a persecuted or neglected religion but had taken the form of a system which represented both the higher social order and a new morality. Princes and tribal chiefs who became converts must have felt that they were being included in what they knew to be the civilised world as well as earning a reward in Heaven. Frequently, when the prince or chief was converted, all his subjects adopted the new religion.

Jerusalem was the first centre of expansion of the Christian faith. When St. Paul started on his missionary journeys, Antioch was the capital of the Middle East, Alexandria the great port of eastern trade and Rome the capital of the western world. Those were the centres towards which missionary activity was drawn. In their organisation the Christians followed the model set by the Roman administration. The bishop, who was responsible for the religious guidance of his flock, had his seat in the district; the metropolitan, higher in rank than the bishop, lived in the provincial capital, and the patriarch at the state capital from which missionary activity was directed. But there was no official hierarchy. The Church as a whole was the Body of Christ and as large as the world of the Christians. The bishops were the most important people. They were religious as well as intellectual leaders and it was not felt necessary to have a supreme head.

Beliefs in regard to the relationship between the Christian community and the State changed with time. St. Paul recognised that the powers that be are ordained by God, and prayers for the emperors and those in authority were customary among the early Christian communities. What the Christians could not accept was the doctrine that religion was an affair of the state. "Men should indeed render money to Caesar, but should render their very selves to God. Otherwise what will be God's, if all things are Caesar's."[2] When Constantine recognised Christianity, he gave the Church the right to receive, hold and administer property like a corporation under the Roman law. The church was also exempted from taxes. When the emperor himself was a Christian and the church the possessor of property, the attitude of the Christians towards the State naturally changed. The Christian king now occupied the position of Augustus and enjoyed in Christian terms the same religious status as the Roman emperor. "The king, beloved of God, will already be a partaker in the heavenly kingdom; for he is crowned with the virtues which are inherent in God and he has received in his soul the emanations that come from God; he has become rational from the Universal Reason, wise by participation in Wisdom, good by fellowship with God."[3]

Christian thought now also came under the influence of the Stoics, who conceived of the universe as a unity pervaded by reason and believed in the world-state. The Roman Empire was the visible symbol of this world-state and was accepted as such by the Christians. In Byzantium, the opinion about the king which we have quoted above continued to represent the Christian view of the king and the state. In the west, however, something had to be done to fill the gap created by the fall of the Roman Empire. St. Augustine presented the ideal of a state that was not made by man but by God, and the bishops of Rome gradually gave material form to this ideal by acquiring wealth and power. Till 230, the language of the Roman Church was Greek, and at the end of the sixth century Pope Gregory the Great denied any claim to superiority over all bishops. But there were others who did make the claim, because they believed in it, and because not only in Rome, but also in the whole of Italy, there seemed to be no power that could be depended upon except the Church. In the seventh century, when the rise of Islam involved the Byzantine Empire in a struggle for survival, the Roman Church became independent. The coronation of Charlemagne as Roman emperor laid the foundation for the ideal of a State which was Universal, Christian and ruled by a Pope and an Emperor.

The Muslim idea of the religious world-state had a different character and came into existence in an entirely different way. To understand it we must first briefly consider the teachings of Islam.

Islam has a body of doctrines. These doctrines have a historical context and cannot be properly understood apart from it. The Prophet was a historical personality, and in the Quran there is continuous reference to human history. Not only this but the revelation begins with the acknowledgement of civilisation, of reading, of writing, of knowledge. From some practices it is clear that there is also reverence for the record in human history of all that has drawn man towards God. The ideal of sacrifice, represented in Jewish tradition by the offering of his son by the Prophet Abraham at the command of God, is preserved in Islam, in the annual sacrifice on the occasion of the Pilgrimage. Idolatry is condemned, and when the Prophet took possession of Mecca he destroyed all the idols in the temple. But the Black Stone, reputed to have been part of the temple of Abraham, who took it from a still older temple, was retained in the Kaaba and must be venerated. All religions have been recognised in principle as expressing the one eternal faith, continuously revealed by God for the guidance of man on the right path. All prophets, whether mentioned in the Quran or not, have to be equally honoured, because they conveyed the message of God. The first man, Adam, is stated to have been endowed with moral sense, and the rise and fall of societies is declared to be due to their regard or disregard for purity, justice and truth. This is a confirmation not only of Jewish and Christian tradition in particular, but also of Zoroaster's teachings about prophets being sent again and again by Ahura-Mazda, and of other similar traditions.

The one, eternal faith which has been continuously revealed and also continuously obscured by the ignorance or wickedness of man, has been called the "Deen". It means belief in God, in a Divine Will constantly expressing itself through nature and man and events occurring in time. Godhood in Islam is a moral and not a philosophic concept, and it has immediate social implications. It is the personal duty of each believer and of each society that professes faith in God to obey the Divine Will, and to strive for the prescribed moral ends. "Deen" also requires belief in revelation. It will be remembered that the Buddha's search for ultimate truth led to his enlightenment under the Bodhi tree. Zoroaster's experience was similar. In the Bible we are told that the Spirit of God descended upon Christ. In Islam revelation is not regarded as supernatural. It is an event that has often taken place in history, and is a means whereby God makes His Will known to the prophet, and through him to mankind. Whatever is revealed has to be believed, but it is asserted that revelation embodies the highest form of reason, and with the injunction to believe there is the equally definite injunction to think.

The doctrines of Islam are few and simple. The Muslim must believe in one God, and worship Him only. He must believe that Mohammad was the Prophet of God, to whom the Quran was revealed, but who was a human being like any other. The Muslim must pray and fast and at least once in his lifetime perform the pilgrimage to Mecca. Equal in importance with prayer and fasting is the obligation to pay the *zakat*, a tax which is calculated at 2½ per cent of savings and capital, whatever its form may be.

A Muslim must regard all men as equal before God. No privilege can be claimed or denied on ground of sex, family, social position, race, language or country. No such distinction is allowed as was made among the Buddhists between the monks and the laymen, or in Christianity between the Church and the laity. Asceticism is forbidden. Historically and socially the novel feature of the Muslim faith is the application of all obligations to all members of the community. This is itself an aspect of the doctrine that life cannot be divided into the spiritual and the worldly, that religion is according to nature and nature consists of both spiritual and material elements. The good life is possible only if this unity of the spiritual and the material is recognised, if man is grateful to God not only for his spiritual enlightenment but for all that He has bestowed to make life possible and agreeable.

Life in society is essential for the practice of Islam, and Muslims have been enjoined to keep their community as well-knit and strong as possible. They could not be only a people professing and practising a particular religion: it was a part of the religion that they should be organised also as a political community. At the same time, a system was evolved whereby any religious group could become a part of the Muslim body politic, retaining its autonomy and determining the extent of its obligations on the basis of an agreement. It was these features out of which was evolved the idea of the Muslim religious world-state.

The religious development in India during this period consists in the propagation of their tenets by the Buddhists, Jains and various sects, and by the consolidation of the beliefs now comprehended under Hinduism within the limits fixed by the six *darshanas*. Some deities emerge into prominence; Brahma, Vishnu, Shiva become a Trinity; worship of avatars is inculcated, and sects whose chief characteristic is a devotional attitude assume a missionary character. Among these the Bhagvatas deserve special mention. They worshipped Sri Krishna. Side by side with the fervour of theology and devotionalism and the speculations of philosophy, we have evidence of liberalism and even of cynicism in the literature of the Gupta period. though the good man is honoured, the Brahman is not esteemed merely by reason of his caste. Life is not looked upon only as a spiritual quest, and the good things provided by nature and human industry get their share of appreciation.

Towards the end of this period there was a movement in India for the eradication of Buddhism as a doctrine and a philosophy. The leader of this partly intellectual, partly religious movement, to which the devotional sects of the Adyars and Alvars also contribued, was Shankaracharya, the famous advocate of monism (*advaita*), whose view that the physical world as well as the world of sense experience is an illusion acquired great currency and influence.

II

The western Roman Empire declined rapidly towards the end of the fourth century, and after 476 it ceased to exist. But at Byzantium the ideas and the experience, the administration and above all the law of Rome were taken over and developed. The eastern Roman or Byzantine Empire was for centuries the richest state of Europe, the strongest in military power and by far the most cultivated. Roman law was codified under Justinian (527-565) and remained a model till far into the modern age, exercising a deep and pervading effect on political and social ideas. The administration was so organised as to increase as far as possible the resources of the state. The emperor was the head and the supreme authority, with the civil government and the army absolutely at his disposal. He appointed the Patriarch of the Church, summoned its councils and issues their decrees, and therefore controlled, if he did not rule the Church. The empire was divided into districts, with a head who was both military commander and civil governor. The army was well-paid, carefully organised and equipped. Justice was administered by professional judges. The civil administration was bureaucratic, and looked after agriculture, industry and trade.

A perpetual drain on the resources of the Byzantine Empire were the struggles with the barbarians to the north and with the Sassanians in west Asia. The Sassanians did not make any contribution to administrative practice or political ideas and merely maintained the traditions of pomp and splendour associated with the king and the court. Khusrau Anushirvan found Persia suffering from tyranny, injustice, corruption, fanaticism and crime. He is reputed to have eradicated these evils and also to have given the country internal peace and security. He fixed the amount of the land tax and allowed payment both in money and in kind. Fruit trees were also taxed, and a poll tax, payable in three instalments, was introduced. He is said to have improved irrigation and built dams, to have guarded the trade routes and looked to the upkeep of the roads and bridges.

Sources for the history of Iran are few. But it is incredible that for the same period of Indian history information should be so scarce. Centuries after a script had been evolved, the writing of history was not taken up. The people were proud of their traditions, but for some reason did not record them. The lives of personalities who attained such legendary eminence as Vikramaditya and Kalidasa are shrouded in obscurity. We cannot, therefore, say anything with confidence about the political ideas or the administration of the Gupta period. All that we have are designations of officers of the central and provincial government, but these designations do not help us to understand clearly what duties the officers performed, or the framework within which they functioned. We can only gather from the fact that there were no internal conflicts or resistance to or approval of measures of government policy that nothing new needed to be done. The pilgrim Fa-hein noted that "the people are numerous and happy; they have not to register their households, or attend to any magistrates and their rules, only those who cultivate the royal land have to pay (a portion of) the grain from it. The king governs without decapitation or (other) corporal punishments."[4] Fa-hien was a deeply religious man, inclined to see only the good side of things, but even if we take him at his word, the Gupta administration must have been easy-going, and government policy would as a rule have taken the line of least resistance. Most probably the prevalence of the caste system and the division of functions which it dictates saved the government from many problems which arose in other countries because of the clash of class interests.

In China, the Han Empire provided a durable basis for subsequent political and social developments by creating the Gentry, a class supposed to be independent and enlightened. The members of this were selected through a system of examinations. It was a kind of civil service into which anyone possessing the required ability could enter. The attitude of the Gentry changed into one of active or passive hostility during the period of anarchy following upon the collapse of the Han Empire, when their interests were disregarded, but they came into their own again under the T'ang dynasty.

The main problem of the T'ang administration was agrarian economy. An attempt was made to equalise all farms, but because the emperor's relatives and the temples were exempted, the growth of large estates could not be prevented. Local government was complicated by the privileges of the landowning class, and there was great diversity in the relationships between the landlords and tenants. The administration attempted to regulate civil and commercial life, and census, registration, tax and labour levies were introduced. In the central administration ministries of home, foreign, economic and financial affairs, justice, armaments and magazines were formed, along with a number of others dealing with the requirements of the palace and the administration of the capital, Ch'ang-an. In the local government, the functions of the civil and military were separated, but generals were placed as military officers in charge not of districts only, but of whole provinces, and were also given the financial administration of the army under their command. This was unfortunate, as it gave too much power to the generals, and the danger was increased when, towards the close of the T'ang period, a Privy Council, consisting mainly of generals, was formed. But the basis of the T'ang administration was stronger than that of the Han, because it was not over-centralised, and all activities were not concentrated in the capital. Loyang and other major towns and various parts of the country participated richly and fully.

T'ai Tsung extended his empire towards Turkestan in the west, and Nam Yueh (the Viet-Nam of our own day) in the south and defeated the Koreans. The kingdoms of south-east Asia were politically oriented towards China, and may have been influenced by Chinese policy, but nothing is known about their methods of administration.

We can now turn to the experiments in political and social organisation implied in the doctrines of Christianity and Islam.

As we have seen, Christianity began as a religion of the poor and its inspiring motive was sympathy and love. But it was also a religion which despised the material world and there were no injunctions as to how social life was to be organised. As Christianity spread, it came under two influences, Hellenistic philosophy and imperial Rome. Hellenistic philosophy led to differences in dogmas and ultimately to serious and sometimes bloody conflicts between sects. The example of imperial Rome induced the formation of the hierarchical organisation of the Church and created the desire to define and exercise authority. Questions of doctrine had to be referred to Councils called together by the Emperor, and the decisions of these Councils could be enforced only through the authority of the Emperor. Constantine gave the Church the right to hold property, and bishops had thenceforward not only to look after the spiritual needs of their flock, but also to manage the landed property of the Church. The bishops of Rome became in course of time the rulers of a large estate, and had to consider their political interest. It was impossible for them not to be influenced by political ideas. On the other hand, after the downfall of the Roman Empire, they had to provide for the security of the city of Rome as well as their own possessions. Assertions of the authority of the Bishop of Rome as Pope over all bishops began to be made, and it was probably as a part of this policy that Charlemagne was offered the crown of the Roman Empire. Because of the decline of Charlemagne's empire under his successors and the demoralisation of the papacy itself, it was only when Otto I (936-973) became emperor that the religious world-state became a question of practical policy. We shall deal with this in the next chapter.

The Muslim community was first organised as a theocracy. This meant in practice that the Prophet guided the community and was himself guided by what was revealed to him. The directive principle was obedience to the command of God. During the lifetime of the Prophet there were no officers and no administrative system, but (a) decisions were taken by consultation and the right of each member of the community to have his opinion heard was recognised; (b) *zakat* was levied for the support of the needy; and (c) agreements were made with Jewish and Christian communities defining rights and obligations in case they became members of the Muslim body politic. The foundations were thus laid for a democratic welfare state entirely religious in spirit but willing and able to include in its fold communities professing other religions on terms that guaranteed their autonomy and the right to profess and practise their religion. Protection from enemies was ensured in return for a tax known as the *jaziya*.

After the Prophet, the head of the Muslim community had three different capacities. He was an elected successor (*Khalifah*), the leader at the public prayers (*Imam*) and the political ruler (*Amir al Mominin*). The government was still nominally a theocracy. The Quran was the final authority; where the Quran was not explicit, the policy and the decisions of the Prophet served as precedents. But the exercise of discretion was also lawful, provided it had the support of the general body of Muslims.

The organisation of the Muslim community under the first four *Khalifahs* continued to have the character of the welfare state. A system of administration was built up, governors and judges were appointed, agricultural classes in the countries that came under Muslim rule were secured against expropriation or enforced sale of land, and a system of affiliation of non-Arabs with Arab tribes was devised. *Zakat* was collected and used to help the needy. The spirit which inspired the administration was in some ways idealistic. The Khalifah Omar is known to have appeared as an ordinary suitor before a judge, and to have objected to the judge showing him respect on account of his being the Khalifah. He is also known to have carried sacks of flour on his own back to the homes of the needy. He was uncompromising in his insistence that no encroachment should be made on the rights of the non-Muslim members of the Muslim body politic, and he officially interpreted a verse of the Quran so as to make it an unconditional obligation that needy non-Muslims should be supported by the Muslim community and by the state.

Political differences became acute after the martyrdom in 660 of the fourth Khalifah, Ali, and are reflected in the sects that arose about this time. There was a view that the Muslims should not seek expansion of power, but devote all their energies to the realisation of the ideals embodied in the teachings of Islam within Arabia. The opposite view, which under Mu'awiyah's leadership carried the day, represented in its idealised form the policy to disseminate Islam over the whole world, but meant in practice a monarchical Muslim government dominated by Arabs. This government could not claim the right to legislate, but it could also not be prevented from exercising the power which it possessed. There being no person or persons entitled to declare the law, the government under the Omayyads, the dynasty established by Mu'awiyah, followed its own policy of doing what appeared to be necessary or expedient. Its deviations from the principles and the practice of the Prophet's days were so obvious and so serious that the more conscientious Muslims did their best to keep away from it. But the idea of a religious world-state is implicit in Islam. This state would have at its head a Khalifah inheriting all the spiritual and political responsibilities of the four Orthodox Khalifahs. It would be a composite state of Muslims and non-Muslims, of all races and all countries, whose rights would be safeguarded and welfare assured according to the directions of the Quran and the precedents established by the Prophet and the Orthodox Khalifahs. This would also be a state in which exploitation, usury and immorality would be forbidden; necessities, such as food grains, would be safeguarded against profiteering, and slavery gradually eliminated.

The Omayyad dynasty was overthrown in 750 because it represented Arab domination and because of an insidious propaganda carried on against it by the adherents of the Abbasids. When the Abbasids obtained power they went out of their way to crush those descendants of the Prophet who were or could become a danger to their authority. But they were also successful rulers, and brought peace and prosperity to the Muslim world. They did not repudiate or evade their functions as Khalifahs or Imams, because they delivered the *Khutbah* and led the Friday prayers.[5] They attempted to establish by argument as well as by force the view that because a large number of representative Muslims directly and the mass of the Muslims indirectly paid allegiance to them by performing the *Bai'ah*,[6] they were entitled under religious law to be regarded as Khalifahs. This view may or may not have been correct, but it was actively opposed only by a small minority, and soon came to be generally accepted and to acquire religious prestige.

The administration of the Abbasids, though it depended like any monarchical rule on the personal qualities of the monarch was, as a system, rational and enlightened. The custom of having a Vizier, or Prime Minister, was taken over from the Sassanians, and this office was given a new character. The administration was divided into departments for the collection of taxes, for the management of the Khalifah's property, for accounts and audit, for the army, militia and police, for protection of clients and slaves, for information (by means of a regular postal service), for record and issue of documents of state, for investigation of grievances, and for payments and grants. Relatively smaller were the departments for public works, and for superintendence of fair dealing in markets, weights and measures, obedience to government orders and behaviour in public. Justice was administered by the Chief Qazi, whose seat was in the capital, and Qazis in towns, the non-Muslims having their own judicial officers. Provincial government was in charge of governors, who were under the strict supervision of the officer-in-charge of information. The larger cities, such as Samarkand, Bokhara, Herat, Hamadan, Basrah, Damascus, had deputy governors, who in their turn appointed committees of merchants with a chief merchant at their head for looking after the commercial life of the town, police officers for maintaining law and order, and judges and other dignitaries.

The power of the Abbasids declined after the middle of the ninth century, and provincial governors began to assume independence. In fact, the Muslim world was so large that it could not be ruled effectively from one centre. But in each of its great divisions the political organisation was modelled on that of Baghdad, and it was considered essential that any ruler who aspired to full legal authority should have his title confirmed by the Khalifah—the recognised descendant of the Abbasids in Baghdad. Even a powerful ruler like Mahmud of Ghazni (998-1030), though he had no fear of the Khalifah and no respect for him, felt obliged to get his claim to his throne and possessions formally recognised. The ideal of the religious world-state with a Khalifah at its head was necessary to maintain the self-confidence of the Muslim world, though the Khalifah may have had no power and no influence over those actually ruling in the different parts of this world.

In western Europe, governments were severely handicapped by feudalism. This was a system of relationships in which protection was given in return for service. The whole land was shared out between the king and his noblemen. The noblemen divided their land among their own vassals or subordinates and these again among others. Lowest in rank were the peasants, or serfs, who cultivated their own land as well as that of their lord, performed military and other service when required, and attended his court when summoned. In return for this they got protection from all enemies outside the lord's estate. Though in appearance there were obligations on both sides, in reality it was a system in which the peasants were exploited by a hierarchy of landowners. From the political point of view, this system led to the creation of two types of authority. There was, first, the public power, exercise by the hereditary or elected ruler in the name of the people as a whole and with a view to the general interest. Secondly, there was the private power of every big landowner over those who lived on his land, and this power was exercised in the landowner's personal interest by virtue of his right of property.

In spite of this limitation, the rulers attempted to improve the law and the administration of justice, to discourage feuds, to promote industry and trade. The Church laboured on behalf of social peace, supported the kings in their efforts to maintain law and order, and set herself to civilise the barbarian society of Europe by organising education. Further, as we shall see, the monastic orders established works of charity, such as hospitals and alms-houses, reclaimed waste land, improved agriculture, and even set up workshops to revive industry.

Feudalism was adopted as a system in western Europe because, after the destruction of the Roman Empire, there was no other means of preventing anarchy. The economic decline of the Roman Empire was due in part to the barbarian invasions, in part to the operation of other forces. Rome and the city-states of Greece were slave-states, and in Rome government was in the hands of the rich. Slavery began to die out from the first century onwards, because the employment of slaves was no longer economic when land could be cultivated by peasants tied to the soil and skilled workmen could be found for industries and made to work directly or through their guilds.[7] The Roman Empire was drained of its gold currency to pay for the import of luxuries from the east, and this, together with the decline in economy, led both the state authorities and individuals to abandon the use of money and adopt a barter system. Public employees were paid in kind and so taxes had to be levied in kind. This made the revival of trade and industry very difficult in Western Europe. In the seventh, eighth and ninth centuries, long distance trade became rare and the circulation of money very limited. Only one to two per cent of the population lived in the towns. But early in the seventh century Venice became an independent city-state and a centre for trade with Byzantium and West Asia; it began to perform for civilisation the same function as a maritime city-state of the ancient world.

Byzantium was, during this period one of the busiest and most important centres of commerce and industry, with a sound economy and a gold currency. Its geographical position was such that it served as a link between Europe and Asia, for the trade routes of south-eastern Europe, West Asia and the Eastern Mediterranean converged here. Unlike Rome, it was a manufacturing town as well, and while its wealth attracted the merchandise of the east, its own industries supplied luxury goods and arms over a wide area. The two most profitable trades, grain and silk, were government monopolies and commerce was strictly regulated. The first model of a rural code, which laid down the principles of a wise agrarian policy, was drawn up at Byzantium.

Contact with Byzantium and Iran brought into Muslim society all the distinctions based on wealth, rank and profession, and introduced the possibilities of class conflict. But Islam also raised the status of the peasant and the artisan, and men who achieved eminence were not ashamed to bear names which indicated that they came from families of tradesmen and skilled workers. Islam also declared that the man who earned his bread by his own labour was the "friend of God," and this added religious prestige to all manual professions.

The Arabs had been participating in the trade between India and the markets of west Asia and the Mediterranean countries, and Islam gave fresh stimulus to their activity. The city of Basrah was founded specially as a centre for trade with India and the east. As the Muslims expanded westwards, they gained control of the carrying trade of the Mediterranean, and industrial commodities, such as textiles, were produced wholesale in many parts of the Muslim world. The security of trade routes was so important that when, early in the eighth century, pirates plundered a ship returning from Ceylon near the coast of Sind, and the ruler did not take any action, it was thought necessary to send an army and conquer Sind.

We have no records of the commercial activity of India that can give us a clear picture. The carrying trade of the Indian Ocean seems to have been first in the hands of the Persians and was then taken over by the Arabs. Broach and other ports on the west coast were centres for the export of north Indian goods. The trade between south India and the Mediterranean countries was both direct across the ocean and along the coast. The natural products of south India were very much in demand in Rome and the export was on a vast scale. Indian shipping was mainly coastal, but the carrying trade eastwards to Malaya, Sumatra and Java may have been an Indian monopoly. The east coast of India was dotted with seaports and the colonial expansion of India must have followed the trade and trade routes to the east.

Chinese economy during the earlier part of this period bears a strange resemblance to that of Rome. By the end of the second century AD, the country was greatly impoverished. The wars against the Huns created a great and constant need for large numbers of horses. When the country's supply was exhausted, they were sought from the neighbouring areas. They were paid for in silk, which was procured by heavy taxation. The second reason for impoverishment was the import of luxury goods from the markets of central Asia, which were supplied by India and the west Asian and Mediterranean countries. These luxury goods were paid for partly in gold but mainly in silk. For some time government revenue was calculated and taxes levied largely in silk. The adverse trade balance had a most harmful effect on the state budget and finances, and the lack of currency made barter common.

The revival under the Sui and the T'ang was political as well as economic. Just as some centuries earlier Shih Hwang-ti had stimulated economic activity by building roads, the canal system was now improved and unified, and it provided a major means of transport, especially of supplies to the big cities, as the canals were deep and broad enough for freighters up to a capacity of 800 tons. The spread of Buddhism also made a great contribution to economic development. Temples and other Buddhist foundations came to be richly endowed with lands and funds. They accumulated large quantities of metal and coined money. Thus they became a source of ready capital and funds or credit. Ultimately, the T'ang government turned against them, and in the ninth century they were deprived of all their wealth.

It is an indication of the highly developed economy as well as of the administrative difficulties in maintaining a sufficient supply of metal coinage that paper began to be used occasionally as currency during the later T'ang period. The practice began with merchants issuing deposit certificates, which came into circulation as means of payment, and it was adopted by the state for its own purposes.

We have seen that trade routes and cities have grown together. Cities have been the live markets for the consumption and the distribution of goods, and trade routes have connected the big cities with each other, the production centres with the sources of raw material and with the markets where manufactures were in demand. In the Roman Empire, peace and economic activity led to an enormous increase in the number of cities. With the decline of the empire the number of cities in Western Europe and their economic activities were considerably reduced. The Eastern empire, however, did not suffer any loss. Byzantium was a large cosmopolitan city with prosperous trades, far-flung commercial relations, and an active commercial life, and there were many other thriving cities also. In the rest of the civilised world cities continued to reflect the progress that was being made in trade and communication. There were cities in China, in the Middle East and in Spain which are believed to have had about a million inhabitants. The expansion of the Muslims promoted industries and the whole Muslim world, from Sind to Spain, was studded with busy and lively cities.

The literature of the period shows that in India city life was highly developed, though the ideal of being close to nature was not given up. It is again unfortunate that except for Ujjain, Pataliputra, Ayodhya, Mathura and a few others, we cannot identify the cities, and the picture we get is of a city life which is not associated with particular cities. From what we know of the administration, cities seem to have had municipal governments with the chief merchants and the heads of the trade guilds in charge. In some cities there were hospitals and other establishments for public welfare.

Industries in the cities were generally carried on by guilds. We know that from the very earliest times manufacturing processes were kept as secrets, surrounded with mystery and regarded as a kind of magic. Later, in the Hellenistic world, we find associations of people engaged in different trades with a kind of corporate life. The functions of these associations centred around the desire to maintain professional status, banquets on special occasions and collections for the payment of funeral expenses. In the Roman Empire, the guilds were recognised, but placed under the control of the state. They all had a uniform constitution and they were forced to work for the state according to orders given to them. The guild-man was bound to his guild, he could not leave it or even marry outside it. The guilds in India must have been sub-castes and their corporate life would have followed the general pattern of caste organisation. Guilds developed in the Muslim world also. We find cities divided into separate wards according to the guilds and professions, and the guilds insisted on maintaining their separate identity.

The condition of education was as varied as that of cities and city life. The attacks of the barbarians and their invasion of Italy in the fifth century meant the destruction of the educational system in Rome along with other institutions of the empire. From the fifth century onwards the Church gradually undertook the function of education, and Rome was the centre from which missionaries were sent to central and western Europe. One may assert that among the principal means by which Roman culture was passed through to the Middle Ages was the Church. The Frankish kings tried to raise the standard of the education given by the Church. They founded new schools and reformed those already in existence by appointing scholars of merit as directors. Ravenna, Bologna, Pavia and Rome were centres of learning. In 796, Alcuin raised the monastic school of Tours in France into a school for ancient sciences. About the same time, the foundation of a centre of learning was laid at Oxford in England. One of the first monuments of learning in Western Europe was an encyclopaedia in 22 volumes compiled by Herbanus Maurus (784-856).

Among the achievements of knowledge belonging to the Hellenistic tradition was the description by Pappos of Alexandria of the working of the lever, the pulley, the wheel and axle and the screw. Pappos also discovered what is now known as Guldin's law concerning areas and volumes of solids generated by rotation of a plane figure about an axis.

Another outstanding achievement was the preparation by Castorius of a road-map of the Roman Empire in the fourth century. In Byzantium, the ancient sciences continued to be studied and it was here that books were first given their present form instead of being written on rolls.

In India this period begin with the development of classical Sanskrit, of which Ashvaghosha was the first and Kalidasa the greatest master. Bhavabhuti and others carried on the tradition, but the standard attained by Kalidasa could not be rivalled. To this period belongs also the first Sanskrit lexicon, prepared by Amar and known as Amarakosha.

Perhaps the greatest achievement of India was in the field of mathematics. Already in the sixth century the minus sign and zero were being used, and numerals had been evolved which were taken over by the Arabs at the beginning of the ninth century and communicated by them to the West. Aryabhatta (born 476) was the first Indian to treat mathematics as a distinct subject. He dealt with evolution and involution, area and volume, progressive and algebraic identities and indeterminate equations of the first degree. As an astronomer he was the first Indian to hold that the earth rotated on its axis, and that the eclipses were not the work of the demon Rahu but were caused by the shadow of the earth or the moon. About this time, the knowledge of Greek astronomy seems to have spread into India, and among the five works mentioned as authoritative in his own time by the astronomer Varahamihira (sixth century), at least three are of Greek origin.

In medical science, considerable progress seems to have been made. Sushruta, who lived in the third and fourth centuries AD, knew of no less than 760 drugs, organic and inorganic, and 1,100 different diseases. He prescribed different means of diagnosis, such as appearance, hearing, smell, taste, etc. Vagabhatta, who lived in the seventh century, compiled a book on the eight branches of medicine. His work shows great progress in surgery, such as stitching of the intestines, operation on the gall bladder and plastic surgery of the nose. About the same time pharmacology became a science separate from medicine.

The great centres of learning in India in those days were Taxila and Nalanda. Of the latter we have glowing accounts from Hieuen Tsang and I'tsing, who were deeply impressed by the scholarship as well as by the number of scholars and the magnificent buildings. But we have no precise account of the general system of education. It seems most probable that the old teacher-pupil family institution continued.

One of the outstanding characteristics of the Gupta period was the cultivation of the fine arts, specially painting and dramatics. Every cultured man seems to have had in his house a drawing board, and a vessel for holding brushes and other requisites of painting. The inclination of the Indian mind to systematise and establish standards and norms is evident from the *Vishnudharmottara*, an appendix to the *Vishnupurana*, which lays down the theory of painting. Dramatic art was systematised in the same way, the types of characters, the plots, the language, the gestures all being prescribed. An extravagance in this direction was Vatsyayana's *Kama Sutra*, which described the various methods of love making.

Chinese literature and science were both influenced and stimulated during this period by the missionary work of Buddhists. We know that a translation bureau was organised soon after Buddhism got a foothold and translations of Buddhist sacred books from Sanskrit were dictated to several Chinese scribes at the same time. It seems these translations were neither literal nor very correct, but still the enterprise was most fruitful. Among the Indian scholars who participated in this work, the most eminent was Kumarajiva. The influence of the Indian style of writing led to new Chinese styles and the musical form of the Indian *bhajan* created the religious chant of the Chinese. Chinese medicine was greatly enriched by the study of Indian medicine and Indian mathematical and astronomical ideas are apparent in subsequent Chinese literature. A learned foundation of this period was the Hanlin academy, established around the year 750.

The great cultural function of the Arabs was to acquire and communicate knowledge. Translation of scientific works into Arabic was begun by the Khalifah al-Mansur (754-775). Harun al-Rashid (786-809) expanded the work and his son, al-Mamun, collected the standard scientific works of many languages for translation. It was he who made the enterprise into one of world significance. The translation of works from Greek, Syriac and Chaldaic was under the supervision of a Christian, Costa, the son of Luke; from ancient Persian under Yahya bin Harun; from Sanskrit under Duban the Brahman. The first observatory was built by al-Mamun, and observations were made concerning equinoxes, eclipses, comets; the precession of the equinoxes and the movement of the sun and other astral bodies was studied; the size of the earth, obliquity of the elliptic and variations in lunar latitudes were calculated. If there had been a break in the observations that were being made, and were continued in the city of Harran under the protection of an enlightened Islamic state policy up to the

Abbasid times, irreparable harm would have been done to astronomcial science. Apart from the astronomers, al-Kindi studied and wrote on meteorology and optics and worked out a complex theory about the lines of force. Imam al-Razi (called Rhazes in Europe, 864-925) was a mathematician, astronomer, philosopher and physician. His treatises on smallpox and measles, apart from other works, were translated into Latin, and his authority was undisputed in Europe down to the seventeenth century. Among mathematicians, al-Khwarizmi (*c.* 825) was the author of an epoch-making work in which the nine numerals and the zero, with the decimal positional system, were used. Al-Khwarizmi also wrote a basic text-book in algebra, which is generally regarded as a Muslim invention.

All the scientific work of this period was done with the encourage-ment and support of the state. Al-Mamun himself was under the influence of the school of thought known as the Mo'tazila, which taught among other things that man was a free agent, that the laws according to which human life had to be moulded could not be changeless. The attitude with which the work of al-Mamun's reign was done was as important as the work itself. But science failed to become associated with the enduring features of Islam, and this was probably a major reason for the indifference shown to it later on, and for the consequent intellectual stagnation.

The spirit of the age is seen at work also in the provision of medical treatment for soldiers, in the foundation of hospitals and homes for lepers and disabled persons, the construction of a network of canals in Mesopotamia for the promotion of agriculture and the building of roads and rest-houses.

III

We have noted already how the institution of slavery and the dislike of manual work among the Greeks and the Romans prevented the application of scientific knowledge to economically useful purposes. In fact, the only definite progress made was in the manufacture of engines of war. The Romans established factories for mass production of pottery and some other goods, but usually the size of factories was small and their output was meant to supply mainly local needs. The downfall of the Roman Empire implied also the collapse of its economic organisation. However, agriculture was soon developed, and water-wheels became common in Europe in the eighth century.

The Byzantine state followed a policy different from that of Rome, and though the only innovation was the culture of silk-worms brought over from China, the silks, fine cloths, tapestry, leather-work, enamel, mining, metallurgy and weapons of Byzantium were famous. In 671, Kallinikos discovered what was known as the "Greek fire," a compound of sulphur, rock-salt, resin, petroleum, asphalt and burnt lime. The art of illuminating books was developed to a high degree of excellence.

In India, the chief articles of export were natural products; among manufactured goods, textiles and ivory work seem worthy of note. Sugar began to be made out of sugarcane juice about AD 300. Skill in India during this period was concentrated on religious objects. It is in the caves of Karli, Ajanta and Ellora, in the gateways of Sanchi and other stupas, that we see the imagination of the artist and the skill of the craftsman at their best.

The achievements of China during this period seem to be most impressive. The Chinese are credited with the invention of the compass, or at least the discovery of magnetic action on the needle, for according to some authorities it was the Arabs who invented the compass.[8] But the horse-collar, the stern-post rudder and printing are undoubtedly Chinese inventions, and had an incalculable significance in the development of civilisation. The horse-collar gradually replaced the band which used to be tied across the breast of the horse and therefore pressed on the wind-pipe. It increased the usefulness of the horse as a draught animal, and in Europe facilitated the development of agriculture and trade. The stern-post rudder made it much easier to steer boats of all sizes, and is a landmark in the development of shipping. The importance of the invention of printing needs no comment. The first book was printed in China in 868. The Chinese appear to have been the first to use iron for other purposes than making tools and weapons, as the first hanging bridges were made there in the third century.

The Arabs learnt paper-making from the Chinese and paper was made for the first time in Baghdad in AD 793, and in Cairo in 900. It took more than 200 years for its manufacture to be taken up in Europe. We have already drawn attention to the effect of Islamic social ideas on agriculture and industry. Natural resources were fully utilised, iron being obtained from the mines of Khorasan, lead and silver from Kirman, porcelain and marble from Tabriz, rock-salt and sulphur from north Persia, bitumen and naphtha from Georgia. The glass and silk industry of Syria, the glass and soap of Basrah, Baghdad and Samaria, the silk, satin and brocades made in different towns were masterpieces of craftsmanship cherished all over the world.

NOTES

1. This seems to be suggested also by Radha Kumud Mukherji, in his *The Gupta Empire*, p. 14 (Hind Kitabs, Bombay, 1947).
2. Tertullian, quoted in Ernest Barker's *From Alexander to Constantine*, p. 455 (Oxford, 1956).
3. Eusebius, quoted in Barker, *op. cit.*, p. 479.
4. The legal punishments for theft, however, were mutilation, imprisonment, confiscation of property, exile and death. *History and Culture of the Indian People*, Vol. III, p. 360 (Bharatiya Vidyabhavan, Bombay).
5. The *Khutbah* is an address delivered to the congregation in the mosque before the Friday prayer. It could be on any subject of general concern or interest, and was usually an occasion for the declaration of policy or expression of the ruler's view. Later it came to have a prescribed form and to be read by the Imam leading the prayers.
6. Formal profession of allegiance.
7. For guilds, see p. 140.
8. Philip K. Hitti, *History of the Arabs*, p. 669. (Macmillan, London, 1946).

33

A Century of Revolutions (1750-1850)

The western world of today is the product of several political revolutions and of an economic revolution, all of which took place between 1750 and 1850. For the rest of the world also, which has been deeply influenced by the events and the political and economic policies of the western nations, the revolutions of this century have proved of decisive importance. We cannot, of course, foretell the future, but so far as the world today is concerned, this century is perhaps the most significant in history. Within it fall the American, the French, two European revolutions (1830 and 1848) and the industrial revolution which changed the character not only, of economic but of political, social and personal life. Within it fall the achievements of Napoleon, Goethe, Beethoven, and of poets, philosophers, politicians, scientists and inventors, which together surpass the work of preceding and succeeding generations.

The political history of this period in Europe begins with the Seven Years' War (1756-1763). In the colonies, the main conflict was between France and Great Britain, in which the political and military power of the French in North America and India was destroyed. The French took revenge for their losses when differences arose between Great Britain and the American colonies and contributed materially to the success of the Americans in their War of Independence.

This war itself was a direct result of the Seven Years' War. The British Government realised to what extent its responsibilities had increased, and how necessary it was to raise revenue in the colonies to meet the growing military and administrative expenditure. The colonies organised constitutional opposition to the laws made by

---

From *World History*.

the British government. The British Parliament asserted its right to make such laws. Opinion against such legislation was mobilised in the colonies, and both sides drifted into direct opposition. Military clashes developed into the War of Independence (1775-1783).

A Declaration of Independence, drafted by Thomas Jefferson, was approved by Congress on 4 July 1776, and on 15 November 1777, Articles of Confederation, affirming the perpetual union of the colonial states and giving to the Confederation the name of the United States of America, were approved by the Congress and sent to the different states of the colony for ratification. France recognised the United States by making treaties of commerce and alliance (6 February 1778), and Spain joined the war against Great Britain a year later. Great Britain realised the danger of continuing a war which could lead to the loss of both territory and trade and, after the surrender of Cornwallis at Yorktown (19 October 1781), decided to make peace. A treaty was signed at Paris on 3 September 1783, by which the independence of the United States of America was recognised, and peace and commercial relations were restored. A Constitutional Convention, meeting at Philadelphia in May 1787, drafted and approved a Constitution, and resolved that it should become operative when accepted by nine of the thirteen states. The ratification by the states, which were not of one mind as regards the distribution of powers between the federation and the states, could be completed only in June 1788.

The revolution in France began with the meeting of the Estates-General on 5 May, 1789. This was an assembly representing the three different "statuses" or "estates" of noblemen, clergymen and townsmen, and had not met since 1614. It was now summoned because the state was bankrupt, but once it had met, it provided the Third Estate, the middle class of the towns, the long-awaited opportunity to assert itself. On 17 June, 1789, the Third Estate declared itself the National Assembly, and when it was learnt that troops had been ordered to Paris, National Guards, consisting of middle class people, were formed in Paris and other cities. The Bastille, the state prison of Paris and the symbol of irresponsible royal authority, was stormed and destroyed on the 14 July 1789 and the Declaration of the Rights of Man and the Citizen was approved on the 26 August. Both these events had a profound effect on the whole of Europe. The National Assembly, now calling itself the Legislative Assembly, carried through a series of reforms, confiscated the lands belonging to the Church, and by the Civil Constitution of the Clergy (12 July 1790) made all priests salaried officials of the state. This created a deep rift among the clergy and among the people, and was one of the main reasons for the king, Louis XVIII's unsuccessful attempt to escape out of France (20 June 1791). The situation made war unavoidable, and the war made the revolutionaries bitter and hysterical. France was formally declared a Republic on 22 September, 1792, and two months later a general offer of assistance was made to all peoples desiring to be free from the despotism of kings. Louis was executed on 15 January 1793, after a short trial.

The initial successes of the revolutionary armies were followed by defeats, and there was a serious revolt among the peasants in south-western France. Extreme measures seemed necessary. The First Committee of Public Safety was formed on 6 April, 1793, and given dictatorial authority. This was the beginning of the Terror, which lasted for about two years. But by the end of 1793, the tide of war had turned in favour of the French. The revolutionaries who believed in killing their opponents killed each other off, and by the middle of May 1795, the hysteria was over and peace treaties had been signed with Prussia, Holland and Spain.

Now followed a period when the achievements of the revolution had to be safeguarded, and it brought to the forefront an artillery officer, of Corsican birth, Napoleon Bonaparte, whose personality was to dominate France and Europe for twenty years. He first won fame as the commander of the French armies in Italy in 1796, and then for his spectacular, if ultimately unsuccessful invasion of Egypt. He captured power soon after his return from Egypt, and ruled France as First Consul from November 1799, till May 1804, and as Emperor till April 1814. He was forced to abdicate and was exiled to the island of Elba, but returned from there on 1 March 1815, and ruled for what are known as the Hundred Days, till his final defeat at Waterloo on 18 June 1815. He was then sent to the remote island of St. Helena, where he died in 1821.

Napoleon is recognised as one of the very greatest military geniuses the world has produced; his achievements as an administrator and legislator are no less dazzling than his military exploits. He was, in fact, the pensonification of the most dynamic tendencies of the French Revolution. He believed that there was a whole world to be set in order, and his plans and visions reveal an imagination such as no political ruler ever possessed. He remade Europe in accordance with what seemed to him reasonable or advantageous. The unification of Germany became possible because he forced the Emperor of Austria to give up his title of Holy Roman Emperor, and reduced the number of German states from over seven hundred to thirty-nine. His domination and his exactions raised the peoples of Europe against him, but wherever he exercised power he set up an example of efficient government. His whole career fulfilled the prophecy Goethe made when he heard of the first success of the revolutionary French armies in 1792: "From here and today there opens a new era in the history of the world."

Napoleon's foreign policy aimed at making France and himself the dominating power in Europe. and for this purpose he defeated and humbled Austria and Prussia, formed the Confederation of the Rhine, and carved out the Grand Duchy of Warsaw. But he realised that success would depend ultimately on the destruction of British power and the overawing or subjugation of Russia. The attack on Egypt, the planned invasion of England, the Continental Blockade (decreed from Berlin in 1806) are illuminating studies in political, military and economic strategy. His invasion of Russia in 1812 was a desperate venture on which everything was staked and lost. But he could say that he was defeated by circumstances rather than the superior wisdom of his opponents.

After Napoleon's abdication in 1814, the powers allied against him assembled at the Congress of Vienna to decide what should be done. The idea, generally accepted at the Congress, that in future differences between states should be settled by consultation was a real step forward. But in practice it came to mean interference in the affairs of states in order to maintain the rights of the rulers and to suppress all movements for political reform. It was because of objection in principle to interference in the internal affairs of states that Great Britain declined to participate in the Congress of Verona (1822). This Congress had been summoned to deal with a popular revolt against King Ferdinand of Spain, and the British Foreign Secretary, Canning, as well as Monroe, President of the United States, felt that this might lead to intervention in the Spanish colonies in America. These had already revolted, Paraguay and Venezuela declaring their independence in 1811, Rio de la Plata in

1816, Chile in 1818, Peru and Mexico in 1821, Brazil in 1822. The provinces of Central America revolted later, in 1823-25. President Monroe enunciated the policy that became known as the Monroe Doctrine. The American continents were to be regarded henceforth as free and independent. Americans would not meddle in European politics and any interference by a European power in the affairs of any country on the American continents would be regarded as an unfriendly act by the United States.

This did not, however, simplify international relations in Europe. France was suspected of aggressive intentions. Russia was a spirit that had been raised to save Europe from Napoleon, and there was a general fear that she would continue her expansion westwards. Prussia was looked upon as the military and diplomatic bulwark against France in the west and Russia in the east. Austria was not lacking in expansionist tendencies, and feared that Russia would take away all that could be taken in south-eastern Europe. Peace depended entirely on a timely adjustment of demands and interests.

The peoples were not supposed to be concerned in these adjustments. The Austrian Netherlands (Belgium), following the example of the French, had revolted against the emperor. The Congress of Vienna decided to unite Holland and Belgium in order to strengthen them against a possible attack by France, and placed them under the rule of one prince. In 1830, the French deposed their king, Charles X, and this revolution stimulated similar movements elsewhere. Belgium separated from Holland, there were widespread revolts in Italy, and Joseph Mazzini (1805-1872) gave a powerful literary and idealistic form to the movement for Italian independence. There was deep unrest in many parts of Germany, and it was followed by repressive measures. The Poles rose in revolt against Russian domination and expelled Russian garrisons, but their freedom movement was soon suppressed. There was a revolution in France again in 1848, and it was the signal for revolutions in Germany, the Austrian Empire and Italy. These revolutions revealed, on the one hand, that the existing governments were not acceptable to the people and acted as a dead weight. They also showed, on the other hand, that the romantic ideals of nationalism that had become current would only replace one type of problem by another. Internal developments in central Europe and Italy henceforth enlarged national into international questions.

The expansionist tendencies of Russia and Austria created what has been called the Eastern Question, the question of dividing up the declining Ottoman Empire among the European nations. At the beginning of the present period (1765-67), we find Russian agents at work in Greece, Crete, Bosnia, Montenegro, inciting the people against the Turkish government. The treaty of Kutschuk-Kainardji (1774) is a typical example of imperialist methods. The Sultan had to promise that he would treat his Christian subjects better, to grant the right of pilgrimage, to protect the Christian religion and its churches, to open the Empire to Russian trade, with all the advantages available to the most favoured nation, to allow Russia to have consuls and vice-consuls in any towns she thought fit, and diplomatic representation at the Court. Russian aggressions continued in spite of treaties of peace, and it was only the jealousy or the self-interest of other powers that prevented her from going to extremes.

In Persia, the decline of the Safavi dynasty was followed by disorder and conflicts among semi-barbarous chieftains. Nadir Shah (1736-1747) established a crude sort of military rule, and carried away a lot of wealth from north India, along with the Peacock Throne of the Emperor Shah Jahan, when he invaded the country and sacked Delhi (1738-39). There was anarchy again after his assassination, and by the time the Qachar dynasty established itself towards the end of the eighteenth century, Persia had become a pawn in the imperialist policies of Russia, Great Britain and France. The interest of the French was temporary, a part of Napoleon's scheme of expansion, The Russians seized the Persian territories north and south of the Caucasus, advancing up to Tabriz (1825-28), while the British made treaties to advance their commercial interests and secure their possessions in India.

British interest in India began with the establishment of the East India Company in 1600, and with attempts to secure concessions, monopolies and trading rights. There was not much of success in this till 1775, when exemption from customs duties and other concessions were secured. The disintegration of the Moghal Empire gave both the British and the French East India Company's officers opportunities to take sides in local and provincial intrigues, and make them a means of establishing their position not only commercially but politically and territorially. The decisive factor was the European superiority in military science. From 1748 to 1763, the French and British fought each other, and ultimately the British were victorious because of their naval superiority. They had now no European rivals in India and could intrigue and fight for their advantage with single-mindedness.

The conflict with the French, which began in south India, spread also to Bengal, where the condition of the government, which had been bad enough before, became very much worse because of the interference, the exactions and dishonest methods of the East India Company's officers and private traders. Mir Qasim's attempt to stem the rot failed, and after his defeat at the battle of Buxar (1764), the Company's officers could do what they liked. The *diwani* (revenue administration) of Bihar and Bengal was taken over in 1765, and these territories were mercilessly plundered and exploited till the appointment of Warren Hastings as Governor in 1772. Warren Hastings fought the Marhattas (1778-1782) and Haidar Ali, who had seized the government of Mysore (1761) and was a power to be reckoned with. Ultimately, because of the conflicts between the Marhattas, Mysore and Hyderabad, the British were able to break the power of the Marhattas, to conquer Mysore and reduce Hyderabad to a moral subjection far worse than military conquest. By a system of Subsidiary Alliances, introduced by Lord Wellesley (1798-1805), it was made impossible for any Indian Prince to remain independent or even aloof, and by 1818 almost the whole of India south of the Sutlej was directly or indirectly under British rule. Ceylon had become a Crown Colony in 1798, a war with Nepal (1814-1816) yielded the present Kumaon Division, Singapore was occupied in 1819 and wars with Burma (1824 and 1853) gave the British possession of Assam and the whole eastern coast of the Bay of Bengal. Sind was annexed in 1843, and the Punjab, after two wars in 1849. In 1857, a movement for setting the country free resolved itself prematurely into ill-organised military encounters, causing bloodshed, bitterness and misery, and the Indian territories came directly under the Crown and Parliament in 1858.

It took the British just a hundred years to appreciate fully the consequences of leaving the commercial, political and administrative policies of their Indian possession in the hands of a private trading company. The Regulating Act of 1774, which was the first attempt to introduce regular procedure in the administration, was accepted by the Company because, though its servants in India and its Directors in Great Britain were amassing wealth, the Company itself was nearly bankrupt. Pitt's India Bill of 1784 was the result of a compromise between the Cabinet and the Directors. The material change in policy was due not so much to legislation as to the social status and personal influence of the Governors-General, which gave to the administration in India a certain measure of independence. The abolition of the East India Company's monopoly of Indian trade in 1813, however, made this arrangement entirely irrational. It was maintained because it was supposed to work. The events of 1857-58 dispelled this illusion.

I

The revolt against the Roman Catholic Church in the sixteenth century was not a revolt against the idea or the ideal of a church. For a time both Protestants and Catholics continued to believe in the possibility of a church civilisation in which every sphere of life would be regulated according to the law of God.[1] But the belief was not strong enough to mould all the new social and economic tendencies, and could not, therefore, take any organisational form. With this belief, the hope of integrating all the aspects of life through the authority of dogma also faded. But the dethronement of the church and of institutional religion did not leave a vacuum. What happened was that belief disintegrated into beliefs, that the need for a concept of the universal order was displaced by the desire to discover the nature of the universe and the meaning of order. Whoever was moved by this desire could set out on his own voyage of discovery. Whatever he claimed to have discovered could be accepted or rejected; the test was logic, evidence, intellectual soundness or emotional appeal.

Two lines of thought had already been marked out in the seventeenth century, one by Descartes and the other by the Deists. Descartes was one of the founders of scientific philosophy, one of the first representatives of the attitude that knowledge is not only essential but the proof of man's very existence. Therefore, in dealing with human affairs, we must think as clearly and objectively as possible. For this reason, Descartes' outlook was secular, and he saw no reason why differences of religious views should interfere with a personal participation in public life. Deism showed the influence of scientific awakening in another form. As a movement it began in England, where a long line of rationalists had attempted to end religious controversy, and to give religion a sound ethical instead of a dogmatic basis. Newton's discoveries gave a strong impetus to the tendency to strip religion of all that reason could not accept or society make use of. Christianity was thus reduced to belief in God and in the existence of a natural moral law. Some writers, applying the standards of their times to historic Christianity, showed in what ways it was irrational. Belief in miracles was one of the main points of attack. Voltaire (1694-1778) made deism into a rational religion, and used it as a weapon not only against the Roman Catholic Church but all forms of Christianity. Rousseau (1712-1778) would also be described as a deist, but his deism grew out of a mystical conception of man, his growth and his destiny. In Germany, Reimarus (1694-1768) and Lessing (1729-1781) were outspoken deists, and promoters of religious tolerance, and Lessing put forward a theory of progressive religious development. Deism in its earlier forms could not serve either as a philosophy or as a theology. But so far as it emphasised the ethical and social aspects of religion, and insisted that religious and scientific thought and intellectual and moral needs should be brought into harmony, it had a lasting influence.

It is not possible here to describe the views of individual thinkers and writers, and these views could not be considered separately and by themselves under the category of belief. We can only take note of features which so many thinkers had in common and which exercised so much influence that they can be regarded as new forms of belief. Outstanding among these was the belief in reason, which many enthusiasts now looked upon as something independent, a source of knowledge capable of replacing all the dogmas and the precepts which religion provided for human guidance. Belief in reason became so intense that the half century ending with the French Revolution has been called the Age of Reason. It was also called the Age of Enlightenment. The belief in original sin, which had such a deep influence in shaping the medieval Christian outlook on life is now transferred from man to society. It was churches, dogmas, traditions, customs that were the origin of evil; man himself was born pure and would remain pure if he were not infected by the evils of society and civilisation: Rousseau placed the state of nature in sharp contrast against civilised society, and though he was aware that nature did not provide for man all that he needed, civilised society did not rise in his esteem. The resultant was an ideal of simplicity, of naturalness, of a life lived according to the desires of the heart. As a member of society Rousseau was in some ways contemptible and in every way disagreeable. But he was a mystic, and within himself he could compose pictures of fascinating beauty, for the painting of which his style was a sensitive and faithful medium. More than any of his contemporaries he gave to the Age of Reason and Enlightenment the vision of a new life, and to educators of the future a new idea of their function.

If man was the embodiment of reason and could mould civilisation in accordance with his idea of the good, it was inconceivable that he should have no rights. The Preamble to the Constitution of the United States and the Declaration of the Rights of Man and of the Citizen provided comprehensive definitions of these rights. The people are collectively sovereign, they are all equal as individuals and entitled to participate in law-making through their elected representatives. They have the right to believe and practise their religion to express their views in speech and writing, to assemble for lawful purposes, to keep and dispose of their property. There were those who, like Edmund Burke (1729-1797), thought it wrong to talk as if men had the power to create governments and institutions out of nothing, merely by the exercise of presumed rights and liberties. Existing institutions, they said, were the result of generations of effort, and must be regarded with reverence. But such ideas could not stem the rising tide of revolutions, which were the expression, in political form, of the doctrine of natural rights.

The new conception of man is seen in its most significant form in the music of Beethoven (1770-1827) and in the writings of Goethe (1749-1832) above all in his play, *Faust*. Beethoven was beyond doubt the greatest of the European composers, not only because of the quality of his music, but because his music reflects the tremendous spiritual struggle that went on within him, the struggle of an artist seeking the highest in his art, and of a man striving to achieve through music something greater than music itself. His fifth symphony is one of the most exalted expressions of inner struggle, of the battle against doom, and of a victory that is eternal. The last of his great compositions, the ninth symphony, reproduces the most significant moods of his life, and ends in an ode to Joy, the ultimate refuge of mankind.

Goethe occupies a unique place in the history of human development. No writer, no student of cultures has had a mind more versatile, more receptive to the most diverse influences, surer in its appreciation of values and more capable of complete identification with them. Kalidas' *Shakuntala* has not been better praised than by him, and in the whole mass of poems written by Muslims in praise of the Prophet Mohammed, there is nothing to compare with the eloquent symbolism of his "Mahomets Gesang." His interest in all the meaningful aspects of life, his power of appraising men and events, his intuitive discernment of the essential in the social changes taking place in his times, the maturity and the soundness of his judgement have no equal. We cannot discuss his writings here, but in his play, *Faust*, where the chief character sells his soul to the Devil in return for the promise of the most complete experience of life, is a representation of "Western" man which is at once the most factual and the most illuminating. For what is most characteristic of western man is his desire to know everything for himself, to experience every variety of emotion for its own sake, without reference to any standard or any judgement other than his own, to determine for himself what he should aspire to become or to achieve.

Reason and Enlightenment, with their optimism, their violence, their supreme confidence in themselves produced a reaction. One form of this was a movement known as Romanticism. Its expressions in literature, art, history, philosophy, religion were so varied that we can only call it a type of sentiment, a particular outlook on life. It comprehends the poetry of Shelley, Keats and Byron, Chateaubriand's interpretation of Christianity, a new attitude of interest in medieval life, laws and institutions, Herder's conception of the people as a spiritual community, with their particular *Volksgeist*[2] and new styles in painting and architecture. The stimulus it gave to literary and cultural activity makes it a movement of great importance.

Among those who deeply influenced the Romantics, specially in Germany, was Spinoza (1632-1677), who lived in an earlier period but whose works became widely known only about a hundred years after his death. Spinoza wrote on politics, ethics, religion, and out of all these he wove a system in which the world as it is, is accepted and a line of thought and action is suggested which brings man, nature and God into complete harmony.

To the age of Reason and Enlightenment belongs also the philosophy of Kant (1724-1804), in which previous philosophical thought is appraised and summed up, and a basis is provided for further intellectual and religious speculation. Kant studied the British philosophers, Locke, Berkeley and Hume; he was an enthusiastic reader of Rousseau. He felt that the analysis of knowledge and experience made by the British philosophers, specially by Hume, reduced experience to unconnected units of sensation. Against this he maintained that experience was always related to a framework of thought; we can say that all our knowledge begins with experience because each experience is related to some other. There is a unity which binds them together. Kant's own philosophy is a criticism of the faculty of knowledge. He believes that we should not dogmatise or raise doubts which are groundless, but subject the nature of reason itself to a sober investigation. For there are things which it can and things which it cannot do. Physics and mathematics, for instance, are fields in which reason can operate effectively. But there are problems, set by reason itself and unavoidable, such as God, freedom, immortality, which reason cannot solve. They belong to the realm of metaphysics. Kant examined and rejected all the proofs advanced in regard to the existence of God, but it followed from the argument that the existence of God could not be disproved either. We have also to admit, according to him, that freedom and the moral law exist. Without them, ordered living would be impossible. In this way, Kant undermined materialism and atheism and made room for faith, without identifying himself with any particular religious doctrine.

The philosophy of Kant became a source from which others drew both inspiration and ideas, even if they did not accept his system as a whole. To the direct line of succession belong those who are known as the Idealists, but he gave both confidence and direction to those who, like Schleiermacher (1768-1834) attempted to harmonise religious doctrine and scientific knowledge. Even Schopenhauer (1788-1860), the pessimist, claims to have reverted to the original teachings of Kant as against the modifications and interpretations of his later followers. Among the Idealists, the thinker who exercised the greatest influence was Hegel (1770-1831). He had a versatile mind, and was able to combine history, logic, art and religion into a system of philosophy where inner experience and external reality become an organic whole and lead to the Absolute Idea, or God. One of his most important contributions is the conception of development through the three stages of thesis, antithesis and synthesis. If we take existing facts as the "thesis," we see that the course of events reveals their incompleteness, and leads to the "antithesis," with a process of reconciliation that produces a "synthesis."

Other systems of thought, which in some ways or for some time operated as beliefs are Utilitarianism, Positivism, Liberalism, Socialism and Communism.

The Utilitarians denied the value of such principles as natural law and natural right, and such assumptions as a Social Contract. They held that all men desire pleasure and dislike pain, that the value of a thing is determined by its utility, and that peace, order and contentment would be attained if the greatest good of the greatest number[3] were accepted as the guiding principle in morals and in legislation. The Utilitarians shared all the confidence and the hope of the Age of Reason, and their standard had some value when applied to the reform of a legal system burdened with customs and technicalities, such as that of Great Britain in the eighteenth century. But Utilitarianism could not be made into a philosophy or a system of belief. It evaporated in the attempts made to give it substance and form.

The same could be said of Liberalism. All liberals professed to be progressive, and their aim in all spheres of life was to remove hindrances and restraints. In matters of belief they were free-thinkers, considering the individual the best judge, so long as his actions did not deny to others the freedom he demanded for himself. In matters of political and social organisation they had the same attitude, their desire being that the policy of the state should confer the largest amount of benefit with the least interference, use of compulsion and authority. But like Utilitarianism, Liberalism could not be given a definite form. Its history is the record of positions taken up on political, economic and social issues by those who called themselves liberals.

One aspect of liberalism was its insistence on the freedom of the individual, and here it had, for about a century, the support of economic theory. The school of Physiocrats in France started from the assumption that all men and all the human powers are governed by moral and physical laws instituted by the Supreme Being. The application of these laws must give satisfaction at the same time to the interests of individuals and the state. A generation later, the theories of the Physiocrats were developed in England by Adam Smith, whose epoch-making work, *The Wealth of Nations,* was published in 1776. Ricardo (1772-1823) and Malthus (1766-1834), who derived their philosophical position from Adam Smith, believed firmly in a natural, invariable law, and Ricardo had as strong a faith as any of the Physiocrats in a divine, pre-established harmony between the public and the individual interest. The definition of this individual interest, which had a divine sanction, was comprehended in six freedoms, freedom from government interference, freedom from monopolies, concessions and privileges, freedom to own and dispose of property, freedom of contract between employer and labourer, between seller and buyer, freedom of movement and domicile, freedom of association. In economic life, these freedoms had meaning and value only for the middle class of manufacturers and businessmen and for the landowners. They were the means of enabling employers to do what they liked, to make women and children work in factories and mines, or to uproot families of farmers and use hired labour instead. The pace of industrialisation would have been considerably slowed down but for the belief that these freedoms were given to the individual by Providence.

Of far lesser significance socially but perhaps of greater importance intellectually was the philosophy of Positivism.

Its founder, Auguste Comte (1798-1857), propounded the Law of the Three States, and in accordance with the characteristic features of the Three States, a Classification of the Sciences. The Law of the Three States is the division of human history into three stages, the earliest or lowest being the theological. This is followed by the metaphysical, with the scientific coming as the height of intellectual and industrial achievement. The Classification of the Sciences places mathematics and astronomy at the lowest level, because they are abstract, and biology and sociology at the top, because they deal with man and with society. These ideas were elaborated in the positivist system of thought. This system exercised a deep influence on the beliefs of the nineteenth century, because it emphasised the physical and material aspects of the social sciences and challenged the value of religion, metaphysics and everything concerned with the supernatural.

While positivism looked at science and industry as human achievement inspiring faith and hope, there were two other movements, Socialism and Communism, which judged life according to other standards. Both Socialism and Communism have a long history as endeavours to organise production, distribution and consumption of goods on lines more in keeping with the ideals of justice and philanthropy. Socialism in modern history begins with St. Simon (1760-1825), a visionary who dreamed of a new order based on love and justice and purged of all selfish competition. Fourier (1772-1837), Robert Owen (1771-1858) and Louis Blanc (1813-1882) brought Socialism closer to reality by proposing schemes that would remove competition and create an economic and social order based on moral principles. But, these schemes were not practical enough to succeed, or to succeed over a sufficiently long period. Communism was placed before the European world as a precise, dogmatic, fighting system in the Manifesto published by a secret society known as the Communist League in January 1848.

> "The history of all hitherto existing society is the history of class struggle... .
> The modern bourgeois society that has sprouted from the ruins of feudal society has not done away with class antagonism. It has but established new classes, new conditions of oppression, new forms of struggle in place of the old ones... In one word, for exploitation veiled by religious and political illusions, it has substituted naked, shameless, direct, brutal exploitation...
> Modern industry has converted the little workshop of the patriarchal master into the great factory of the individual capitalist. Masses of labourers, crowded into the factory, are organised like soldiers... . They are daily and hourly enslaved by the machine... . The more openly this despotism proclaims gain to be its end and aim, the more petty, the more hateful and the more embittering it is...

> But with the development of industry the proletariat not only increases in number; it becomes concentrated in masses, its strength grows, and it feels that strength more...
> All previous historical movements were movements of minorities, or in the interest of minorities. The proletarian movement is the self-conscious independent movement of the immense majority, in the interest of the immense majority...
> The proletarians have no country...
> National differences and antagonisms between peoples are daily more and more vanishing, owing to the development of the bourgeoisie, to freedom of commerce, to the world market, to uniformity in the mode of production and in the conditions of life corresponding thereto.
> The supremacy of the proletariat will cause them to vanish still faster...
> The Communists everywhere support every revolutionary movement against the existing social and political order of things...
> The Communists disdain to conceal their views and aims. They openly declare that their ends can be attained only by the forcible overthrow of all existing social conditions. Let the ruling classes tremble at a Communistic revolution. The proletarians have nothing to lose but their chains. They have a world to win.
> Working men of all countries, unite!"

The theory of class struggle, of the means of production being the determining factor in the organisation of society, of the developments that are to lead inevitably to the final revolution, the victory of the masses and the dictatorship of the proletariat, is known as the theory of historical materialism. As a system of philosophy, communist teaching calls itself dialectic materialism. It is an application to economic and social life of the dialectical method of the German philosopher, Hegel, who believed that human development took place through the interaction of opposites. These, we have seen, he termed Thesis and Antithesis, their interaction resulting in a Synthesis, which in the onward movement of life itself became a new Thesis. The dialectic materialism of the Communists is supposed to provide the answer to all questions, to be logically perfect. But the forecast of events made in the Communist Manifesto has turned out to be wrong in many substantial respects. National differences have not disappeared, the position of the working class has not grown worse, the accumulation of capital in a few hands has not taken place. The churches and religions have not grown weaker. In the latter half of the eighteenth century, people did become intensely anti-clerical, and even the Roman Catholic Church was so affected by this attitude that in 1773 the Society of Jesus was dissolved. But it was re-established in 1814. The National Assembly of France confiscated the property of the Church, and placed the clergy on the same level as the civil servants. But Napoleon had to come to terms with the Pope in order to reduce the hostility of the Catholics to the Revolution, and the Romantic movement in France deepened religious sentiment. New beliefs did not displace the old, they only created a diversity which made uniformity impossible.

II

The eighteenth century in Europe, the end of which is marked by the French Revolution, is also known as the age of the Enlightened Despots. Frederick the Great of Prussia, Catherine II of Russia and the Emperor Joseph II of Austria-Hungary are considered the most outstanding and the most typical examples. But it is only in Frederick the Great that we see the fact of power combined with the ideal of service, with a high regard for the rights of his subjects and with a confidence in his own judgement which enabled him to stand alone. He was a despot who could not make his people fully understand his motives, his ideas and his ambitions, but he succeeded in winning their affection, their loyalty and their admiration. It cannot be said that benevolent despotism succeeded as a type or as a method of government, and the idea that the ruler was the fittest person to lead and guide the people did not survive the French Revolution. Certain traditions and loyalties did, however, survive. They were among the chief reasons for the continuance of monarchies as constitutional monarchies.

The American and French Revolutions impressed very deeply on the minds of people the idea of government according to law and constitution and in the interests of the people. Napoleon created in France the first typical modern government, an agency acting according to reason and expediency, not hampered by tradition. He drew up codes of civil, commercial and penal laws, which served as models for several countries of continental Europe. The government of the United States was a complete example of democracy. It was to many a source of inspiration, but distance as well as difference of circumstances and historical development prevented it from becoming the model for European nations during this period. France had a monarchy with defined powers and a constitution from 1815 to 1848. But till 1830 the powers of the king were extensive enough to upset the working of the constitutional machinery. There was a legislature consisting of two chambers, and the government was carried on by a ministry representing the majority in the legislature. The franchise was very limited. The constitution framed by the revolutionary National Assembly in 1791 had fixed such a high property qualification that only about 50,000 people in the whole of France had the right to vote. The franchise was extended later to 1,00,000 in 1815, and to 2,00,000 in 1830. But even then it included only the upper middle class, and in a legislature representing a small part of the population, the majority could not really represent the views of the people. One of the reasons for the fall of Louis Philippe's government in 1848 was its obstinate resistance to the demand for the extension of the franchise.

Parliamentary government was well established in Great Britain by 1750, but the extent to which the king could control and direct administrative affairs depended in theory as well as fact upon the desire of the king himself. George III (1760-1820) formed a party known as "the King's Friends," and set up a ministry over which he had great influence. Ministers and ministries began to resign in case of an adverse vote in Parliament, but it happened also that members of Parliament holding radically different views joined the same cabinet. They were not responsible to any electorate; their constituencies did not represent the actual distribution of the population. There were such extreme cases as a large industrial town having no representation, and a member being "elected" from a constituency that had few or no inhabitants. Public life was the public exercise of personal influence.

The Federal and State constitutions of the United States of America, originally, like all constitutions, rough drafts incorporating political principles that were considered fundamental. They had to be amended, as ideas changed or practical difficulties arose. Authority of all kinds was subject to checks and balances; it was believed that unless the executive, the legislative and the judicial powers were separated, there would be no freedom. The federal constitution divided powers between the Federation and the States, between a President having sole executive authority, elected for 4 years, a Congress consisting of two houses, one representing the people and the other the States, exercising legislative powers, and a Supreme Court having final authority in questions concerning the interpretation of the constitution. A strict division of the different functions of government is impossible to maintain, and the constitutional history of the United States may be summarised as an attempt to maintain the original separation of powers while providing the opportunities and creating the conventions for necessary coordination and cooperation between the administrative and legislative authority, and bringing legislation and the exercise of authority more and more in correspondence with public opinion.

One of the most significant features of political life that appears during this period, which can be traced very largely to the American and French Revolutions, was that government acts and policies were subjected to constant criticism, and public opinion could be mobilised in such ways that governments had to yield to it. What was formerly the concern of individual politicians or political groups now becomes, or is made to become the interest of the mass of the people. Newspapers and pamphlets, public meetings, demonstrations, armed risings now become the means of the self-assertion of the people. The particular means used depend on the measures of resistance the government takes. In the United States the use of the vote for and against a person, a party or a policy was usually decisive from the very beginning. In countries where the electorate could not influence government directly enough or soon enough, other means became necessary. In England, till the Reform of 1832, the danger of armed risings was usually enough to force a change of government or the revision of a policy; in France armed risings were also resorted to. Where the system of government was not representative, armed rising seemed to be the only effective means of expressing the wishes and of gaining acceptance of the demands of the people.

Those who have similar interests or views tend to band themselves together, to form parties. In England, after the revolution of 1688, there were two groups, Tories and Whigs, which were contending for power. They were at first parties of members of Parliament only, and of the relatively small class of nobility, landlords and successful money-makers. As a larger number of people began to take interest in the affairs of government, they became parties representing opinion in the country. But it was only after the end of the Napoleonic wars, when laws which affected the interests and the lives of whole sections of the population, such as the Corn Laws of 1815, began to be passed, that party policies began to be canvassed in the country. The Reform Bill of 1832 was symbolic of the decisive importance of public opinion. It abolished fictitious constituencies, and though it did not introduce a system of representation on the basis of population, and retained property qualifications that seriously limited the franchise, it made the electorate much more effective. Important measures of reform followed, such as the abolition of slavery in the British Colonies (1833), the Factory Act (1833), the New Poor Law (1834), the Municipal Corporation Bill (1835). Working men began to organise themselves, and an agitation for the extension of the suffrage to all adult men, known as the Chartist Movement, was begun. Parties were formed in the United States soon after the Constitution was passed. They did not identify themselves with particular interests and policies even to the extent that the Whigs and the Tories of the eighteenth century did, but their contention for power introduced a system of canvassing the electorate. This canvassing became even more important after 1829, when manhood suffrage was introduced. In France, parties tended to multiply. There were opposing groups like the monarchists and the socialists, but in most cases there were shades of difference that made it difficult to identify them with particular economic or social interests.

In Great Britain and the United States the attitude towards government was determined very largely by the interest of those who benefited from free enterprise in trade and industry. This attitude affected government policy and also the form taken by economic organisation. But already during this period an opposite interest asserted itself, and demanded legislation for its own advantage. This was the agricultural interest. Manufacturers desired the fullest freedom in order to employ the cheapest labour, to procure the cheapest raw material and to work under the most favourable conditions, and both manufacturers and traders needed free access to the markets. The United States enjoyed the reputation of being the land of both opportunity and free enterprise. Great Britain was the first among the European countries to develop the system of mass production, and the first to acclaim the principle of free trade. This, as Frederick List (1789-1846) showed, was less a matter of intellectual opinion than of national interest, since Great Britain was industrially the most advanced country in Europe, and free trade would perpetuate this supremacy. But in Great Britain landlords and farmers desired to get the highest prices for corn, and their interest militated against the tendency of free trade to lower the cost of labour by lowering the cost of bread. They asked for protection, for prohibition of the import of corn or for such import duties as would keep the price of corn in the country sufficiently high. The use of legislative power for the protection of agricultural interests is well illustrated by the British Corn Law of 1815, which prohibited the import of corn, and was modified with great difficulty in 1828 and 1841. But it was not only agricultural interests that needed protection. Countries with less developed or nascent industries needed to be protected against competition with countries where industries were more developed. The principles of free trade and protection thus came to play a very important part in the formation of political parties. Apart from being economic issues, they also indicated the attitude towards the functions of government, free traders trying to prove that the common interest lay in the government interfering as little as possible in economic and social life, and their opponents insisting that government should use its legislative and administrative power and undertake all the responsibilities necessary in the common interest. The further stages of this conflict and its result in the form of legislation become evident in the next period.

The attitude towards war underwent a revolutionary change, and armies acquired a new significance and a new organisation. We have seen how the professional army came into existence, and how its administration and armaments were improved. During the French Revolution, when the country was in danger in 1793, we see for the first time the phenomenon of a nation in arms. The system of mass levies or the conscripted army was introduced, all able-bodied citizens being called upon to enlist in the army. This made it possible to have very large armies, and, as in Prussia when Napoleon's domination became unbearable, a sentiment could be created that would not only ensure enlistment of a large percentage of able-bodied citizens, but make these citizens into fairly good soldiers. Even Napoleon's victories, however, do not prove the value of the conscripted as against the professional army, because of the high percentage of those who evade enlistment when the means of enforcing it are not sufficiently effective, and also because conscripts are harder to discipline. In Prussia a system was evolved in which conscription was combined with rigorous training, recruits being first disciplined and kept in active service, then being put on garrison duty, and finally being allowed to return to civilian life, but listed as reserves. This system was elaborated and perfected in Prussia, but most of the other countries retained the system of having professional armies.

Napoleon's tactics gave a new significance to artillery, but the only invention of this period which is of importance is the needle-gun, a far more efficient weapon than the guns fired according to the old methods. The equipment required by the large armies made the manufacture of armaments a matter of great economic significance, and brought war and industry closer together than they had ever been before. The results of this development are even more evident in the succeeding period.

Economic interest acquired a new and permanent significance because of the Industrial Revolution, which was perhaps the most important of the revolutions that took place in the eighteenth and nineteenth centuries. It began in England about the middle of the eighteenth century and advanced slowly and in a rather haphazard way in England and on the European continent. It consisted basically in groups of inventions in the textile and in the iron and steel industries, and in the invention of the steam-engine with a rotary movement by James Watt in 1782. The number and size of the factories increased considerably, but it was the application of steam-power to production that marks the fundamental change. The first factories using water-driven machinery were erected along the banks of rapid streams, and this limited their expansion. Steam-driven machinery did not suffer from any such drawback. It was not affected by changes of climate, it was regular and controllable and could be erected at any site that appeared favourable for the transport of raw material and of finished products. But because of the need for coal, industries began to centre round coalfields. Steam-driven machinery and coal thus became the symbols of the Industrial Revolution.

A revolution in agriculture accompanied the revolution in industry. This also began in England, where the movement for enclosing land for sheep-breeding or farming reached its height between 1760 and 1820. The main incentive to the development of agriculture was the need for more food created by the growing urban population, and "the growth of a market economy, the quest for profit, the commercialisation of agriculture quickened scientific discovery." At the same time, animal husbandry developed into a science. Robert Bakewell (1725-1795) was one of the pioneers in this field. Before his time, sheep were valued for their wool, hides, and manure. He bred them for meat by careful selection of breeding stock and by inbreeding.[4]

One of the major results of the growth of industry was urbanisation. More and more people were drawn to the towns. If we take English cities as an example, the population of Bristol increased by 1760 from 29,000 to 1,00,000, of Birmingham, Sheffield and Liverpool from 4,000 to about 50,000. of Manchester from 6,000 to about 45,000. Another result was the growth of a new social class, which acquired wealth through ingenuity, self-reliance and aptitude for business. It was also a class distinguished for lack of sensitiveness and fine scruples. It seized the position and the prestige which had so far been the possession of the nobility, and opened the gateway to democracy.

The Industrial Revolution also created the proletariat, the worker depending entirely upon employment in mine or factory, while his employment depended upon the fluctuations of the market. Till the Factory Act of 1833 began to be enforced, the condition of women and children working in mines and factories was indescribably wretched, and the crowding of the poor in the slum areas of towns produced conditions in which the family and family morality were undermined.

There was continuous improvement in the means of transport. Roads with hard surfaces were made and passenger services by coach were organised. The invention of the locomotive and the steamship brought the speed of transport into line with industrial developmenit, increasing the rate of distribution and enabling the supply of goods to the most distant markets. A regular trans-Atlantic service of fast sailing ships was organised in 1816; the Peninsular and Oriental Line in 1839 established a regular steamship service between London and Alexandria, which connected with East India Company ships coming from Indian ports up the Red-Sea. The first important trans-Atlantic steamship line began operating in 1840. This expanded the area of commercial interests made the security, if not the monopoly of trade routes essential, and brought into the relationship between nations the spirit of competition which was the driving force in industry and trade.

Communications improved with transport. There had been till now some method or other of conveying letters, documents and parcels by post, but it was different in each country, and sometimes varied from city to city. A penny post had been introduced in London city in 1680, following the institution of a similar postage in Paris by Louis XIV. Postage for other cities depended on the distance and was charged from the receiver. In 1840 Rowland Hill succeeded in persuading the British Government to accept his proposal that postage should be charged by weight and not by distance, that it should be prepaid by the sender affixing postage stamps, and that, for all letters up to a certain weight, there should be a uniform penny postage for the whole country. Other countries soon followed Great Britain's example, and uniform national systems opened the way for international agreements.

If we consider education during this period, we find two forces at work. There is, first, the interest of the rulers and the ruling classes that the poor should remain content with their lot and the rich become more useful to the state and to industry and trade. The Prussian School Codes of 1763 and 1787 represent the first planned attempt to provide elementary education to the people, with rules regarding the age of compulsory admission, the curriculum, teacher education and inspection. The Code of 1763 gave too much control to the Church; in 1787, elementary education passed almost entirely into the hands of the government. In France, the Church dominated education at all levels till the Revolution, and it did so in the interest both of itself and of the state. In England and the United States, where the, "rulers" were the middle classes, elementary education was organised by private religious and philanthropic societies. The controlling force in secondary education was either the state, as in France during and after the Napoleonic period, or the economic interest, as in Great Britain and the United States, where education was considered to have value because it fitted men for business and industry. The universities were watched and suspected in France till the Revolution, and more or less neglected in Great Britain and the United States during this period. In Prussia, on the contrary, the foundation in 1809 of the Frederick-William University in Berlin was an acknowledgment of the idea that the function of the university is to cultivate the mind so that it becomes fully representative of the national character and culture, and to provide intellectual resources, strength and stability to society and the state.

The influences determining the content of education were religion, desire to create contentment, humanism and the requirements of industry. Religion was the interest of the Church or a particular religious community, such as the Quakers or the Methodists, or of those who believed that the moral values necessary to make a man honest and hard-working could only be acquired through religious instruction. Those who established schools for the poor in different parts of Great Britain often provided soup and other nourishment to the very poor children, in the hope of fostering contentment. The influence of humanism appears only in secondary and higher education, in the importance attached to Latin and Greek. In the universities, the study of science, specially of the natural sciences, was taken up only gradually. The ideal of the French Encyclopaedists to eliminate superstition, persecution, intolerance, to create a society governed by just laws and free from poverty, disease, slavery and war influenced people's minds but not the system of education. This period is, however, also the age of Rousseau, Pestalozzi (1746-1827) and Froebel (1782-1852). Rousseau was the first to emphasise the emotional aspect of human nature and to assert its value. Pestalozzi was among the first to make experiments in methods of education. The spirit with which he opened and conducted his schools and the ideas enshrined in his writings, made a deep impression on his contemporaries and are studied with reverence till today. Froebel was the originator of the Kindergarten, which is based on an ideal of harmony between man and nature, and between the individual and society, and of an unfolding of latent qualities and aptitudes that leads to personal fulfilment.

Scholarship made great advances during this period. There was a renewed interest in the Middle Ages, partly as a reaction to the idealisation of Greek and Roman culture in the Age of Enlightenment. The new spirit of nationalism, symbolised as the Volksgeist, prompted, the study of the national language, of folklore and of customary law. Sir William Jones initiated the study of Sanskrit, and the relationship between Sanskrit, Greek, Latin and the Germanic languages served as the foundation for the science of philology and opened a vast field of scientific study of languages and races. We have mentioned in the previous section the great importance acquired by the science of economics. Monumental works on history were written and the foundations laid for historical criticism. Grotefend (1775-1853) deciphered the cuneiform script (1802) and Champollion (1790-1832) read the Egyptian hieroglyphs. This made it possible to study the ancient civilisations of Mesopotamia and Egypt.

In the natural sciences, great progress was made. Leyell (1797-1875) put the study of geology on a scientific basis. A new science, palaeontology, was created by the study of fossils. Lavoisier (1743-1794) established the nomenclature now used in chemistry, and showed that it could be ordered in a law of the combination of elements. Following upon his work, the structure and types of molecules began to be determined, and structural formulae laid, down; gases were studied, oxygen, nitrogen and many compounds of carbon and other substances were isolated. Ordinary gases were liquefied. Electricity was considered interesting,[5] but had not found any particular use in the early eighteenth century. It had been discovered that it was capable of transmission through metal conductors, and a distinction had been made between conductors and insulators. Towards the end of the eighteenth century, the quantitative study of electricity began, a battery was made by Volta in 1800, the relationship between the electric current and magnetic effects was investigated, and Faraday laid the foundations of electro-magnetism. The first electro-magnet was constructed in 1825, but for reasons mainly social and economic, the electrical industry took about fifty years to develop. From 1800 onwards, it was generally accepted that light was a wave motion, and the velocity of light was measured fairly accurately in 1829.

Greater knowledge was acquired of the human body also. By 1800 it was recognised that it consisted of different kinds of material, such as muscle, membrane, cartilage, etc. and these were called tissues. In 1838-1839, the theory that all living organisms are cells or communities of cells was put forward in a simple form, and later it became clear that in every cell there is an essential living stuff, which was called protoplasm. The process of digestion was first thought to be a sort of combustion in the body. But Liebig (1803-1873) discovered that proteins, carbohydrates and fats were constituent elements of plant and animal tissues. This gave the right direction to further research. The brain was also studied. Bell (1774-1842), in 1820, discovered that the sensory and motor nerves were separate, while in the 1830s Johann Muller discovered the law of specific nerve energies. It was soon found that certain nerves regulated the rate of heart-beat and the flow of blood through the vessels.

The introduction of vaccination marks the first great step in the advancement of public health. Small-pox was the most universal and dreaded of diseases before the nineteenth century. The Turks seem to have begun the practice of inoculation by infecting children with matter from a very mild case of small-pox. The practice was brought to England in the early eighteenth century. In 1798, Edward Jenner discovered that an attack of cow-pox protected against small-pox, and soon the practice of vaccination was introduced.[6] This was the first step in the remarkable progress made in inoculation against disease.

III

The Industrial Revolution, which began about the middle of the eighteenth century, was the result of continuous application of skill and inventiveness to methods for the increase in production. It was not a revolution in the sense of being a sudden and unexpected appearance of an inventive faculty or of an organising ability. Men had exercised their minds for the improvement of production techniques before also, and we have seen that the factory system came into being before the invention of machines and the application of mass production processes. But there was now an urge to produce as much as possible because of the new opportunities of procuring raw material, marketing goods and making profits. In fact, new markets came first, inventions followed.[7] The urge to make the fullest use of opportunities made existing disadvantages obvious. One of these was shortage of fuel, another the shortage or undependability of water-power. The search for a new type of fuel and the desire to have it available in ever-increasing quantities led to a number of inventions and technical devices. The limited area in which water-power could be utilised, as well as the difficulty of increasing the power itself even where it could be had, induced the search for a new source of power. We have seen that the new fuel that came more and more into use was coke and coal. The existing coal mines had to be exploited fully and new ores discovered. As mines had grown deeper, the problem of devising a means for pumping water out of them had become more acute. The first application of steam-power was made in pumps. Other inventions and devices were also the result of a continuous endeavour to increase the output of the coal mine. The first rails, of wood and then of iron, were laid to facilitate haulage of coal, the first locomotive was used for pulling loaded wagons of coal. The utilisation of coal led to another series of improvements and inventions. Coal as a fuel and steam as a source of power had to compete against charcoal and water-power. As furnaces, and smelting processes, where coke and coal were used as fuel, improved, wood and charcoal were eliminated, and as the steam-engine proved its superiority, it began to be adopted instead of the old sources of power. Inmprovement of the steam-engine depended on the production of better iron, on precise workmanship, on greater knowledge of the fundamental sciences of chemistry and physics. Technological needs stimulated scientific study. We find, therefore, laboratory techniques being evolved and precision tools and instruments being placed at the service of the inventor.

We must not assume, however, that things happened by themselves. Behind all the inventiveness and the expansion of industry was a new spirit also, which is evident not only among the more famous and successful inventors, engineers and industrialists but also in persons of averagae ability. An illustration of this is an obscure machine factory set up in 1837 at Elbing, a small town near Danzig, whose establishment was advertised as follows in the local newspaper:

> The undersigned manufactures steam-engines, Watts' machines as well as condensation machines with expansion

> high pressure machines, iron water-wheels of all kinds, horse-drawn Persian wheels, hydraulic presses, rollers, apparatuses for dehydrating sugar in rooms with low air pressure etc. He also undertakes to set up whole establishments, such as oil mills, saw mills, sugar-beet factories and takes the liberty to mention that he has completed the courses of the Royal Industrial Institute of Berlin, done two years' practical work in the same Institute, and thereafter journeyed to London through the Rhineland for further training.[8]

It is significant that the first to benefit from inventions was the textile industry. Here the incentive was the large demand in Great Britain and the European and American continents for textiles; the opportunity was the availability of cotton from India and America, and Indian textiles provided both patterns and the challenge of competition. John Kay invented the flying shuttle in 1733, Lewis Paul and John Wyatt introduced roll-spinning in I738, James Hargreaves made the spinning jenny in 1764, Richard Arkwright the water-frame in 1796, and Samuel Crompton a spinning machine, called the "mule" ten years later. Improvements continued to be made. In 1785 Dr. Edward Cartwright made the first power-driven loom, which has further improved in 1853, A self-acting "mule" was invented in 1827. Across the Atlantic, the first ginning machine was made in the United States in 1793, which increased considerably the speed with which plucked cotton could be utilised for spinning. Interest in chemistry was reflected particularly in the manufacture of textiles. Study of the glass-colouring mineral, manganese, led to the discovery of chlorine, and its utilisation for bleaching. In this same process, the production of sulphuric acid supplied a much-needed substitute for skim milk sours that had been used so far. Soda, manufactured hitherto from expensive substances, now began to be made from salt. Industry thus supplied chemistry with new problems and new substances, while itself benefiting from advancement in chemical knowledge.

Between 1763 and 1769, James Watt (1736-1819) perfected his steam-engine. He grasped the need for economising heat and of converting the action of pulling a pump-rod, which was all that engines up to his time could do, into the turning of a wheel. The first change he made was to introduce double action, having two pistons instead of one and making them move alternately. The second improvement he made was to stop the admission of steam when the piston had travelled over but a part of the course, and make the expansion of the compressed steam complete the stroke. Between 1801 and 1825, quite a number of locomotives were constructed and used for pulling trucks on wrought-iron rails, which had begun to be manufactured in 1795. The engines moved at a very slow pace. But they could be used for other purposes also, and they opened the way for the utilisation of steam-power in the textile and other industries.

Progress in the iron industry was essential for improvement in machinery. The production of cast iron increased, more and more wrought iron became available after the introduction of puddling and the invention of grooved rollers. The employment of crucibles made steel more homogeneous. Furnaces became more efficient when a hot blast began to be used instead of a cold one, and more economical when the gases that escaped while smelting iron began to be utilised. The first factory for the production of rollers and cylinders was established in England in 1754, the first drilling machine was made in 1770, the planing machine in 1776. Between 1790 and 1800; machine-made tools became available. The early cylinders of steam-engines were not sufficiently accurate in bore. They improved considerably in efficiency when a new method of boring, first used for cannon, began to be applied. Wheel cutting machines, hydraulic presses, blowers, steam-hammers, heavy screw-cutting lathes, and machines for producing nails also began to be manufactured. Templets for the reproduction of machine parts began to be made from 1830. It is interesting to note that the clock-makers had taken the lead in concentrating on precision. Machinery borrowed directly from their equipment was added to the chisels, gouges, drills, dies, vices now used by those who worked in iron. Screw-cutting lathes were improved to ensure precision. Methods and tools were devised for mechanically dividing the graduated limbs of instruments and rules, and dilatometers and comparators were made for measuring the thermal expansion of metals.

Technical improvements in the means of transport followed closely upon developments in industry. Apart from hard roads, canals were also made primarily for transport of heavy goods, barges and boats being towed by horses. The first steam-boats were built in 1787, and trams drawn on rails by horses began to be used in England from 1795. The first steam tramway was operated in Philadelphia in 1804, and steam-boats began to ply on the Hudson from 1807. But the next great step, after Watts' steam-engine, was the improvement of the locomotive by Stephenson (1781-1847) in 1814. It revolutionised transport on land. After the first trial run in 1815, locomotives began to be manufactured, and railway services were started in France and the U.S.A. in 1820 and in England in 1830. With the use of iron for shipbuilding (from 1818), and the invention of the screw propeller (1836), transport by sea also developed rapidly, and the first Atlantic crossing by steamship was made in 1819.

This development of postal services has already been mentioned. The Semaphore system of telegraphic messages was invented in France in 1794, and was rapidly adopted in other countries. The present system was invented by Morse (1791-1872) in the U.S.A. in 1832, and the first telegraph line was laid between Baltimore and Washington in 1844. Various types of printed literature could become a widely used means of communication with the invention of lithography 1797), of a paper-making machine (1805), of the cylinder printing machine (1811), which increased by eight times the output of the press, and of the use of wood shavings for the manufacture of paper (1843). The first steel nibs were made in 1750 and the first fountain-pen thirty years later.

Mechanical inventions which gradually changed the whole character of warfare were the shell gun, first made in France in 1824, the needle-gun, manufactured in Germany (1836), the revolver, made by Colt (U.S.A., 1836), and the discovery of nitro-glycerine as an explosive. Experiments were also made during this period in the production of torpedoes. Miscellaneous inventions that were of great significance in different ways were the iron plough (U.S.A., 1797), sulphur matches (1825), and the sewing machine (1846-1850). Gas from coal began to be used for lighting from 1807, and within twenty years the streets of London, Paris and Berlin were gas-lighted. Davy (1778-1829) invented the arc lamp (1801) and the safety lamp for use in mines (1815). A Frenchman, Rene Laennec, invented the stethoscope, (1819) now used by every physician, and an American dentist first used ether as an anaesthetic (1846).

After the discovery in 1776 of hydrogen and its properties by Cavendish (1731-1810), the idea of flying was taken up, and the first balloons were made in 1783 and 1784. An attempt to cross the English Channel in 1785 failed, but in 1836 a balloon flew from London to Weilberg, in Germany, a distance of about 500 miles. Flying was to remain a romantic ideal till the internal combustion engine had been perfected, but what the spirit of adventure would contribute to flying had already been foreshadowed.

NOTES

1. Tawney, *op. cit.*, p. 32.
2. *Volk*—people, *geist*—spirit, mind, genius.
3. This phrase was first used by Beccaria (1738-94), in his book, *On Crimes and Punishments.*
4. Friedlander and Oser, *Economic History of Modern Europe,* pp. 35-37 (Prentice-Hall, Inc., New York, 1953).
5. After the invention of the Leyden jar, the king of France organised the electrification of his whole brigade of guards, who were made to jump in unison by shocks from batteries of Leyden jars.
6. Taylor, *op. cit.*, p. 197.
7. *History of Technology*, Vol. IV, p. 148.
8. *Elbinger Hefte* (1954).

34

Profiles of Some Great Cultures

The cultural map of the world has been constantly changing, and we cannot fully understand any one part of it unless we see it in the context of the whole. If we look at the map of Europe in AD 1800, we find that Charlemagne (Charles the Great) had just founded a state known as the Holy Roman Empire. He was crowned at Rome by the Pope, who was the head of the Western Christian, later called Roman Catholic Church. There was another Empire, with its capital at Byzantium (later called Constantinople and Stamboul), and its own Church, which came to be known as the Eastern or Greek Orthodox Church. The Scandinavian countries—Denmark, Norway, Sweden—and Europe east of the Elbe and north of the Danube had not yet been converted to Christianity, and the converted peoples were constantly in danger of attack. To the south of Christian Europe and dominating the Mediterranean Sea, lay the strong and expanding Muslim states. Most of Spain was also under Muslim rule. There were constant conflicts in all parts of this world, but it was also held together by commercial and cultural bonds.

The chief centres of production and, therefore, of civilisation were Byzantium, and the cities of Syria, Egypt and Spain. Syria and Egypt were also of great importance because goods that came from India and Southeast Asia passed through them. The Abbasid Empire, founded in AD 750, controlled these routes and was for about two hundred years the richest state of the world. The decline of this Empire and of other Muslim states bordering the Mediterranean was followed by the attempts of Italian cities like Venice and Genoa to capture the Mediterranean trade and also to

---

From *Education and Traditional Values.*

imitate and surpass the manufactures of Byzantium and the East. The Italian cities were not strong enough by themselves to seize the production centres of the eastern Mediterranean, and it was largely due to their intrigues that the Popes and Christian kings of Europe fought the long and devastating series of wars known as the Crusades. These wars had the effect of acquainting European kings and noblemen with the standard of living in the Muslim states, which was at the time much higher than the European. It would be most interesting to trace the influence of Arab dress and manners on the medieval European way of life.

The cultural map of the world at any time repeats to a considerable extent the map of the immediately preceding ages. The Roman Empire, which began as the city-state of Rome around 600 BC and included ultimately all the countries bordering on the Mediterranean, left two ideas firmly implanted in men's minds, the idea of a 'universal', efficiently administered state, and the idea of a law which meted out equal justice to all. The western half of the Roman Empire was constantly overrun by barbarians in the fourth and fifth centuries, and finally succumbed in AD 476. The foundation of the Holy Roman Empire in AD 800 marked the revival of the idea of a Christian world-state, which was to be as well-administered as the Roman Empire. A world-state of the same kind, but based on Islam, was the Abbasid Empire established in AD 750. Muslim rulers did not have the right to legislate on any matters comprehended in Muslim religious law, called the *shariah,* and it is interesting to note that Muslim religious law was based on the interpretations of the Quran and the Hadis (record of acts and saying of the Prophet Muhammad) by learned men, just as a large part of Roman law was based on the opinions of eminent lawyers. Roman law was codified by the Emperor Justinian (527-565). Muslim religious law was codified along the same lines between AD 750 and 850. The Muslim idea of a world-state was based on the concept of a universal religion and a ruler who would be the successor to the Prophet (*Khalifah*), the religious head of the community (*Imam)* and the chief administrator (*Amir al-Mo'minin*). Since there was no church and no separate organisation of the religious, the political ruler became all-powerful and matters of religious law continued to depend very largely on the opinion of the learned, as collected by four schools, known as the orthodox, the Maliki, the Shafi, the Hanafi and the Hambali. The Christian ideas of the world-state was also based on the concept of a universal religion, with Christ as the head and with authority divided between the Pope as the spiritual and the Emporer as the temporal (or worldly) ruler. It was assumed that Pope and Emperor would act in complete harmony, but this did not happen. There was, instead, conflict between Pope and Emperor over the question as to which of them possessed final and overriding authority. Lawyers of the Church took up the study of Roman law, and the principles laid down by it were first used as arguments by the scholars of the Church to prove that the highest authority vested in the Pope. Supporters of the Emperors also studied Roman law and used the same arguments to prove their case. It was because of this discussion that the theories of a law of nature, a law of nations, natural rights and sovereignty became important elements of European political thought and served as the foundation of the modern European state.

A more important formative influence on Western civilisation were the thinkers and writers of ancient Greece. But the European peoples came into contact with the culture of ancient Greece later and in an indirect way. The works of Plato and Aristotle were first studied in Muslim centres of learning, particularly in Spain, and this led to the growth of a tendency to introduce philosophical ideas into religion and formulate beliefs in a manner consistent with logic and reason. This tendency spread from the Muslim to the Christian centres of learning. An outstanding example of this is the prevalence of Averroism in the University of Paris and among Christian thinkers. Averroes is the Latinised form of the name of the Spanish Muslim philosopher, Ibn Rushd (1126-1198), who taught among other things that the universe was eternal and human beings mortal. His teachings took such root that they had to be combated by several Christian writers, among them St. Thomas Aquinas (1225-1274), who effected a reconciliation between Christian beliefs and Greek thought as apprehended by the Muslim—and through them the Christian thinkers. By the end of the fourteenth century, the number of people in the prosperous cities of Italy who got educated outside the institutions of the Church had grown, Latin began to be studied and then Greek. After 1453, when Sultan Muhammad II took possession of Constantinople, a large number of people who could teach Greek fled to the Italian cities, and the study of Greek became an intellectual fashion. About the same time, books began to be printed, and side by side with religious knowledge there developed a learning which was secular in character and spirit, and which could be subjected to criticism. This was the beginning of humanism, of knowledge which was human and not divine in origin, which centred around man and depended entirely on human effort for its advancement. The content of this knowledge was all that could be learnt from the writings of the ancient Greek and Roman poets, historians, philosophers and scientists, and the first means of increasing it was to recover as much as possible of the old literature in whatever form it could be found and print and publish it. The art and architecture of the ancient Greeks and Romans also began to be studied, imitated and adapted. The result of all this study and diffusion of knowledge has been called the Renaissance, or the intellectual and artistic rebirth of the European peoples. The Renaissance began in Italy and spread to France, central Europe and England.

A very important aspect of the Renaissance was interest in the methods of production and a search for better techniques. Books on technical subjects began to be written and printed from the fifteenth century, and a scientific basis was given to processes knowledge of which had hitherto been handed down from father to son or master to pupil as a 'mystery' or trade secret. In the fifteenth century the manufacture of firearms was begun, and because success in war depended on superiority in arms, the iron industry made rapid progress. Trade with Byzantium and the Muslim countries promoted accumulation of capital, and Italian merchants got around the religious prohibition of usury by forming companies or houses and lending capital for industrial and sometimes military enterprises. We must always bear in mind that there was a close relationship in Europe between the advancement of knowledge, industrial development and increase in wealth.

There was no conflict at first between the Roman Catholic Church and the new learning. Popes as dignitaries of the Church patronised artists and raised no objections to the ideas expressed in the poetry and literature of writers influenced by humanism. But the new ideas were bound to influence the attitude towards religion. Erasmus (1467-1536) evolved what he called the 'philosophy of Christ', and his *Manual of a Christian Soldier* was translated into many languages and very widely read. But Martin

Luther (1483-1546) and Calvin (1509-1564) were reformers rather than intellectuals, and their successful revolts against the Roman Catholic Church divided the Christians into three camps. Rulers, for political reasons, supported the Roman Catholic Church or the Lutherans or Calvinists, and for about a hundred years (1555-1648) there were disastrous wars of religion. The Roman Catholic Church now became hostile not only to those who opposed its authority or rejected its beliefs and practices, but to all those who put forward new ideas. Galileo (1564-1643) was taken to task for declaring as a scientific proposition that the earth revolved round the sun, and would have been burnt as a heretic if he had not recanted. Gradually, the people were divided into two camps, those who adhered to the Church and the established authority. In France, during the eighteenth century, an intellectually alert and vital people were oppressed by the combined power of the Church and the king. Writers like Voltaire (1694-1778) and scholars of the group known as Encyclopaedists tried to undermine blind belief by stimulating the exercise of reason and providing so much of what they regarded as real knowledge as to make men intellectually independent of the Church. Political opposition to absolutism culminated in the French Revolution, which began in 1789, and which provided opportunity for the assertion of the rights of man, as an individual human being and as a citizen. These had been proclaimed already in the constitution of the United States of America (1777), and the two together formed the basis of democratic ideology. The Revolution of 1688 had established parliamentary government in Great Britain, and government through elected representatives of the people became the basis of the democratic state.

In the meantime, scientific knowledge had grown, Galileo invented the simple telescope, Newton (1642-1727) the reflecting telescope, von Guericke (1602-1686) made the first pump and demonstrated the power of the vacuum. Newton, as is well known, formulated the laws of motion and of gravity. Science was ably seconded by skill, and during the second half of the seventeenth century, instrument-makers of fine and accurate craftsmanship could be found in every big European town. Indispensable measuring instruments had already been invented, the Vernier scale in 1631 and the micrometer in 1638.

Economic and political rivalry were the most potent means of stimulating industry and the application of scientific knowledge to the techniques of production. The scientific attitude and the spirit of competition became the distinctive features of western civilisation. The scientific attitude consists in the acceptance only of what can be proved by adequate evidence and is capable of practical and useful application. The competitive spirit is seen in the ungovernable impulse to acquire more and more of wealth and power, and in the tendency to judge men by the success they achieve in the race against all rivals to amass money and goods. A great change in the methods of production, known as the Industrial Revolution, began in England about the middle of the eighteenth century and spread rapidly to the European continent. It led to the growth of large manufacturing cities and enormous business concerns; to the development of means of transport and communication; to living conditions in which the old ideas of family life and morality had no place, and also to comforts and amenities which no one had even dreamed of before.

The history of Eastern Europe followed somewhat different lines. The organisation of the Eastern or Greek Orthodox Church was such that, while it was subject in matters of doctrine to a general council of representatives, the Emperor had executive power and could control the Church. The Church, therefore, was a means of support for the state. This characteristic was as determining influence in the history of peoples who were converted to Christianity by missionaries of the Greek Orthodox Church and helped to create the absolute authority of the Tsars of Russia.

The first centre of culture and political authority was Kiev. After the Tatar invasions of the thirteenth century, the Romanoffs, whose seat was Moscow, gradually expanded their territory and power. Tsar Peter the Great (1689-1725) made St. Petersburg (now called Leningrad) his capital, and introduced European industries and ways of life. The Empress Catherine II (1762-1796) extended her dominion to the Black Sea and the lower Danube, and raised Russia to the position of a European power, with a dominating influence. European statesmen realised the enormous war potential of Russia. Napoleon's attack on the country in 1812 was the climax of his attempt to get Europe completely under his power, and the

Crimean War (1853-1856) was intended to stop Russia's advance southwards. The political ambitions of the rulers of Russia far exceeded the industrial development of the country, there was cruel suppression of ideas and movements of reform, and when Russia collapsed during the war of 1914-1918, there was a revolution which led to the establishment of a dictatorship of the proletariat, of a state administered and controlled by the Communist Party. Stalin, the General Secretary of the Party and absolute ruler of Russia—called, after the revolution, the Union of Socialist Soviet Republics, planned the industrial development of the country from 1927 to 1953. Whether this planned development is superior or not to what the Western nations have achieved through free competition is a matter on which no judgement can yet be passed.

We have seen that the Muslims studied Greek thought and were instrumental in transmitting it to the western peoples. They also acquired knowledge of Indian mathematics and astronomy, and they cultivated and developed these sciences also on their own. Translations were made of Greek, Persian and Sanskrit works. Al-Kindi wrote on meteorology and optics, al-Razi (known as Rhazes in Europe, 864-925) was esteemed as a mathematician, astronomer, philosopher and physician; his works were translated into Latin and his authority in medicine was undisputed in Europe down to the seventeenth century. Al-Khwarizmi was the author of an epoch-making work on mathematics in which the zero, decimals and the nine numerals were used. He was also the author of a basic textbook on algebra.

But science failed to become associated with the enduring features of Islam. In the conflict between orthodoxy and the rationalism represented by Greek thought, orthodoxy was victorious, and independent enquiry came to be regarded as essentially irreligious. The autocratic, monarchical state, which had no basis in religion, was accepted and supported by orthodoxy, with the result that no experiments could be made in political organisation. Administrative reforms were carried out, as by Sulaiman the Magnificent (called the Lawgiver by the Turks, 1520-1566) and Akbar the Great (1556-1605), but the principles according to which authority could be possessed and should be exercised never became subject of speculation and discussion. State could be large, well-governed and prosperous, but everything depended on the personality of the ruler. Arts and crafts were patronised and industry was encouraged, though no significant improvement was made in the methods of production; social grace and personal refinement were cultivated to a high degree. From the thirteenth century onwards, the distinctive feature of Muslim life was mysticism or sufism, which exercised a profound influence on literature and the general outlook and attitude of the people. The rapid industrial advance of the West undermined the economy of the whole Muslim world, causing political disintegration and social backwardness everywhere.

Index